The author is indebted to Steve Bacon, a Trustee of the Wilts & Berks Canal Trust, for his work in verifying the accuracy of the book's content. The Wilts & Berks Canal Trust is registered charity no. 299595 - a waterway society based in Wiltshire, England, whose mission is the restoration of the Wilts & Berks Canal.

A Kindle version is available. The Kindle Reader or App allows images to be reproduced in colour and at a higher resolution than possible in a monochrome paperback book.

The Characters

Sam Hart – Lindsay's father
Sylvia Hart – Lindsay's mother
Lindsay – my wife
Jonathan – my son
Jo– Jonathan's girlfriend
Jennie – Jonathan's girlfriend, then wife
Suzanne – Lindsay's sister
Nick Hamer – Suzanne's husband
George – Suzanne's friend
Philip – Lindsay's brother
Liz – Philip's wife
Dominique – Philip's daughter
Nick – Lindsay's cousin
Diana (Dinny) – Nick's Wife
Virginia – Lindsay's cousin
Robert – Virginia's husband
Sandra – Friend
Steve – Married to Sandra
Jemma – Friend
Andy – Married to Jemma
Di – Friend
Dave – Married to Di

Narrowboat Insights

Peter M Hills

Published by New Generation Publishing in 2025

Copyright © Peter M Hills 2025

Second Edition

ISBN: 978-1-83563-503-2

www.newgeneration-publishing.com

New Generation Publishing

Contents

Introduction

Over 15 years or so, I went from being a complete boating novice, never having been at the tiller of any kind of craft, to experienced skipper who accumulated over 1,500 hours at the tiller. What follows are descriptions of just about every scenario, good and bad, that the family and I encountered around canals and rivers all over England and Wales. Of course, liveaboard continuous cruisers amass thousands of hours at the tiller – most are prepared to share their knowledge with less experienced travellers in the same way I hope to do within these pages.

I have not described all the trips we went on – just those where there was a story to tell in which the crew and I had learnt something about navigating our inland waterways.

Interest in narrowboating as an activity holiday has grown over recent years, helped by TV and video productions. The current trend began in 2011 with a four-part series on BBC4 featuring canal walks with Julia Bradbury. In 2014, Timothy West and Prunella Scales' first series 'Great Canal Journeys' was broadcast, attracting an audience of 1.5 million. They went on to make ten series, the final one in 2019.

In May 2015 Cassian Harrison's film 'All Aboard' was broadcast on BBC4. The film recorded a two-hour journey from Bath top lock to the Dundas aqueduct on the Kennet and Avon canal. It was one of a series of 'silent' films, captioned but with no commentary. The first showing attracted over 600,000 viewers.

Since then, there have been four series of Robbie Cumming's 'Narrowboat Diaries' broadcast on BBC4. A fifth was on the 'Yesterday' channel in June 2024 over ten one-hour episodes.

Robbie, a single-handed boater, gives a warts and all commentary on his solo life on board narrowboat 'The Naughty Lass'. It's not a bed of roses and in at least one respect fails to show how tough single-handed boating can really be. He cuts corners by appearing to exit each lock without shutting the gate(s). I'm told that the producer does it for him but nevertheless, it creates the wrong impression for boaters new to the game. It is poor practice like that which this book aims to point out and why the book is called 'Narrowboat Insights'.

In June 2024 Channel Four broadcast a 20-part series called 'Narrow Escapes'. It featured an agreeable collection of narrowboat owners and their businesses. There were cake makers, a pizzeria, a flower seller, a hotel boat, a comedian, a couple doing their own narrowboat fit-out, a part-time cocktail maker, a bicycle repair workshop and a children's entertainer. There were first-time liveaboards enjoying marina life, brand-new boat owners and an experienced narrowboat skipper who took his family across The Wash.

One of the narrowboats featured a young couple part way through a tour of the canal network. They joined a flotilla of boats navigating the River Thames tideway from Limehouse basin to Teddington Lock. The trip was organised by the St Pancras Cruising Club based in Limehouse basin. I assume the skippers had all been briefed about the tidal Thames and were experienced boaters. However, our young couple witnessed a near disaster when one boat, going upstream with the tide, got too close to a bridge abutment, found they had no steering and were very nearly capsized by the inevitable collision. Their boat rode up and then rolled about 60 degrees and could have sunk in seconds in deep water. A perfect example of being let loose on a 15-ton vessel with no understanding of the situation about to emerge.

My hope is that this book can provide that understanding. What follows is deliberately full of detail. I could have provided a comprehensive list of do's and don'ts but that would hardly be an interesting read. I could have cut some of the detail but that would have said goodbye to the background of the insights. So the details are woven into real-life adventures, enabling a reader get the most from the narrative. And to go on to become a responsible, safe, competent traveller around the network.

Chapter 1
The Canal Revolution

Prior to the coming of canals, the only methods of moving goods, livestock or people over land were Shanks' pony, horseback, packhorse, horse and cart or horse-drawn carriage. Over millennia, trackways, bridleways and footpaths became embedded within the landscape.

Boats powered by teams of rowers or ships powered by the wind and rowers had navigated oceans, estuaries and rivers since time began of course.

By 1750 the Industrial Revolution was under way, essentially powered by the development of the steam engine – which needed coal as its fuel source. Francis Egerton, 3rd Duke of Bridgewater, had coal-a-plenty under his land, but that had to be mined by hand and then transported to the cotton mills of North West England. He could not do that efficiently by land-based transport or by the river network, most of which was either unnavigable or unreliable or downright dangerous or all of these.

He did make use of the Mersey and Irwell Navigation initially but rapidly discovered the then failings of river transport. He had seen the Canal du Midi in France and then conceived the idea of constructing his own inland waterway and using flat-bottomed boats, barges, to move his coal.

By 1762 civil engineers John Gilbert and James Brindley had put that idea into practice and had built the Bridgewater Canal – the first in Britain. It ran for 41 miles with initially ten locks and was a huge commercial and financial success.

Britain was the first country to develop a nationwide canal network, extending eventually more than 4,000 miles. Canal building continued through the 1950s until finally killed off by the railway network. But 2,000 miles of restored canal and navigable rivers remain accessible today.

Chapter 2
The Beginning

It was springtime in 2005 and with my 60th birthday later in the year and about ten years since we had to abandon some wonderful horse-riding holidays, I suggested to Lindsay that we try out a narrowboat holiday. I had seen these impossibly long, thin, colourful and frankly ludicrous-looking boats during my travels around the UK demonstrating our business's auction software. Lindsay's father, Sam, had recently died and I thought we could invite Sylvia along – it might help her get over his passing.

Our riding holidays were most certainly adventurous. Maybe cruising the canal and river network would create a new set of memorable experiences.

It began with a one-day Helmsman's course from Stourport-on-Severn Marina. I had no experience of driving a boat of any kind, let alone a vessel of length 62 feet and weighing 15 tons. And since on the first trip I was going to have my mother-in-law on board, plus my sister-in-law and her dog Bagins, I thought a bit of tuition would be prudent.

In my professional life I had decades of experience of working on systems for big ships, small ships and little boats. These included nuclear submarines, destroyers, frigates and fast patrol boats. I went on sea trials trying to sink trawlers and cross-channel ferries, but I knew nothing of boat handling or the rules of the road at sea or on inland waterways.

That day out from Stourport was an eye-opener. There were three trainees on board a narrowboat owned by a British Airways 747 pilot. He would be our instructor, our captain, for the day. We started with a few basic knots and the importance of the centre line[1] on a narrowboat. Then pushing the bow off, walking to the stern, stepping on and getting away.

---

[1] All narrowboats have three mooring/handling lines. One is attached to a stud at the bow, one at the stern and a centre line attached to a stud on the roof. That stud is placed at the centre of gravity of the boat – if the craft were to be lifted out by a

Stourport Marina was exceptionally cramped, and we were all incredulous it would be possible to manoeuvre a 62-foot steel tube without hitting something. Our instructor did that effortlessly while we just watched drop-jawed.

I asked about a mother-in-law overboard procedure. First engage neutral, he said, which stops the propeller. Then suggest she stands up – I had not realised that canals were so shallow.

While manoeuvring to navigate our way out of the marina we discussed getting on and off a narrowboat. We had just all got on by pushing off the bow, walking to the stern and stepping onto the rear deck – which is always level with the canal bank. Our captain then said that on a boat that is not moored (i.e. tied to a bollard or rings or mooring pins), getting off must always be from the rear deck – never by jumping off the bow. The bow of a narrowboat is typically two feet above the bank and any jump from there will produce a horizontal force that will make the boat move smartly away from the bank – resulting in you doing the splits and ending up in the water with a cracked head!

We went north out onto the Staffordshire and Worcestershire Canal via York Street Lock. The canal is a 'narrow' type, with locks just wide enough for a single narrowboat to pass through. York Street Lock is deep – it raises or lowers the canal by some 12 feet. It has a single top gate and a pair of chevroned lower gates that were leaking like a sieve. Those gates were first visible as our captain drove the boat under York Street, where he stepped off and secured the boat to a bollard using the centre line and the boatman's hitch knot he had demonstrated earlier.

A boat had gone through ahead of us, leaving the lock full of water. The first task was to make sure our bow doors were shut. All four of us walked under York Street, then up to street level and then to the pair of lower gates. Each gate had a huge black wooden balance beam attached, painted white at each end. It was the first time I had seen one of those up close. Each gate had a hefty winding mechanism that would drag a sluice,

---

crane using just the centre line (a ridiculous concept but stay with me) it would be perfectly balanced with bow and stern level with the horizon.

A narrowboat in a turn pivots around its centre of gravity. In most situations, the centre line is all that is needed to control the boat from the towpath. We will cover the exceptions later in this book.

called a 'paddle', up from the bowels of the structure, allowing water to flow out.

We three trainees each had a windlass to be used to crank those paddles up or down. The instructor explained how each gate paddle should be partially opened initially, ensuring the boat below the lock would not be hit by a torrent of water. Once the outward flow had stabilised, we opened the paddles fully, allowing the lock to drain completely.

Our 747 captain then explained a couple of bits of protocol. It's essential he said to ensure both lower gate paddles are closed before walking up to the single top gate[2] and opening its paddles. The protocol is to always wind down (never drop) the lower gate paddles before opening the lower gates. He said we should get into a habit of doing that. And never ever leave the windlass attached to the winding mechanism, where it could spin off and cause serious damage to one's head.

That done and with both gates open, I was tasked to go back to the boat with the captain, undo the centre line hitch, walk to the bow and push off, then walk back to the stern, flick the centre line back on board and drive the boat under the road and gently into the lock.

My God, it was dark down there, slimy, wet brick walls towering above the waterline. I was mighty nervous, but the captain was with me and demonstrated how to stop before colliding with the concrete cill at the far end, using a flick into reverse. He then explained how to position the boat in the chamber, using the engine, while the boat rises in the lock. I was going to be the first of the group to do this.

The two lads up top then closed the two chevroned gates behind us. A ladder clamped to the lock wall had miraculously appeared from nowhere, quickly grabbed by the instructor, who managed to shin up without getting covered in green algae. Three heads appeared at the far end, followed by a thumbs-up from the captain. I reciprocated and the

---

[2] Actually, most top gates whether flat or chevroned have 'Ground Paddles'. The sluices are not sited in the gates themselves but in channels underground. This allows water to enter the lock with far less turbulence than if they were on the gates. However, some canals do not follow this rule and operating their locks requires greater care or even special procedures. That aspect will be covered later in this book.

trainees gently opened the two ground paddles, one at a time, keeping their eyes on me all the while.

The inflow of water did initially push the boat forward (not back), but that was easily controlled. We rose majestically up to canal level, the crew shut both ground paddles and pushed open the single top gate. I drove the boat around to the landing stage, waiting for them to close the gate and join me on board. The captain said we must always close the gates(s) on exit from a lock[3]. The only exception would be if there were a boat waiting to come straight in.

We each had a session of steering the boat. The instructor had already explained how a narrowboat turns around its centre of gravity, which could be up to 36 feet away. Move the tiller to the left, the stern moves over in that direction and the bow moves to the right. We all did splendidly as we moved slowly north towards Kidderminster – at least at the start. What became evident, though, was as soon as steering became critical, such as passing another craft, we eventually each made the mistake of pushing the tiller the wrong way. Our instructor demonstrated

---

[3] Most inland waterways have locks. They are there to allow boats to move upstream or downstream. Water levels on rivers are maintained by weirs – essentially solid walls placed in a waterway to maintain a minimum water level upstream of the weir. A lock usually sits alongside a weir to allow craft to get past.

Most canals have flights of locks – one lock after another. Each lock has two sets of gates – an upper set and a lower set. Each flight will usually be an uphill one or a downhill one – never one lock up followed by one lock down, unless going over the summit. Navigating a flight of locks is a bit like sailing up or down a mountain built from water. A boat will always be either moving up towards the summit or down from the summit.

The stretch of water between each lock is called a 'Pound'. Pounds can be short, barely more than a maximum boat length. They can also be long, many miles – the longest pound on the Kennet and Avon canal is 15 miles.

Rivers have natural water sources. A canal *can* have a river as its water source but most have a reservoir of some sort. Those reservoirs are sited at the canal summit. Each time a boat moves through a lock, one lock's worth of water eventually flows out of the reservoir and is lost. It is both sets of lock gates that stop that mountain of water from draining away completely.

And for that reason, unless advised otherwise, it's good practice to shut a lock's exit gate(s) after leaving, having made sure all four paddles are firmly closed.

how a narrowboat could stop quickly, well within its own length, via judicious use of reverse.

York Street Lock

Back down into Stourport Basin from the Staffs and Worcs Canal. Note how the single top gate has two 'ground' paddles while the two lower mitred gates have one 'gate' paddle each.

© Copyright Roger Kidd

We went through Falling Sands Lock and on to Caldwell Lock, with each of us taking turns to be steerer and lock-side crew. We did not wear life jackets. Most boaters don't on canals, we were told, but we must always wear them on rivers.

We were shown the turning procedure at a winding hole (canal speak for a turning point) near Kidderminster. In our case this involved turning the boat left through 90 degrees and gently placing the bow on the bank. Then, with the boat still in forward gear - hence keeping the bow on the bank - and pushing the tiller arm hard to the right, the stern will be driven to the right. Next, at about 45 degrees to the bank and now facing the other way, using reverse to pull the bow off the bank and back towards the other side. Finally, into forward gear using the tiller to straighten up and away home.

We then went through the narrow downhill lock procedure. The first thing that struck me was how easy it would be to go in too fast. Downhill locks can give the impression of running over a cliff edge. We were shown how we must keep the boat forward of the rear concrete cill - marked by a white line on the brickwork. And ensure the bow and stern fall at the same rate. If there were any issues, the lock-side crew should quickly wind down both paddles, thereby stopping the flow of water out of the lock, and then take stock.

Back in the marina, the captain made us go through the broad-beam lock (where two narrowboats can fit side-by-side) and down into the lower basin. And then back again and finally return to our berth where it was my turn to be at the tiller.

The procedure there was to come in to the berth slowly at an angle of about 30 degrees and let the bow gently kiss the bank. Then a quick burst of reverse to stop the boat. Then push the tiller arm in the direction you want the stern to move, apply gentle forward gear and wait until the stern moves over to touch the bank. Finally, put the engine in neutral and with centre line in hand, step off and secure the boat to a bollard or mooring ring. I almost did a perfect bow-first landing but, at the last moment, turned the tiller the wrong way.

We all had a great day. We all got our RYA Helmsman Certificates. But with hindsight, we needed more days. These could cover boat handling and some practical issues. For example, open water 360-degree turns, manoeuvring in reverse, boating in windy conditions, going slowly past miles of boats moored on both sides, dealing with shallow water, de-fouling the propeller, tunnels, boating on rivers and so on. However, we will deal with all these later in this book.

It occurred to me later that driving a narrowboat is akin to steering a shopping trolley. If your trolley, one of those with fixed front wheels, or a wheelbarrow for example, is hard up against the frozen veg on your left and you need to turn right to get to ready meals, you won't make it. You will need to reverse and get into centre-aisle. As you then turn right, you will have space for your stern to swing out left onto an arc that will take you to that chicken arrabbiata.

For anyone reading this and contemplating canal boating for the first time, get down to your local supermarket or garden centre, grab yourself a big wheeled trolley or wheelbarrow and 'drive' it up and down the aisles – keeping both to the left-hand side and to the right-hand side and driving it around every corner. Turn right from the left-hand side. Turn left from the right-hand side. Squeeze past other 'boaters'. Reverse away from obstructions.

Take note of how the stern of the trolley needs to behave. If the back of the trolley needs to go left, you will push the tiller left. If the back of the trolley needs to go right, you will push the tiller right.

Unless you have never been supermarket shopping before, you already know how to control that trolley. *And therefore, you know how to steer a narrowboat. You just didn't know you knew.*

Chapter 3

Llangollen Canal September 2005

Llangollen Canal

© Copyright waterwayroutes.co.uk

Map 01

The very first trip I planned was a week on the Llangollen Canal in North Wales. I had asked Lindsay's sister Suzanne and husband Nick Hamer if they would like to come with us. They accepted and I made an early booking with Black Prince Narrowboat Holidays, who have a base at Chirk Marina.

Then dreadful news. Just a couple of weeks before we were going to set off, Sue phoned to say Nick had been diagnosed with lung cancer. She was not sure whether they would be able to come along now. However, it turned out that Nick was very keen, and Sue thought it would take his mind off the next few weeks when he would be undergoing further tests.

We came out of Chirk Marina on a 70-foot Black Prince narrowboat with a semi-trad stern. My mother-in law, sister-in-law, her dog

Bagins and brother-in-law Nick accompanied Lindsay and me. We turned west and, after a short bout of zigzagging, found our sea legs. We crossed the Chirk Aqueduct. Then our first problem. The Chirk Tunnel. The training day hadn't mentioned tunnels. I knew from the (Pearson's) guide book that it was only 460 yards long, but the far end was just a tiny circle of light in the middle of a well-buttressed black hole. However, I knew the ropes, headlight on, wait for the circle of light to indicate the tunnel is empty then set off.

I was steering but could not see a thing. Nick was on the stern with me. Bagins was sitting between his legs. The headlight was next to useless, so we turned on all the cabin lights. It was dripping wet. It was smelly. It was noisy. It was tight. It was slow going. It took every ounce of concentration to keep in the centre channel. The circle of light would become a pinprick every now and again and I felt like I was driving into a brick wall.

Bagins was a big black lump of a thing. He didn't like the dark or the noise. We couldn't see him. He howled all the way through. It was a sound that reverberated around my head for the entire week.

Next up, the Pontcysyllte Aqueduct – now a World Heritage site. Just Nick and me at the stern, feeling very exposed. The remaining crew, including Bagins suitably tied down, were in the cabin with their hands and paws over their eyes.

Words cannot do justice to the visual and aural sensations experienced over those 307 metres, gliding serenely over the valley of the River Dee some 40 metres below. I had been concerned about steering the boat within that narrow trough, but in fact the boat steers itself simply because it is a tight fit in the channel. And it is impossible to go too fast, not that one would want to anyway – that tight fit means the boat has to push large quantities of water along ahead of it in order to make any progress at all.

The Pontcysyllte Aqueduct over the valley of the River Dee

Note how thin the edge of the boat channel is. The towpath is on the right-hand side.

We made it to Llangollen by mid-afternoon, had a teacake and coffee, then turned around to face eastward and moor overnight at Trevor.

On that first day we certainly learnt a thing or two. Priority at tunnels, lift bridges, shallow water, tight turns particularly after the aqueduct, one-way systems and nowhere convenient to moor for the night.

One lesson learnt was after a particularly nasty encounter with another boater who clearly hated those who hire. Particularly novices. She was never a novice – she came into the world as a fully-fledged boater. She got into a rage because my 'use the engine to balance the boat in a lock' technique that I had been taught, and Nick was using, took too much time for her. Lindsay eventually dispatched her with a wild-eyed outburst of "Everyone's a bloody expert."

However, her technique, reluctant as I was to admit, was better for narrow uphill locks. She entered the lock, cabin bow doors closed, and gently put the bow against the single top gate. She then engaged tickover, which

11

kept the bow on the gate while the boat rose in the lock. This does not stress the gate because of the water pressure from the other side. And it works really well – so much so that we have used it ever since, aware of course that the crew need to ensure the bow does not get jammed on the way up. It's not likely to though because on most narrow canals, although not all, the top gate is flat. But it's a pity she had to be so nasty in imparting such a useful technique.

As a novice boater I had not yet experienced the optical illusions that crop up without warning. It was a beautiful late September evening around 7pm. We were travelling east, so a setting sun was low on the horizon behind us. We were looking for somewhere to moor for the night, preferably near a pub so we didn't have to cook a hot meal. The boat was meandering through glorious countryside on dead calm waters. There were tall trees on both banks trying to form overhead arches. I suddenly got a jolt, like I had been struck with an arrow. The boat was going over the edge of a waterfall. I literally leapt into the air with shock and slammed us into reverse. Nick, on the stern with me, turned his head and stared. What the hell was wrong? When I recovered some composure, I looked ahead and realised that I was seeing a reflection of the sky and landscape in crystal clear still water. An infinity pool in fact. We laughed.

As an engineer I always had to be prepared for any eventuality, so I went on this first adventure armed with retractable Stanley knife, plumber's wrench, torch, bungees and all manner of unnecessary stuff. I kept the knife on my belt.

We were making our return past Chirk Marina. Sue wanted to walk along the towpath for a while to give Bagins a break – he was being a real pain. The dog wanted to be off the boat if he was on it and on the boat if he was off it. Sue put him on his lead, which Lindsay slipped over the T-stud on the bow. Nick was steering as we approached the marina entrance. I had stepped off the stern and walked to the bow, which had drifted out a little. Nick regained control, the bow came in, but the boat was still going too quickly. Suddenly, Bagins decided that was the time to leap off. He fell between boat and bank with his lead still around the T-stud. He became a living fender. Either a sausage dog or a strangled dog – soon to be a dead one. Quick as a flash, and without thinking, I whipped the knife off my belt and slashed his tether.

Lesson learnt for future trips – something along the lines of boats and dogs don't mix.

Lindsay and Jonathan at Grindley Brook Lock

On that first trip we experienced our first boat failure. We had moored for the night at Grindley Brook, facing east, at the top of the three-chamber staircase lock there. The next morning after breakfast, we noticed the front cabin carpet soaked in water.

I phoned Black Prince, who despatched an engineer straight away. He arrived about three hours later and got to work. Of course, I had ideas about the boat sinking, but it turned out there was a leak in the fresh-water tank under the bow floor. Water was accumulating in the bilges, hence the wet carpet. Nothing could be done to fix it; we just had to keep on using the bilge pump and hope we could get back to base on time at the end of the week. We lost most of a whole day of our schedule. I did later wonder if that leak would be fixed in time for the next crew handover or would the boat have to be withdrawn from service – leaving the new crew with a different boat, or maybe no boat at all.

The next morning, we got away early and had a great day, ending up near Hindford, Oswestry. We moored right outside the Jack Mytton Inn. This is a famous canal-side pub with a long, not to say infamous, history. It has extensive gardens and at that time was a high-quality restaurant. I had the best fillet steak ever in that place, then walked 20 yards to the boat along the towpath for a good night's rest.

Because of that leak, we didn't get as far down the Llangollen Canal as we had hoped. We stopped at Ellesmere to pick up Jonathan and girlfriend Jo. But made time for a proper family lunch on my 60th birthday when we moored just outside Ellesmere, where there are a series of wide, picturesque lakes – so-called 'meres'. It was a glorious sunny afternoon. We had a great spot in the shade, so it was cool inside the boat with a gentle breeze flowing through. We all crammed together in the lounge area at the front of the boat – Nick, Sue, Sylvia, Jonathan, Jo, me and Lindsay, plus Bagins of course. Out of the fridge came pies, meats, pickles, salad stuffs, cheeses, beer, water and so on. Out of the kettle, tea and coffee.

We stayed by that mere for a couple of hours, then upped mooring pins and set off for Wrenbury.

I realised very late that teaching others to drive a narrowboat causes considerable delays to any set schedule. Nick was very good, but sister-in-law Sue didn't really take to it. As we approached the Wrenbury lift bridge, she ended up at the bow with the two other ladies. This was our first experience of an electrified bridge. There are plenty of manual lift bridges on the Llangollen; this one would not involve strenuous cranking but was going to hold up traffic if we dallied. Lindsay and Nick got off the boat and went to investigate the bridge control console. I stayed at the stern, ready to drive under as soon as it had lifted.

It would not lift. The barriers came down, but the bridge stayed closed. I could see the cars beginning to queue on either side and could feel my anxiety levels rising rapidly. After what seemed an eternity, Nick collared a passer-by who told him that he had to insert the British Waterways key, turn it and hold it one way while simultaneously pressing another button. An interlock system. At last it went up and I drove through accompanied by cheers and jeers from the watching masses. However, it is a tight turn past the ABC boatyard at that point and I was now frazzled and going too fast – not to mention I'd forgotten that the bridge had to come down and the crew had to get back on board. So to the delight of all those watching, all those in cars parked either side of the bridge, the rest of the crew and the boatyard personnel, I didn't make the turn and drove the boat straight into a mass of overhanging vegetation, where we disappeared from view. Sister-in-law didn't think much of that, haranguing me later.

We had hoped to get to the bottom of the Hurleston flight before turning back, but after a mile or two, we came across a winding hole and decided to turn around and look for a pub. This was my first experience of 'winding' a narrowboat on my own. To this day I don't know the true origin of the term 'winding' or even how to say it. There are so many opinions. Is it 'winding' as in 'there is a strong wind today' or 'winding' as in 'winding our way down a twisty track'? Did boat people of yore use the wind to assist in turning around or did they use a wound-up rope to gradually pull a boat round? However, I knew what to do because on the training course we had used the winding hole near Kidderminster.

The next day we returned to Grindley Brook and its staircase of three lock chambers. Our aim was to get back to Chirk Marina. It was a Sunday, and the place was packed with boats and people. There was a queue for the lock that began at the two locks below Grindley. Staircase locks are always manned by Canal and River Trust (CRT) lock keepers because of the danger of flooding should a crew get the sequence wrong. The CRT team were operating on three boats up then three boats down sequence – the most efficient, water-saving procedure for three chambers. I manoeuvred the boat into the bottom chamber as soon as its last occupant came out. Jo and Jonathan closed the gates behind us. The top two chambers would have been empty of boats but full of water. CRT opened the paddles above me, and water flooded in from the chamber above – but a little too fast for my liking. I had been taught to balance the boat in a lock using the engine but, on this occasion, the turbulent water pushed me back. I surged forward again and bounced off the front gates.

It was then I noticed that all the gates at Gridley were mitred pairs. I'd not met that before. All the top gates in all the locks thus far, without exception, had been single and flat.

Jonathan was up on the lock edge, reminding me (yelling actually) of the 'put the bow on the front gate' technique and to use the engine to keep it there. I hesitated because I didn't know of the risk that the boat's bow might get caught in the 'V'. However, it worked, and the boat rose quite smartly in the lock, riding the front gates all the way up. When the water levels equalised, CRT opened the gates so we could proceed into the next chamber. That process was repeated for the next chamber, while another boat came into the lower one we had just vacated. We made it to the top chamber without further yelling or incident, collected the crew and set off for one more overnight stop before getting back to Chirk Marina.

The next morning, we dropped off Jonathan, Jo, Nick and Sue at Ellesmere. That left just Lindsay, Sylvia and me on board. Sylvia tended to stay in the warm in the main cabin – appropriate on that day because it was cold and exceptionally windy. This became another of those days where a big lesson would be learnt. Wind, no not that kind – the howling kind. (Although the former kind within the confined space of a narrowboat cabin needs to be avoided if at all possible.) Narrowboats weigh some 15 tons, so one would think that a bit of a gale would not be a problem. You would be wrong. It's typically 60 feet of slab-sided steel which acts like a gigantic flag and although it can't flap like a flag, it can sail like a sail, pushing the boat sideways.

A lot of the Llangollen, travelling west, after Ellesmere is up high on an embankment. On that day the wind was howling across the boat. Without prompt action, the boat would have ended up pinned to one or other canal side and never get off. Being pinned to the non-towpath side could be disastrous because the boat would end up buried in shallow water, in amongst all the offside vegetation that's both above and below the waterline.

That prompt action was instinctive, I am pleased to say. The wind[4] was blowing powerfully from the port side. It was necessary to point

---

[4] One of the trickiest situations in windy conditions is having to wait, or loiter, for another boat to pass by. If there is a cross-wind coming from the right, it will try to push your boat onto the oncoming craft. If there is a cross-wind coming from the left, it will try to push your boat onto the offside of the canal where mud or underwater vegetation and lumps of rock will ground the boat. The only advice I can offer is to try and keep the boat moving. Do not let the boat be pushed onto the offside where the only remedy may be to use the long pole and push out the stern. Use small forward or backward movements combined with left and right tiller

the bow into the wind and sort of crab along – moving forward with the boat almost diagonally across the canal. In places, especially on bends, the boat got right across the canal and almost jammed up at both ends simultaneously. If the wind had been any stronger or the canal any narrower, we would have been stuck with no option but to moor up and wait for the weather to improve.

However, we did make progress and got back to the Jack Mytton Inn by late afternoon. Sylvia made us tea – Lindsay and I had got very cold – and we then went into the warm of the pub for a meal. It got dark around 7.30pm in September and after our meal we clambered back onto the boat, played some cards and then turned in for the night. However, in the dark, I had not noticed there were no fenders down the towpath side of the boat. As soon as the engine was turned off, it became evident that the wind was playing havoc with the mooring lines, even though we had been able to tie up to mooring rings, leaving the metal hull crashing about onto the concrete canal edges. My God, it did make a racket, and although Lindsay and I could probably have got to sleep, Sylvia really could not cope. No other choice then than to step outside into the dark, into that howling gale and lashing rain, loosen off the lines, push the fenders down the boat side and re-tighten the ropes. The boat still moved around but without the sound.

We made it back to Chirk Marina the next afternoon – on time, having had a great week on the water and having learnt a few of many good lessons.

---

movements to try to keep the boat in position around a small figure-of-eight track. Bit like trying to balance an egg on a flat plate. With practice it works very well but do expect a few gentle scrapes as you learn the technique. Narrowboating is after all a contact sport.

Chapter 4
Four Counties Ring 2006

Our next trip was the Four Counties Ring. This time on a 70-foot Black Prince narrowboat with a cruiser stern. The Four Counties Ring takes in the counties of Cheshire, Shropshire, Staffordshire and West Midlands. Highlights include the Industrial Canal Heritage of the Stoke-on-Trent potteries region, the wealthy pasturelands of Cheshire and the stunning remote sandstone cuttings of Shropshire. This route, which is 110 miles long and includes 94 locks, is a favourite with holiday boaters. The ring traverses parts of five canals – Wardle Canal, Staffordshire and Worcestershire Canal, Shropshire Union Canal and the Trent and Mersey Canal.

We had cousins Nick and Dinny along, together with Sue and Nick Hamer, Bagins and Sylvia. We decided to do it in a week, which actually turned out a bit of a stretch.

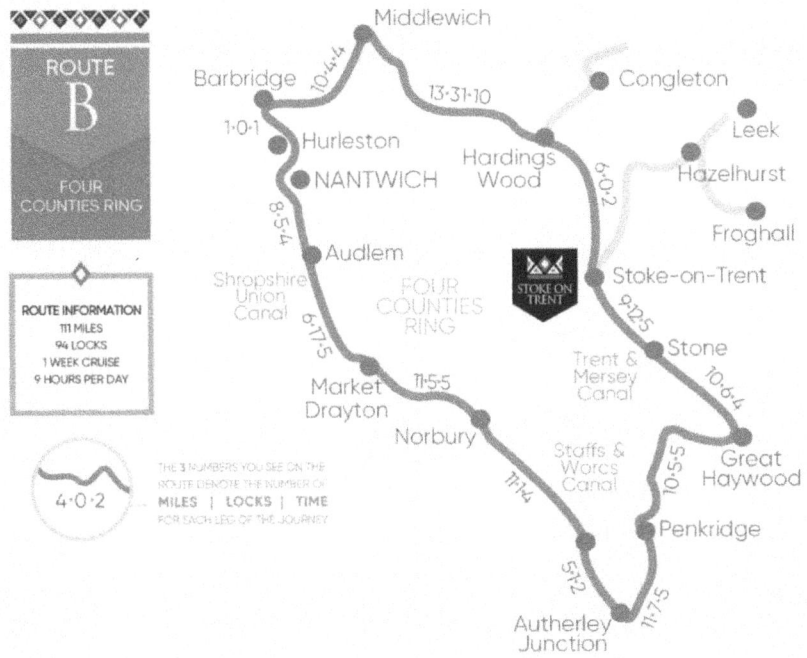

Map 02

We began from Etruria Junction just outside Stoke on Trent, where there is a Black Prince hire base. Immediately there was a problem with the boat – it had a list. I checked the bilge, which was dry, and then realised that one of the three loos on board had not been pumped out. So about halfway round came our first experience of toilet pump-out machines. These are easy to use but not pleasant to be around. And in 15 years of boating, we have never again had to seek one out.

The first challenge was to navigate the Harecastle Tunnel, just north of Etruria. Harecastle Tunnel is on the Trent and Mersey Canal in Staffordshire between Kidsgrove and Tunstall. The tunnel, 1.5 miles long, was once the longest in the country. Its original purpose was for the transport of coal to the kilns in the Staffordshire Potteries.

There were two working tunnels originally. The first, completed and in operation by 1780, was designed by James Brindley. It had no towpath.

Boats were propelled through by 'legging', where crew members laid on their backs on boat roofs and used their feet to push on the canal roof. Within 20 years, however, the tunnel had reached capacity and by 1830 a new tunnel designed by Thomas Telford was in operation. This one had a towpath allowing horses to pull narrowboats through, plus many internal branches off to coal local mines. The two tunnels operated a one-way system with each tunnel taking traffic in one direction.

Harecastle Tunnel southern portal

© Copyright Roger Kidd

The Brindley Tunnel subsequently suffered serious subsidence and was closed in 1904. The Telford Tunnel operates today but with severe restrictions. It was wide enough when built for two narrowboats to pass inside, but nowadays that is not possible and a one-way system operates. Boats go through in batches – a northbound batch and then a southbound one, and so on, closely controlled by CRT supervisors.

Ventilation was always a problem and now a set of huge fans push foul air out of the tunnel.

The southern entrance, called a 'portal', is a strange place. Getting there requires passing through the industrial bits of Stoke on Trent, some derelict and some modern. Nick started at the tiller. He was a bit meandry to start with, not surprising since it would have been a year since he last drove a narrowboat. As we approached the tunnel, the water turned an orange colour, a consequence of groundwater containing iron oxide leaching from the tunnel walls.

At the entrance we were met by CRT staff who beckoned us over to the landing stage side. We were to be the first boat through that day. We were given a good talking to, safety stuff mainly, and warned about the meanders inside the tunnel. They advised we should don waterproof gear, including hats, since the tunnel leaked like a sieve, they said.

Before we got into the tunnel, we switched on the headlight and all internal lights. Nick was at the tiller with me alongside him on the boat's rear counter. Everyone else was in the cabin in the dry. The boat moved forward into the dark. Then a massive crash echoed behind us as steel doors closed over the entrance. A howling gale appeared from nowhere as the ventilation fans came on. We were in pitch black apart from our own cabin lights, reflecting on walls literally running with water.

My God, what a hellhole. Nick (Hamer) had trouble keeping the boat in the middle, away from both walls, not helped by constant tunnel meanders left and right. We could see almost nothing ahead and at times thought we were about to run into a dead-end. There were still fumes in there and a constant soaking deluge from the roof. It was just Nick and me on the stern, but I could do little to help him steer – I would be no better at it than him.

We then met a section where the boat could not be kept straight. It hit the left wall, bounced back and hit the right wall while all the time ploughing on in the dark at 1.5 miles per hour. The engine note kept changing, an indicator of varying depth. Suddenly there was a God-almighty bang and a startled yell from Nick – the tiller arm had hit the sidewall as he tried to correct the boat's path and broken off. We had no steering and Nick very nearly had no hand. He quickly realised that it was just the wooden bit that had gone and that he could still steer using the short metal stub arm.

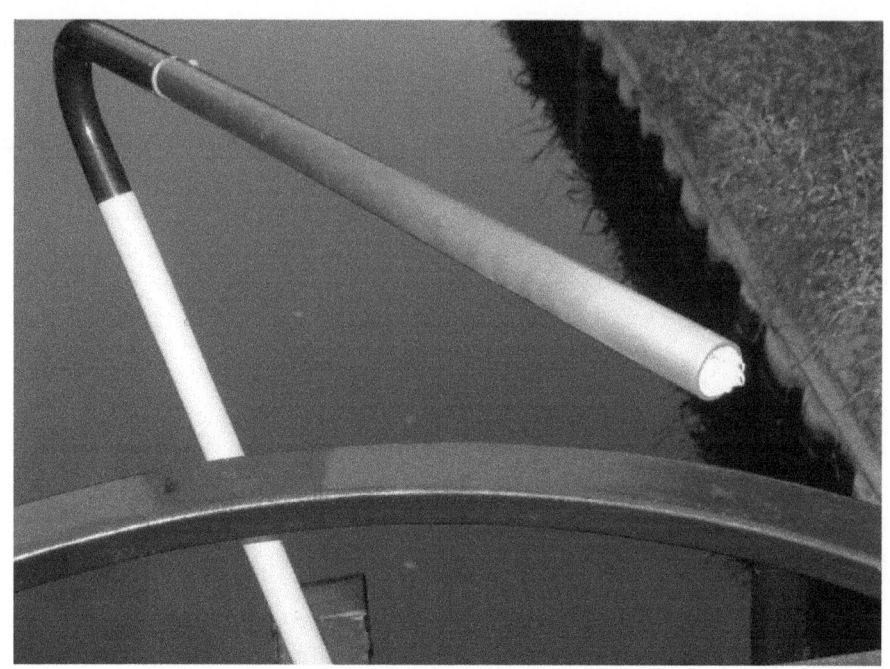

Tiller arm damaged in Harecastle Tunnel

The tiller could still steer the boat but needed much more force. That was not a problem at a mile and a bit per hour but would seriously delay us if we could not do 4mph on the straight bits out in the countryside. We had no choice but to continue onward. At times the tunnel roof was so low that Nick and I had to squat on our haunches to avoid getting our heads knocked off.

We finally saw a pinprick of light at the far end. We had been in there for well over an hour, were both soaked and couldn't wait for some fresh air and light. I recall that once out we moored up as soon as we could, made a hot drink and ate cake.

Heartbreak Hill

The next challenge was a series of 31 locks over 13 miles that would take over ten hours of boating time. So on that first day we would go through about half of them and then moor up overnight. Boaters from yore called them Heartbreak Hill locks, but their proper names are the Cheshire locks. They are narrow locks but, uniquely, are paired with two locks side by side. Most have working pairs, but some are chained off or literally derelict.

There was nothing special to report during that descent, apart from the lock gear being well maintained and easy to operate. But we were all still narrowboat novices and we did learn a lesson. It went like this: some of the pairs are close together. We were exiting one pair, making sure all the paddles were down and in the process of closing the lower gate – we were going downhill you see. The boat was out of the lock, waiting. We then heard a manic hooting from another boat coming towards us. The skipper was gesticulating wildly but was too far away for voice communication. We all waved back, which caused him to wave and hoot even more vigorously. I could see he was yelling at us because his jaw was going up and down and his tongue kept popping out of his mouth. But the wind was in his face, and we heard no sounds. As he got nearer, I could see he was single-handed. By then we had closed the lower gate and were just getting going. Suddenly I realised that his manic calling was to tell us to leave the gate open so he could sail right in. Nick and Nick leapt off and reopened it. His boat came in like a bloody express train – he absolutely apoplectic and the colour of a ripe cherry.

Somewhat shamefully we got on and out of his way poste-haste. The lesson learnt was that on a long flight of locks, it's a joy to see a boat coming out of a lock, so you can wait for it to pull clear and then sail right in. That situation is known as a lock being 'in your favour' as opposed to being 'against you'. The joy is heightened if you are a single-handed boater simply because of the time and effort it saves. The lesson is to be sure to always look around and be aware of approaching craft and assist if necessary.

Shropshire Union Canal

We set off early the next day – it was going to be a long one. We shared out time at the tiller with Sue and Nick, then Nick and Dinny, then me on my own – Lindsay did not want to drive the boat that much.

We navigated the remaining Cheshire locks and approached the junction with the Wardle Canal. I made a mess of the tight left turn there. I managed to tee-bone the abutment of the bridge over the entrance – it was exceptionally windy, and I lost control of the bow. But it was very early in my boating life. We cruised up the Wardle and then turned south onto the Shropshire Union Canal at Barbridge.

Boating down the Shropshire Union is a glorious experience. A lot of the canal is in the bottom of a deep cutting which makes the tall trees seem gigantic. And all the bridges have arches high in the sky as if they are on stilts. The 'Shroppie', as is known locally, is a narrow canal and it takes care driving through those narrow bridge holes. The temptation is to slow right down and glide through, but that does waste so much time. A narrowboat weighs over 15 tons and doesn't slow or accelerate quickly. After a while, having got one's eye in, they can be taken without slowing too much, especially if there is a lookout on both sides. We sailed past Hurleston Junction. This is where the eastern end of the Llangollen Canal begins and where we had tried to get to the year before. We have got to know that junction well over the years. Then on to Audlem – a famous boating town. That turned into a bit of an event.

Audlem

We found ourselves in the lock outside the famous 'Shroppie Fly' pub at the foot of the Audlem 15-lock flight. We had opened the gates. I put the boat into forward gear and increased the engine revs. Nothing happened. More revs. Still nothing. We all looked at each other and after a while decided we would bow-haul the boat out of the lock and tie up. We dispatched Sylvia off to the pub with her book while we pondered. Nick thought there might be a problem with the prop so, with the boat tied up, I engaged forward gear and peered down into the engine compartment. Sure enough the prop shaft was rotating. It had to be either a fouled propeller or some damage under the water.

The next step was a bit of security. I stopped the engine, took the keys from the ignition and handed them to Nick – or was it Nick? I found the Stanley knife and some wire cutters and opened up the engine room cover. The weed hatch[5] was somewhere in the depths at the stern. I

---

[5] All narrowboats have a weed hatch at the stern, accessed from the engine compartment below the rear deck. The weed hatch allows the boat's propeller (prop) to be inspected from above and cleared of weed and other obstructions. Clearing a prop is a dirty, cold and arduous task for which long arms, wire cutters and sharp knives are a necessity. There is a danger element too – the hatch is held in place by

lowered myself down but could not find enough space for my feet so back up and off with the shoes. I had to be careful because there was oil and hot stuff down there. I could reach the weed hatch cover, which I unscrewed and removed to reveal a tank of murky canal water. However, there was no room to bend down and I realised I was going to have to reach a long way into the canal so back up, strip off to my vest, back down and try somehow to kneel. But it was oily, so back up, find a couple of tea towels on which to kneel and back down.

I eventually got my arm into the water up to my armpit and began to feel around the prop. It was completely wrapped up in frayed mooring line. The water was icy. Nick or Nick passed me the knife and I began hacking away. I guess we were there for about 20 minutes. Bagins the dog had been getting restless. Sue let had him off his lead so he could mooch around. I never noticed him behind me.

I managed to pull out about ten feet of rope and finally clear the prop. I straightened up somewhat gingerly, turned round to pull the rope onto the deck and was confronted by yellow teeth, stinky breath, an excited but ugly black face, two huge yellow slits for eyes and a very long slobbery tongue. That tongue then got stuck in to give me a vigorous slapping and slurping. A huge dose of doggy slobber, in my eyes, in my ears and up my nose. It went on forever – I had been bent double for so long I could not get away. I was offered no help – the crew were also bent double, tears rolling down their faces.

---

a horizontal steel bar. This must be carefully replaced and tightened after the prop has been de-fouled. Failure to do that will sink the boat.

One way that might prevent a trip down the weed hatch is to first stop the boat and put the engine in neutral. Then put the engine in reverse and apply maximum power for a few seconds. In many situations, that will unwrap what was around the prop, allowing the boat to continue.

Always wash up after being in the water, especially if using tools has resulted in a cut.

Bagins

I was in the bathroom for quite a while. Once we were ready to get going, me cleaned up, keys back in the ignition and with Sylvia cheerfully reading and chatting to new friends in the pub, we decided we would tackle the 15-lock ascent up the Audlem flight. We had lost some time and since this can be problematic on a hired craft, we decided we would try a bit of 'lock-wheeling'.

During World War II, goods were transported by boats operating a scheduled 24/7 service between London and Birmingham. 'Lock-wheeling' was an important part of keeping to the agreed schedule. It recognises the fact that a crew member can go ahead of the boat as many locks as they wish, setting (i.e., emptying the lock if going uphill or filling the lock if going downhill) each lock in your favour as they go. It doesn't matter if another boat comes past in the opposite direction because that boat must have left each lock once more in your favour. This procedure does take a bit of getting one's head around. On the London to Birmingham run, especially at night, lock-wheelers would use bikes to go miles ahead on stretches where there were no wharfs that could put a boat ahead. Of course, what you can't do is to open all the lock gates along the way!

Audlem is a flight of narrow locks. We had to empty the first before I could drive in. Nick closed the rear gates and then went round to open the paddles. We had agreed he and I would eyeball each other during the entire flight, for I was concerned about being on my own when the boat was rising in the lock. Sue and Lindsay went ahead emptying each lock ready for us. Of course, had a boat come down before they started, their efforts would not be necessary – other than opening the next set of gates so we could sail straight in. We got to the top in no time, moored up and then walked back down to collect Sylvia. She was being chatted up and had not noticed how long we had been gone.

Over the next few days, we passed through Market Drayton, Norbury, Autherley Junction, Great Heyward and on to Stone. We had turned north now and were heading back to the hire base at Etruria.

We had arranged to meet two of Nick Hamer's adult children at the Star Inn in Stone. I dropped everyone off the boat at the lock outside the pub and then went on to find moorings within the town. That was the first time I had been on a narrowboat on my own. It was a warm, calm September evening and that little journey has stayed firmly in my mind over all these years. It was so peaceful, just gently drifting up the canal looking for space to moor. Just me, and 15 tons of 70-foot narrowboat.

Stone is a famous canal market town. The first meeting of the Grand Trunk Canal Company (later the Trent and Mersey Canal Company) was held in the Crown Inn, Stone, on 10th June 1766. At this meeting *James Brindley* was appointed Surveyor-General, *John Sparrow* Clerk and *Josiah Wedgwood* Treasurer. In 1767 it was decided to locate the headquarters of the canal company in the town. The arrival of the canal in Stone changed the town, to quote from a contemporary source, "from a sleepy market town into a busy inland sea port".

Nick Hamer, Sue, Lindsay and Sylvia

We got back to Etruria on time. Nick and Dinny had got off a few days earlier. It had been a great adventure on a waterway completely different from the Llangollen the previous year.

Squadron Leader Nicholas Hamer

Nick Hamer's lung cancer had been confirmed by this time and he was to undergo treatment, followed by palliative care over the next three years. He died in 2010. Nick was a flight engineer officer in the RAF at the time he retired. He could speak fluent German, having been brought up in Belgium. He was a member of the UN's nuclear inspectorate. He played an important role in reporting on Russian and East German military activity in Berlin before the fall of the Berlin Wall in 1989.

I liked and respected Nick Hamer. He was not the arrogant military officer type I often met in my professional life. He was knowledgeable on many subjects, especially antique art, but listened to learn about those he was not. He was sociable, of course, and a smoker and that killed him in the end. He loved boating with us. It was a new experience for him. I'm sure that would have continued had he been given the chance.

Chapter 5
Monmouthshire and Brecon Canal May 2007

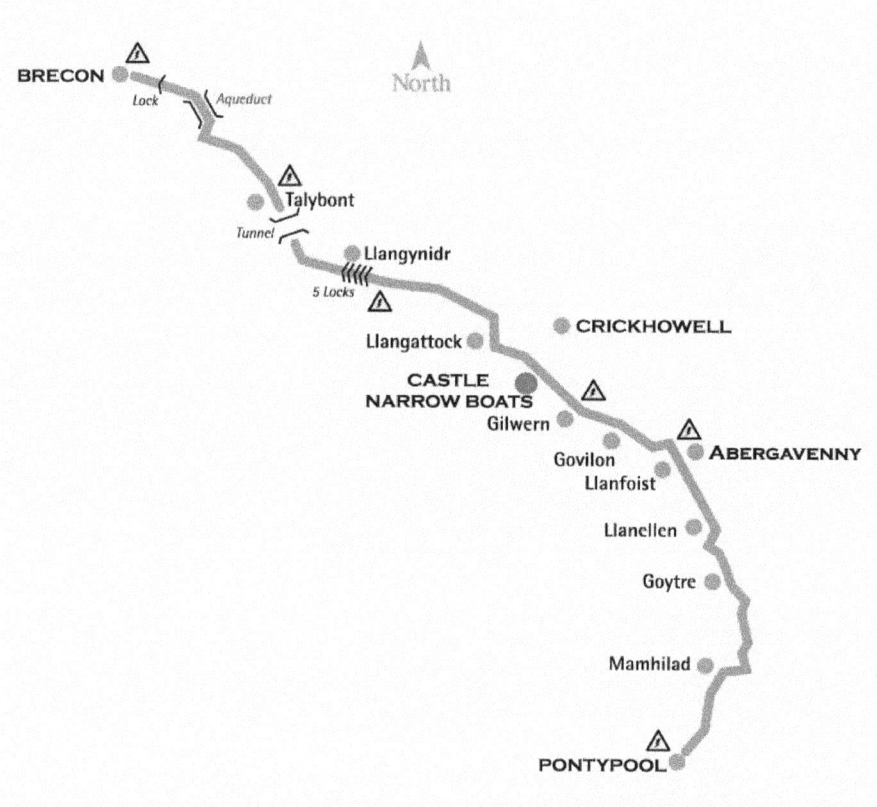

Monmouthshire and Brecon Canal

© Copyright Castle Narrowboats

Map 03

The Monmouthshire and Brecon Canal covers 33 miles of beautiful, rural Welsh countryside from Brecon to Pontypool, much of which lies within the Brecon Beacons National Park. There are only six locks, but a number of lift bridges, a tunnel and an aqueduct over the scenic River Usk.

This was to be the first narrowboat holiday that Lindsay and I would experience on our own. The canal raised a number of challenges, not the least of which was that it didn't have a great deal of water.

We collected the boat from Cambrian Cruisers, just south of Brecon. She was a masterpiece of design I have to say – one of the best layouts we have experienced. She was the first cruiser-stern design we had met. Our other boats had semi-trad sterns that were somewhat enclosed, with not much space for more than three on the rear deck (the Counter) at one time.

The first noticeable thing was how much the boat rolled as we got on board and as we moved around. That was a portent of what was to come, in that the boat was designed to have a very shallow draft – i.e., there was only about a foot and a half under water, thus making her top-heavy. The reason for that design soon became evident.

We set off from Talybont and headed north, through one lock and on into Brecon for an overnight stay. Brecon Basin is a fine spot, great moorings on rings and immediate access to the town. We found a rather good Indian restaurant within a few minutes' walk. The canal's water supply comes from a weir on the River Usk and then via a 2,000-metre culvert into Brecon Basin – the canal's high point.

We had hired the boat for just four days and anticipated getting to the end of the canal and back in that time. It's a little under three miles from Brecon Basin to the first lock at Brynich. The canal then crosses the River Usk on an aqueduct. We stopped to admire the views and eat doughnuts.

View from the aqueduct over the River Usk

We then met the electrified lift bridge at Talybont. I was a bit nervous about the procedure there, having had that kerfuffle at Wrenbury on the Llangollen. I moored up and then held the boat before the bridge and let Lindsay off so she could, bravely, go and investigate. In the event, she coped admirably. The traffic stopped, the bridge went up, I got back on board and steered the boat underneath, then moored again on the far side. She let the bridge down, restored the roadway, ran back to the boat and we got under way feeling a bit chuffed. That didn't last long.

Next up was a short but very wet tunnel. Then the problems – you see the canal is very twisty and very shallow. That was why the boat had a minimal draft. And I had not yet learnt the golden rule never to cut the corner on a bend – always steer the boat right around the outside of a bend or at the very least as close to the outside as possible. We immediately became grounded on the mud.

Generally speaking, the best way off any mud is backwards, the way you got on. We tried reversing, but that just sucked the boat down further. The only way out was to use the long pole to push the bow sideways into deeper water, plus hang off the side so the boat lists. So I went forward onto the bow and pushed with the pole while Lindsay hung off the side of the boat at the stern, simultaneously applying just enough engine power to push gently sideways and forward. It worked, but we had to have that pole near to hand for the entire week.

There are then five locks in quick succession at Llangynidr. The final 23 miles from Llangynidr to Pontymoile Basin, north of Pontypool, are lock-free.

It was springtime, leafy, peaceful and gorgeous with all the trees and hedges in bud. The canal follows the contours of the hillsides for most of its route, giving lovely views into the valleys below. After boating through Llangattock, Gilwern, Govilon and gawping into residents' often spectacular gardens, we reached Llanfoist near Abergavenny. This is a most magical location, almost tropical forest or the nearest possible in the UK. The canal sits in a valley with tall mixed deciduous trees on either side and with shafts of dappled sunlight wafting across the water.

We were only out for four days, but because of slow progress through shallow water, we were not going to reach the canal's terminus. I realised we had to turn around soon after Llanfoist – but no winding hole in sight. Lindsay wanted to go further, but I was nervous we would get committed and not be able to return the boat on time. In the event I found a spot slightly wider than the boat and managed to change direction via a 20-point turn.

Returning through Llanfoist, there is a tricky bit of boating required. The canal makes a 90-degree turn to the left under a small canal bridge. We did that well enough but then found ourselves up against a hard wall on our left, heading towards a dead-end and a fibreglass cruiser moored ahead. Now, 15-ton steel narrowboats and plastic cruisers do not like meeting up. With the stern just out from under the bridge, I had to bring the boat to a dead stop. Lindsay then went up to the bow and pushed it sideways using the pole – sort of a human bow thruster. We waited patiently while the boat gently drifted through 90 degrees to the right and then got under way. We got back on time.

Chapter 6
Warwickshire Ring September 2007

This time we hired for two weeks because the Warwickshire Ring entails 190 locks over 130 miles. Cousin Nick and wife Dinny came with us, as did mother-in-law Sylvia.

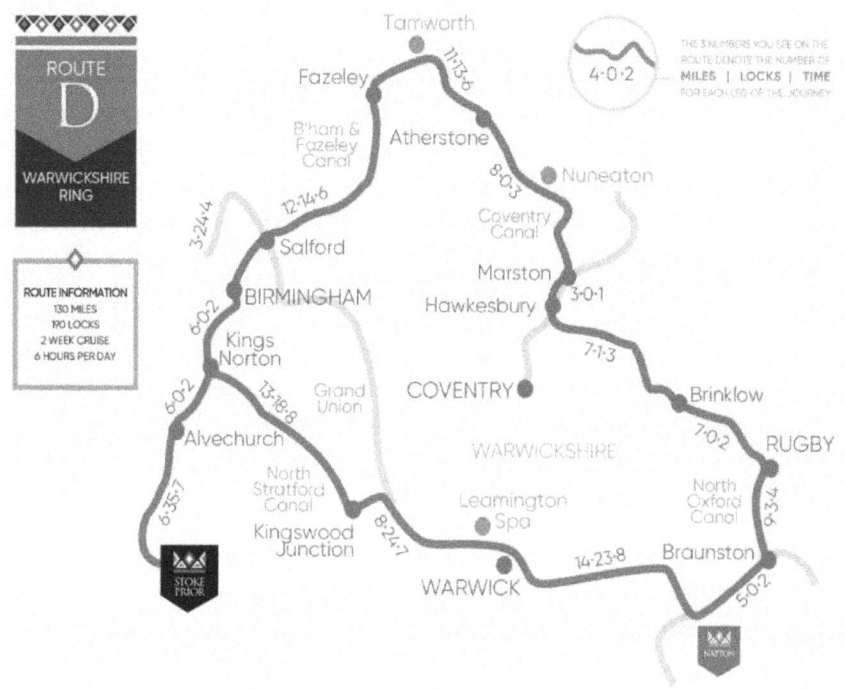

The Warwickshire Ring

© Copyright Black Prince Holidays

Map 04

Again, a 70-foot Black Prince narrowboat which we collected from Wigrams Turn Marina at Napton, near Warwick. This trip presented some new challenges, not the least of which was to be a long flight of wide locks (Hatton) on the Grand Union Canal. Our previous boating holidays had been on narrow canals with narrow locks for boats with a maximum beam (width) of 6 foot 10 inches and length 72 feet. The Grand Union Canal is for broad-beam boats of up to 12 feet wide and 72 feet in length. Locks are 14 feet 2 inches wide and can fit two narrowboats side by side or one broad-beam boat. So you can see, locks on broad canals are a lot bigger than narrow locks and that raised the question of the best way of handling the boat in a Grand Union lock.

The pair of gates at the top of each wide lock are much bigger and heavier than their narrow lock counterparts. Water flow from the paddles (usually ground paddles) is much higher and turbulence going uphill can be an issue. Once a paddle is opened, water flows in fast and under the boat, hitting the bottom lock, bouncing back and pushing the boat forward. This effect is much stronger in a wide lock, so had to be thought about in advance.

And think about it I did. Worried myself a bit if the truth be known. Boats can be sunk in wide locks if the captain and crew are inexperienced or not paying attention. A narrowboat in a narrow lock can only move forward and back. A narrowboat in a wide lock can also move sideways across the lock, ending up on the wrong side. One of the nice things is that a narrowboat can get in or out of a wide lock with only one of the gates opened – saving a great deal of work. So one does not want to end up on the wrong side. See note 14 on page 298.

I had learnt a little on the visit to the Mon and Brec last year, where the canal is a narrow canal but wider than in the rest of the UK. It can take boats up to a beam of 9 foot 2 inches. A narrowboat of 6 foot 10 inches can therefore move sideways in locks. What I learnt was to keep the centre line with me at all times on lock side or towpath so that the boat can be pulled over if need be. And that is how we set out to tackle the wide locks of the Grand Union. When going uphill, the centre line would be thrown from below up to the canal side, ready to pull the boat over once it had risen in the lock. When going downhill, the centre line would be thrown onto the ground so that a crew member could use it to keep the boat to one side as it descended the lock. The line would be pulled back onto the boat before exit from the lock.

Actually, as we got more experienced in wide locks, we learnt to use the short pole at the stern to control sideways movement. Nevertheless, we always had the centre line to hand on or off the boat – wise thing to do.

We collected the boat, did the usual handover procedure from the Black Prince team and set off to find the marina exit – it's huge. Then turned left to begin our uphill climb towards Birmingham.

The first locks we met were at Calcutt – a flight of three but not too close together. Sylvia stayed in the bow and was in charge of chucking the bow line up onto the lock side. I stayed at the tiller while the rest of the crew managed the gates and paddles. Nick emptied the lock and opened one gate and I sailed in, staying in the longitudinal middle of the lock, with the boat against one wall. Just me and Sylvia on board. She chucked the bow line up to Dinny, who wound it loosely round a bollard – OK to do that because the rope was going to get shorter as the boat came up in the lock. Then Nick and Lindsay opened one paddle – slowly was the name of the game. The boat started to move forward, which I controlled with the engine. When one paddle was up to three-quarters height, Lindsay opened up the other, considerably increasing water ingress rate. But that was OK, the boat remained controllable throughout and we rose gently up to lock side. The boat did drift across but was quickly hauled in using the bow rope and the centre line, which I could cast onto the path.

We were then quite adventurous on that first afternoon in going on to tackle the Stockton flight of ten locks, which raise the Grand Union Canal by about 50 feet. Each lock is on average some 400 yards from its neighbours, meaning the crew could walk from lock to lock, preparing each for the arrival of the boat. Sylvia and I were the ones on board. We made good progress. Handling the boat in these uphill locks was uneventful and with the sun now setting behind us, we moored up by the canal towpath and made dinner. It looked like my fears of wide locks had been unfounded.

The next day we navigated the nine locks of Long Itchington followed by a lengthy section past Royal Leamington Spa. Nick and Dinny took turns to drive the boat – both were very good – Nick a natural, with Dinny excellent but once or twice pushing the tiller the wrong way, making us veer off towards the bank and giving all of us on the bow a fright. We moored for the night right by Tesco, hoping it would not attract too many joy riders liking nothing more than casting boats adrift in the small hours.

Warwick Castle

The next day we left the boat and took a taxi to Warwick Castle just a few miles away.

Warwick is a medieval castle developed from a wooden fort built by William the Conqueror during 1068. The original wooden motte-and-bailey castle was rebuilt in stone during the 12th century. In the 14th and 15th centuries it was home to the Neville's – one of the most powerful families in England. And specifically, home to Sir Richard Neville, known as 'The Kingmaker' and his brother John Neville. Both men had daughters called Anne Neville – one became Queen of England when she married King Richard III and the other Anne was my eighteenth great grandmother.

None of us had been to the castle before and I didn't know then of the historical connection. We split up and made our way round separately. It was hugely impressive I have to say, and for that reason I've included brief descriptions of each of the major features.

Great Hall

The Great Hall is the largest room in the castle. It is approximately 12 metres high, 19 metres long and 14 metres wide including the window bays. It was first constructed in the 14th century, when a fire would have been in the centre of the room with a hole in the roof to let out the smoke, and the walls contained small narrow windows and some arrow loops. The original hall would have been similar in size and grandeur, but the current Great Hall was rebuilt in the 17th century to provide a grand entrance for those visiting the Earl of Warwick. It was largely restored in 1871 following a great fire which destroyed the old hall. Today the Great Hall stands as a romantic reinvention of a medieval hall and was designed to reflect the vast history of the castle. It holds the remnants of the Earls' famous weapons and armour collection that was acquired throughout the 19th century. It contains equestrian armour, pole arms, rifles, parade armour, and a suit of child's armour, amongst many other treasures.

Within the Great Hall is the Kenilworth Buffet, one of the most impressive items in the collection. It was made for the Great Exhibition of 1851 by Cookes and Sons of Warwick, who were awarded a prize medal for their craftsmanship. The buffet is made from a single oak tree which grew at Kenilworth Castle and was cut down in 1842. In 1852 the buffet was presented to George Greville, Lord Brooke, as a wedding gift from the people of Warwickshire.

State Dining Room

Francis Greville commissioned this room in 1763. It was designed and built by some of 18th-century England's finest craftsmen. This room has seen some impressive dinner parties and distinguished party guests over the years. Some of the most illustrious guests include Queen Victoria and Prince Albert, who had lunch here in 1858, Edward, Prince of Wales, later King Edward VII, and Queen Elizabeth II and Prince Philip, Duke of Edinburgh, who completed their visit with lunch in this room in 1996. At the far end of the room hangs a famous portrait of King Charles I on horseback with his Master of Horse, Chevalier Saint Antoine. It is one of a handful of virtually identical pictures produced in the studio of Sir Anthony Van Dyck.

Red Drawing Room

The Red Drawing Room is the first of the state rooms and primarily served as an anteroom. Its red lacquer panelling and enclosed space was designed to realign the expectations of guests before passing through to the lavish rooms ahead. The room is primarily filled with portraits and artefacts from the 16th century.

Cedar Drawing Room

This room is named after its intricate 17th-century cedar panelling which was completed in the 1670s by William and Roger Hurlbutt. It is at the heart of the state rooms and was used for hosting grand festivities over the centuries, including banquets and ballroom dancing. The room has a distinctly Italian style. The plaster ceiling, originally designed by James Pettifer, was gilded in the 19th century to replicate the baroque ceilings of the Renaissance, and the room was filled with impressive items collected by the 3rd Earl of Warwick throughout his grand tour of Europe. The five chandeliers in this room date from the mid-15th to the late 19th century.

Green Drawing Room

This room is aptly named to reflect its green painted panelling. The room functioned largely as a private gentlemen's room for travelling aristocrats to rest and play in the comfort of this tranquil space. The beautiful coffered ceiling, made up of octagonal sunken panels with central motifs, was inspired by the ceiling of the Temple of Bel in Palmyra, Syria. Unfortunately, the temple was destroyed in the conflict in Syria in 2015, so this ceiling has become more poignant since that event. The ceiling was installed in the 1750s by Francis Greville, 1st Earl of Warwick. Within the room is a mysterious secret door which hides a 14th-century escape. This hidden stairway and passage lead down to the River Avon below.

Queen Ann Bedroom

The Queen Anne Bedroom was formerly known as the State Bedroom and was renamed in 1773 after Queen Anne's furniture was given to Francis Greville, 1st Earl of Warwick, by King George III. The bed had been part of the bedroom suite in Queen Anne's State Bedchamber at Kensington Palace. Anne died of a stroke in her bed at Kensington Palace in 1714, and this bed was almost certainly her deathbed. The incredible tapestries surrounding this room were created by Franciscus Spiringius in 1604 in Delft, Belgium. They illustrate the gardens of a medieval palace, and the detail is extraordinary, with flowers, animals, insects, objects and people all intricately woven into the design. It is probable that the tapestries were acquired by Sir Fulke Greville.

Blue Boudoir

This small and intimate room was redecorated by Daisy Greville, 5th Countess of Warwick, in the 1890s to convert the private dressing room into a ladies' boudoir. Daisy sought a room in which to host the ladies during a party whilst the men occupied the Green Drawing Room. The blue silk that adorns the walls is from Lyon and reflects Daisy's love of French style and culture. This is added to by the display of Marie Antoinette's silver-faced clock.

River Island

This is an island on the River Avon where we watched brave 'knights' face each other during a mock battle, followed by a longbow competition and finally jousting. It also houses the trebuchet, a huge stone-throwing machine used to batter castle battlements. The machine is an accurate replica, and I can vouch that it hurls huge boulders a very long way.

Trebuchet Machine at Warwick Castle

The most famous use for the island was in the 1890s when the 5th Countess of Warwick housed her exotic menagerie of animals on the island. Some of the more unusual animals included Japanese deer, peacocks, an emu, monkeys, an ant bear and a baby elephant.

One of the most iconic elements of Warwick Castle is the stunning peacocks that roam in their garden home. This part of the garden was designed by the Victorian landscape gardener Robert Marnock and consists of a number of topiary peacocks, manicured hedges and beautiful pond and fountain. Running gently down to the river is the Pageant Field, flanked on either side by trees, such as the Cedars of Lebanon, which is a great space to sit and take in the beautiful surroundings. Overlooking their garden home is the conservatory, which was built in 1786 by local man William Eborall. It was originally built to house the Warwick Vase, a magnificent piece of ancient Roman pottery excavated near Tivoli in 1771, which is now on display at the Burrell Collection in Glasgow. However, a full-size replica can still be found in the conservatory.

The Chapel

The chapel was commissioned by Sir Fulke Greville in the early 1600s. It was the meeting place of the Earls of Warwick and their families every Sunday until the mid-20th century. The stone screen divided the family from their household staff. Over the years, weddings, christenings and funerals have taken place here.

Gardens, Towers, Battlements

Since the entrance to a castle was likely to be a common target for an attacking force, it was necessary for the defences to be as effective and deadly as possible. The first defence attackers would face was the Barbican. The Barbican was an exterior walled passage which had a drawbridge and extended out into the ditch to provide the Gatehouse with more protection. Soldiers would be faced with the first iron portcullis and a barrage of crossbow bolts. The attackers would then find themselves in a dark narrow roofed passage with arrow slits on either side and, worse still, murder holes above, from which stones, waste and boiling substances would rain down upon them. This was followed by an open-air space known as the killing zone, above which waiting soldiers would fire down arrows onto the advancing army. For the few that made it through these treacherous defences, they would then have to struggle towards the Gatehouse. They would be confronted by yet another portcullis, another set of murder holes and another door.

The Towers and Ramparts were largely constructed during the 14th and 15th centuries when the castle was under the ownership of the de Beauchamp family. The family spent vast amounts of their fortune on their construction. They were intended to protect those within the castle walls and symbolised the power and importance of the castle's earls.

The first mention of the gardens is during 1576, which coincided with the visit of Queen Elizabeth I, and consisted of a series of coloured gravel pathways and formal patterns of herbs and shrubs. Between 1604 and 1628, Sir Fulke Greville's renovation of the castle saw the planting of new gardens which were without parallel in this part of England. However, they were dug out during the Civil War to act as a further castle defence. It wasn't until the 1750s when Warwick Castle transformed into a stately home that the development of the gardens became a priority.

Under the instruction of the 1st Earl of Warwick, the gardens were transformed under one of Britain's greatest landscape gardeners, Lancelot 'Capability' Brown. It is believed that Warwick Castle was Brown's first independent castle commission, and his achievements here won him praise and national recognition. Although there have been many changes since Brown's time, the overall layout is still ultimately his and continues to be maintained by the passionate grounds and gardens team.

Mill and Engine House

There has been a mill at the present site since the late 14th century. It was originally used to grind corn. In the 17th century an engine house was built for pumping water into the castle for domestic needs. In the 18th century the mill's half-timbered structure was largely rebuilt in a more fashionable Gothic style. In 1880 a fire gutted the mill and destroyed the machinery except for the waterwheel. It was shortly after this disaster that the electricity generating plant was installed – in 1894. The electricity was first officially powered up for the 5th Countess of Warwick's birthday.

Dungeon

This is listed as an interactive experience and indeed it was. The dungeons were a gruesome sight, with a number of torture machines and devices on show. However, the visit was ruined for me by numerous cackling 'actors' jumping to life or emerging behind pillars – more annoying than frightening and detracting rather than adding to the experience.

I came close to laying out one such actor who startled me from behind. In a reflex self-defence move, I pinned him one-handed to a pillar with a judo strangle hold. It was the first and only time I have ever been called upon to use my Judo training (London Judo Society 1956–1961).

We all came together in the late afternoon for tea and cakes at the castle café, then taxi back to the boat for an evening meal and conversation. Tomorrow would be a big day.

Hatton Locks

Halfway up the 21 locks of the Hatton flight

Up early, we set off to get through Cape locks, before tackling the Hatton flight – 21 chambers over two miles, raising the Grand Union by 150 feet. This is the third greatest number of locks in a single flight in the UK. Only Tardebigge (narrow) and Cain Hill (broad) have more.

I knew it would be best to share the locks with another boat but had not done that before and was uncertain of the protocols involved. Much to the annoyance of Lindsay and Dinny, I turned down an offer from another crew of four fit and tanned young men who offered to share the locks with us. I let them go on alone but very nearly lost the two girls, leaving Nick and me and Sylvia on our own.

The gates on double locks are heavy, with a chevron pair at each end, unlike narrow locks which only have a chevron pair on the uphill side. However, the ground paddles were smooth and easy to crank, unlike Cain Hill – more of that later. We all took it in turns to steer the boat in and out, open and close gates and operate the paddles.

Each lock is separated by a short pound (that's a section of canal linking two adjacent locks), which means it is possible to moor between locks and take a break, unlike Cain Hill in Devizes, which has side-pounds, inaccessible by boats, so once committed, you have to keep going.

We completed Hatton in about six hours in total, including a stop for tea and toast halfway up. Then lunch once we made it to the top.

Kingswood Junction

After Hatton came the Shrewley Tunnel, just under 400 metres long and on to Kingswood Junction. This is an important place for inland waterways folk.

We got off the boat and wandered a few hundred metres up the link channel to have a look at the Stratford Canal and its narrow locks. Those locks all have small bridges with elegant ironwork – example above. The route from Kings Norton to Kingswood Junction was the scene of one of the first campaigns by the fledgling Inland Waterways Association, when Tom Rolt announced in 1947 that he intended to navigate along the canal. The railway company had to jack the bridge up to allow his boat to pass, and the event was widely reported in newspapers, gaining useful publicity. The route from Kingswood Junction to Stratford was reopened in 1964 by Queen Elizabeth the Queen Mother, having been taken over and restored by the National Trust.

Knowle Locks

The next challenge was a five-lock flight of wide locks at Knowle. We reached Knowle around mid-afternoon. It was dull and overcast, threatening rain with a howling gale into our faces. It was very cold steering the boat in that. At Knowle, the Grand Union takes a 60-degree turn to the left, leaving the wind coming from the right.

The first lock was handled well since we were protected from the wind by the lock infrastructure. We were still going uphill and in fact would be doing so all the way into Birmingham. Nick was driving the boat as it emerged from the lock – the rest of us were lock side. The Knowle locks have side-ponds, rather like Cain Hill in Devizes, and are close together. The wind caught hold of the bow and pushed the boat left. Nick carried on out of the lock and the whole boat got swept into the side-pond. He could not get back. It became difficult to turn around. The wind was too strong. Nick made many, many valiant attempts but was alone on the boat with Sylvia on the bow, meaning we could not help. It was becoming distressing when Dinny had a flash of inspiration – and we all learnt a lesson. She yelled out to Sylvia to throw the bow line onto the bank.

None of us realised how simple it was to pull the boat round from the bank side, even in a howling gale. Using the rope, we got the bow into the lock infrastructure below the bottom gates, allowing Nick to use engine power and full right tiller to push the stern over against the wind while the bow was held immobilised by the rope. Lindsay and I had prepared and emptied the lock and opened both lower gates, giving Nick a good prospect of driving in.

We fairly shot up the next four locks by working as a team. We were being pursued by another boat, having an all-female crew, who seemed to think there was some kind of race in progress. We let them go past at the top, while we all had tea and conversation.

That night, we moored at the fabulously named Catherine-de-Barnes. That village grew from a small heath in the manor of Longdon, which merged with the manor of Ulverlei to form Solihull. The name Catherine-de-Barnes derives from Ketelberne, a 12th-century lord of the manor. The village has been known colloquially since the 19th century as Catney Barnes, often abbreviated to Catney. (Text courtesy of Solihull.gov) We walked a short way to The Boat pub, where I had a very good fillet steak. Made a change from French onion soup and beans on the boat the previous night.

Under M6 Spaghetti Junction

Who would know that there is an extensive canal network under the M6 motorway? I didn't until I studied the route planner for the Warwickshire Ring.

We left Catherine-de-Barnes early because today was going to be arduous. Nick and I were at the stern as the views changed from rural to urban and then industrial. We were chatting away when all of a sudden there was a loud bang from beneath, making the stern jump sideways. We looked back to see a battered and bruised shopping trolley surface in our wake. The boat chugged on calmly through Tyseley and then Small Heath. There were no locks to deal with until we met the flight at Camp Hill. At this point the Grand Union becomes less grand – the locks are narrow once more. The cost of making them wide was prohibited in 1844 when a new 'cut' was commissioned to provide a route to Salford via Bordesley Junction. And we were at the summit of the Grand Union now, so Camp Hill would be downhill.

The Camp Hill flight was not an experience one could enjoy. It was cold, windy, overcast and spitting with rain – only adding to the gloomy and desolate-looking surroundings. The canal skulked under dirty, old, sometimes subterranean, bridges. There was rubbish floating in the water, and the canal walls were covered in a century and a half of grime and detritus. The lock hardware looked like it was ready to fall apart, gates covered in weed, winding gear hanging on by a thread, sticking out at crazy angles. And as we chugged from lock to lock, the landscape was of derelict buildings, waste ground littered with all sorts of unmentionables, probably drug related in places – basically the whole area looked like it had been abandoned as if hit by a bomb.

At Bordesley Junction we turned right and made our way through the five downhill narrow locks to Nechells, where there is a cinema complex. Nick and Dinny left us there and clambered over a fence into the cinema, where they planned to call a taxi for the train home. It had been great having them along.

We could see the looming presence of the M6 ahead, its complex superstructure towering into the air – essentially hovering above us like one of those Martian tripods from H G Wells' 'War of the Worlds'. I had to make a hairpin turn to the right onto the Birmingham and Fazeley Canal at that point but made a complete Horlicks of it, nearly ramming the bank ahead. I let Lindsay take the tiller while I went up to the bow and used the long pole to push the boat around. However, the pole got stuck into the mud and I very nearly went in.

There was just Lindsay, me and Sylvia on the boat now. We moored for the night just before the Curdworth Tunnel. It was not a formal public mooring space and in what looked like a dodgy area, but it was outside a pub. We had a good meal, were not disturbed by the local rabble and slept soundly.

The next morning saw us about halfway round the Warwickshire Ring – four more days to go. We set off, still heading north, towards Fazeley. Until we got there all the locks would be downhill and narrow. Downhill locks are easy to navigate. Fill the lock, open one chevroned top gate and sail in, taking care not to go in too fast and hit the far gate. If the drop is large, that situation can create an illusion of you and the boat going over the edge. Close the top gates, open the lower gate paddles and gently sink into the ground. There is never any turbulence if water is flowing out of a lock. Just need to be careful to keep the stern of the boat forward in the lock so that the stern does not get hung up on the cill of the upper gates. Boats have sunk in such circumstances.

At that point we joined the Coventry Canal and began the long turn south past Tamworth and through Atherstone. There are 11 locks in the Atherstone flight, now going uphill. It took us about four hours to get through them and we were short of water. We delayed lunch until the next water point[6], which was an old British Waterways wharf at Hartshill. Lindsay and I got off the boat and tied up to the water point using just the centre line. Sylvia stayed on the bow of the boat, chucked over the hose and unscrewed the water filler cap. However, Lindsay was trying to secure the bow with a rope around a bollard, but it slipped off and the bow began to move away from the wharf side. She tried to hold onto the boat's gunwale. Unfortunately, with hand on the boat and feet on the bank, she very nearly reached the point of no return and could have fallen in. To go in the water between a 15-ton narrowboat and a concrete bank is not to be advised. Sylvia tried to catch her daughter and in doing so gashed her hand rather badly on the boat's steel handrail. Lesson learned – never, never lean over or jump from a boat that is not secured to the bankside.

We patched Sylvia's hand, had a late lunch, filled the water tank then got under way although considerably delayed. After Atherstone then past Hartshill, Nuneaton, Marston and then to Hawkesbury Junction, there are 14 miles of lock-free canal. At this point the Coventry Canal joins the North Oxford Canal – separated by a 'Stop Lock' of about six inches drop. We moored for the night at Ansty and walked a short way for dinner at the Rose and Castle pub.

---

[6] Water points are places along the canal network where boats can moor up, usually on rings, and take on water. A tank full of water lasts around a week depending upon how clean the crew wish to keep and how many loo flushes they make. An absolute no-no is to use the water moorings as a lunch stop, or worse, an overnight stay. Those welcoming spaces are a frustration though – I've stopped in one so many times, tied bow and stern lines, only then to be yelled at and realise I'm going to have to move on.

The following day would be lock-free on the North Oxford Canal from Ansty to Rugby. The boating guide indicated a number of public mooring sites on the outskirts of Rugby, but we could not find a space. We had to keep going, but the boat had developed a problem – it didn't want to go. I parked eventually just past Tesco. We all got off the boat to find an evening meal, which we could only do via scrambling down a steep embankment into the rear of a Harvester. Sylvia was not too enamoured with this, but we had no choice. The next morning, I called Black Prince who, several hours later, sent an engineer.

Another lesson learnt. There was nothing wrong with the boat, just weeds wrapped around the propeller. Stopping the boat then giving it a powerful dollop of reverse would have unwrapped the weed and had us on our way.

The next day would be our final full day. The Oxford Canal follows the line of the 300-foot contour and so there are few locks. We got held at the Hillmorton flight of three locks where I let Lindsay off the boat to investigate the delay. I decided to keep the boat in the stream but had not noticed a strong crosswind. It was a while before she came back but, in that time, I learnt by accident how to steer the boat in reverse – a technique that would become invaluable in future years.

We moored overnight in Braunston – that very famous canal town. We got there early, then wandered up to the canal shop to buy a few bits of memorabilia. Then an early start the next day to get the boat back to Napton and Wigrams Turn Marina. Two week' boating, many lessons learnt, a thoroughly enjoyable adventure.

Chapter 7
Welford Arm of the Grand Union Canal
May 2008

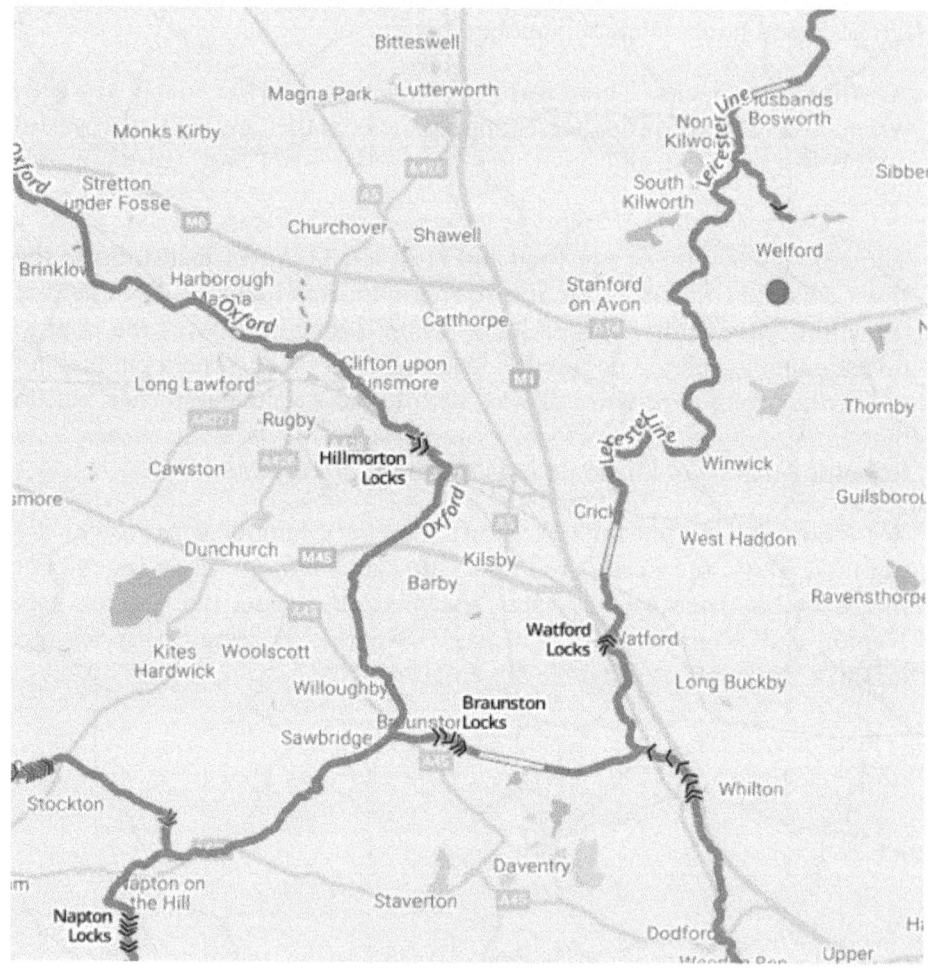

Napton, Braunston, Watford and Welford
© Copyright Ordnance Survey
Map 05

We hired once more from Black Prince Narrowboats based at Wigrams Turn Marina.

This was going to be a short, pleasant trip of just four days in glorious spring sunshine. Err, no. It was absolutely freezing, with Braunston, our first destination, shrouded in fog. We got through the first six locks, with Lindsay doing all the work and me driving the boat. Then the short Braunston Tunnel, wet and dank. Another mile or so and we turned left onto the Leicester Arm.

I wanted to do this trip because there are a pair of interesting, indeed historic, locks at Watford and Foxton. They are both narrow staircase types but very different from the Grindley Brook staircase we met on the Llangollen.

Looking north, the four-chamber staircase locks at Watford

The Watford flight are three single locks followed by a four-chamber staircase. They are situated just 400 metres, as the crow flies, from Watford Services on the M1 motorway. Both sets of locks have unusual side chambers, not accessible to boats, that receive water from a chamber being emptied or fill a chamber that is empty. Up to four boats can be ascending the staircase at any one time – or four descending at any one time. Each chamber has two sets of paddles – one painted red and one painted white. The operating procedures is 'Red before white and you'll be all right. White before red and you'll be dead.' Not actually true, of course, but getting it wrong will lose a lot of water and irritate a lot of people. Watford locks have a full-time lock keeper in attendance at all times and are chained shut an hour before sunset each day.

After Watford we had to negotiate the 1,528-yard Crick Tunnel. That was another dark, dank, smelly, like damp socks, experience. Water dripped or often poured from walls and roof. I had often wondered what would happen if two boats were in a tunnel at the same time, each coming from a different entrance. Well, we found out – we were about one third in when I thought I saw the exit portal in the distance. It was just a pinprick of light that kept disappearing and then coming back. To my horror, I realised it was the headlamp of a boat coming the other way. The light got bigger and nearer. I slowed to a near stop because I was dazzled by the light. I assume they did the same. Both boats crept closer, getting slower and slower. Eventually, I saw their bow. There was just room for us to pass, but only by pulling the stern side fender on board.

We moored at Crick Wharf for the night as we had arranged to meet Jonathan and his new girlfriend, Jennie. Lindsay was not well so, while nice to see the kids, my mind was on her.

The next day we left late because Lindsay had abdominal pain. It was going to be about four hours driving before we got to our destination at Welford. It was a stinker of a day. Freezing cold, lashing rain, howling gale in our faces. There was nothing to do but continue since we could not turn around. My hands froze on the tiller. Lindsay spent most of the time curled up on a bunk in the warm below. My waterproof, high-quality Gore-Tex jacket leaked like a sieve. After what seemed like an eternity, I turned the boat into the Welford Arm itself and then through one final lock and on to find a mooring in the marina.

Having tied the boat securely, Lindsay and I set of to walk the few hundred yards to the pub. We squelched along a muddy, pitted towpath, making slow progress in that howling gale. It was now about 4pm and we were looking forward to a warm room and hot food. However, the pub looked dark and closed as we approached, and our hearts sank. It was open, but they had suffered a power cut – there was no electricity for their heating system or cooking meals. We were like drowned rats, leaking great puddles of water onto their carpets.

The landlord and landlady were wonderful thereafter. They helped us take off sodden top clothes and gave us towels to dry our hair. They did have a gas range and cooked us a fry-up with tea, coffee and toast. They really took pity and spoilt us rotten. We thanked them, paid the bill and got back to the boat about 6pm. The weather had decided to cooperate, Lindsay felt better, and we had an early night.

The next day saw us make our way back to Braunston, where we moored for the night. The boat had to be back at Wigrams Turn Marina by 9am the next day. We had to be off and gone by 9.30. It meant an early start – but it was a glorious morning, and we were sorry we had no more time.

Chapter 8
South Oxford Canal September 2008

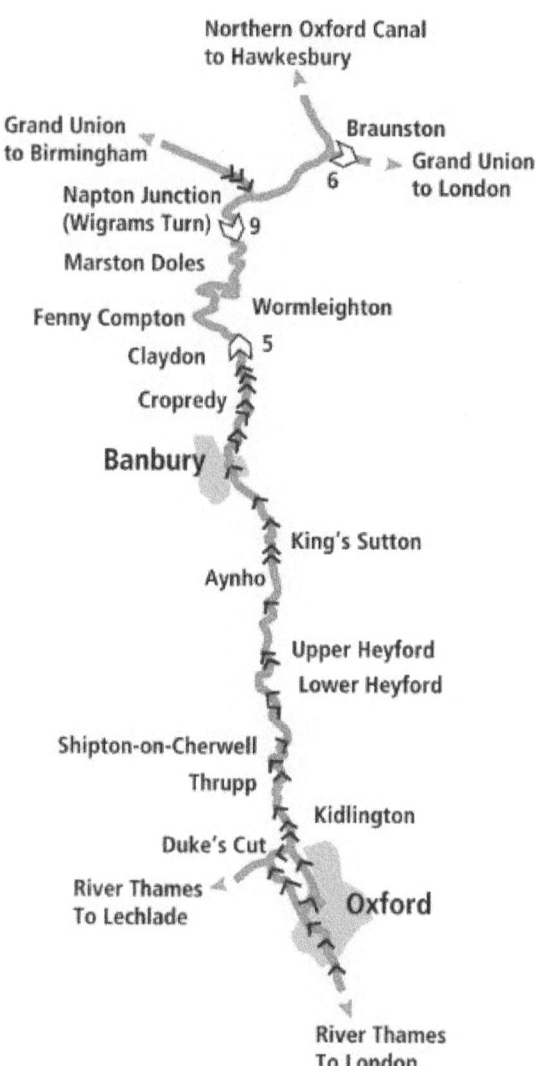

Northern Oxford Canal
to Hawkesbury

Grand Union
to Birmingham

Braunston

Grand Union
to London

6

Napton Junction
(Wigrams Turn) 9

Marston Doles

Fenny Compton

Wormleighton

Claydon 5

Cropredy

Banbury

King's Sutton

Aynho

Upper Heyford

Lower Heyford

Shipton-on-Cherwell

Thrupp

Kidlington

Duke's Cut

River Thames
To Lechlade

Oxford

River Thames
To London

South Oxford Canal
© Copyright Kelsey Publishing
Map 06

The first time we visited the River Thames was towards the end of a trip down the South Oxford Canal that began at Wigrams Turn Marina, near Napton, where we had hired from earlier that year. We initially thought we might have to cancel because the Thames locks were red-boarded, and the River Cherwell had been too high. (The Cherwell and the canal merge for a short section below Aynho.) However, the levels receded just in time, and we set off on a Black Prince narrowboat with Lindsay and Sylvia on board. We headed south. The canal was exceptionally twisty. It had been built to follow a specific contour and so minimise the number of locks. It also played with one's mind when apparently following another boat ahead and half an hour later seeing the very same boat behind.

Sandra and Steve joined us at Aynho Wharf. Steve drove the boat most of the day since he and Sandra were going to leave us when we reached Thrupp that evening. The short Cherwell River section was twisty but so smooth, allowing the boat to glide easily on deep clear water.

We arrived at Thrupp, where we were joined by son Jonathan and his girlfriend Jennie. What a lovely spot that is – good visitor moorings, excellent pubs, immaculate towpath, heritage properties and excellent boating facilities. Steve, Sandra, Sylvia, Lindsay, Jon, Jennie and I had a family and friends meal in The Boat Inn at Thrupp that evening. And that's just one of a multitude of things about holidays on a narrowboat – how they provide a unique opportunity for close social contact and conversation.

Steve and Sandra left us that evening. The next day saw the boat continue south into Oxford. At Isis Lock we stopped to put on life jackets as the Thames was next. Huge 'danger' signs and other warnings alarmed Jennie. She thought we would be going straight on, over the weir. I assured her we would be making a sharp right-hand turn under the railway bridge and onto the river proper. Nevertheless, she gave me one of those looks.

The plan was then to head upstream through Godstow Lock and then King's Lock before turning right into Duke's Cut and Duke's Lock and back onto the Oxford Canal and Thrupp.

This was my first experience of the Thames. I was aware that the locks we would meet would be electrified and manned by resident lock keepers. I was also aware of the very specific in-lock procedures required

55

of boaters. Boats had to be secured by both bow and stern ropes and the engine turned off. I had studied the Environment Agency rulebook about the Thames. In particular, the marking of channels using buoys. A buoy with a red can, similar to Tommy Cooper's red fez, on top must be kept to port going upstream. A buoy with a green triangle on top must be kept to starboard going upstream. Then the reverse going downstream.

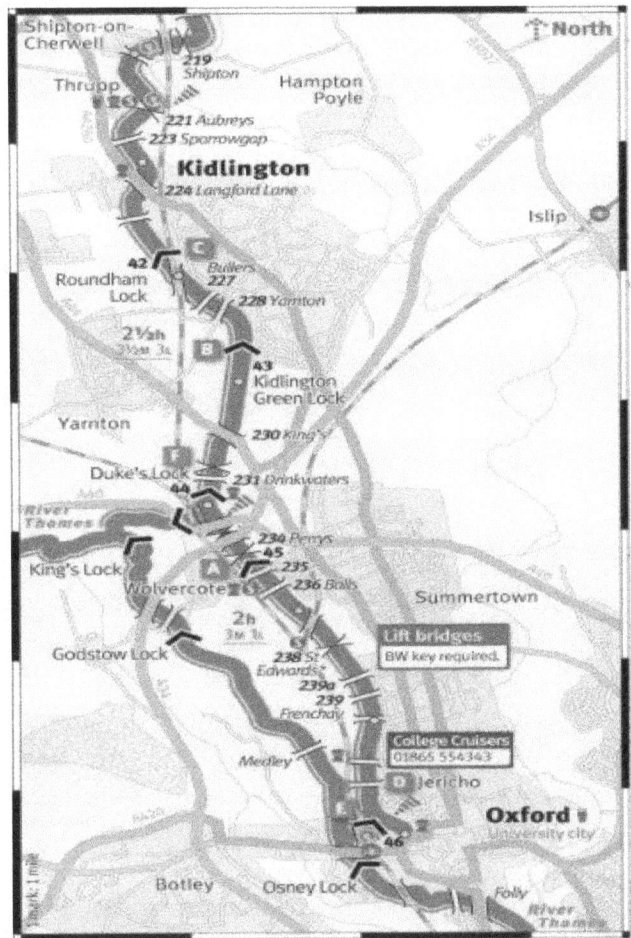

Thrupp into Oxford and back via King's Lock and Duke's Cut

Duke's Cut connects the South Oxford Canal with the River Thames via the Wolvercote Mill Stream and Duke's Lock. It is named after George Spencer, 4th Duke of Marlborough, whose land the waterway crossed.

Map 07

We turned right after Isis, under the railway bridge and prepared to make another right turn onto the Thames. I had nominated a spotter on the bow as I gently nudged out into the stream. Big mistake. I had forgotten the red boards from the previous week – the river was still flowing fast. The bow was immediately swept to the left. I was going to have a shopping trolley moment. The boat should have been hard over to the right, giving me a chance to counteract the wayward bow. I quickly increased power and got the stern over, but it was not enough. We shot across the river and the three ladies on the front disappeared from view into a tangle of shrubbery. They were not too pleased.

Jonathan and me at the tiller on the River Thames

However, under the bushes, the bow had gently collided with the bank and held fast. The stern drifted with the stream, and after a burst of reverse, the boat more or less completed a 90-degree turn all by itself. We were now pointing upstream.

It was a hot sunny day, and the Thames was magnificent – wide and flat with the flood plain stretching seemingly for miles across the meadows. We moored up just below Godstow Nunnery and got out the gangplank so Sylvia (I know what you were thinking there) could set up a picnic on the grassy bank. We all had lunch in the sun and then set off towards Godstow Lock, obeying a number of the aforementioned red and green floating buoys, then on to King's Lock, where I caught sight of my first Thames weir – they are huge! We moored on the landing stage opposite the weir waiting for the lock gates to open. The weir stream was pinning us to the landing stage, and it took a big shove on the bow and a sprightly walk back to the stern before we could get away and into the lock. After

King's we made a right turn into Duke's Cut and on into Duke's Lock and a left turn back to Thrupp. We were now back on the South Oxford Canal. Jon and Jennie got off the boat there, where a taxi was waiting to take them back to their car. I'm not sure Jennie enjoyed the experience, but hey, it's not for everyone. We were certainly pleased she came along.

I made our way rather gingerly back to Thrupp because the banks were lined both sides with boats and the canal was twisty. It was the first time I had experienced such tight conditions. When we got to Thrupp Village, another crew pulled our boat into a narrow space for us – it was the first of many times we experienced courtesy and willingness to assist other boaters.

Thrupp back to Wigrams Turn Marina

Oxford Canal on the 120-metre contour south of Napton

© Copyright elevationmap.net

Construction of the South Oxford Canal began in the late 1700s but quickly ran into financial trouble. Economies were necessary. Wherever possible, wooden lift or swing bridges were built instead of expensive brick ones. Deep locks were used wherever possible, with single gates at both ends instead of double gates. The latter are not a problem for the boater though because this is a narrow canal – those gates are not too heavy despite their size.

The South Oxford Canal was built to follow specific contours, adjacent to the River Cherwell, all the way to Banbury and on to Cropredy. That section was later straightened, but then the money ran out, leaving the section south of Napton as originally built. That's the bit that still play tricks with your brain. Following a contour minimised the number of locks required but greatly extended journey length.

We set off north with Sylvia, Lindsay and me on board.

Our first test was the electric lift bridge at the north end of Thrupp. It is a large structure sited on a 90-degree bend going left. Lindsay needed to get off and use the British Waterways (BW) yale key to unlock and operate the bridge. I wanted to turn sharp left once through, then pull into the bank to collect her. However, there was a brisk wind blowing from the west. A narrowboat side-on operates like a big sail, making it difficult to get the boat to turn left. I had a few goes at getting through but each time got caught by the wind and pushed right. That meant reversing back under and trying again. Or give up, put the kettle on and wait for tomorrow. I'm sorry to say, Black Prince, I got through by deliberately scraping the left side of the bow and right side of the stern against the brickwork, giving the boat enough left-pointing bias to be able to power through and finally beat that wind.

I then just hovered mid-stream into a howling gale while Lindsay closed the bridge. It was then simple to bring the bow into the towpath while she walked round and leapt nimbly on.

The canal follows the path of the River Cherwell for the next 30 or so miles, finally leaving the river at Cropredy. Part of the Cherwell is canalised from Shipton Weir Lock to Baker's Lock just south of Enslow. The difference in water height between the Cherwell and the canal is small, averaging just 2 foot 5 inches (74cm). This can vary considerably, and the lock protects the canal from seasonal changes in the river flow and height.

Because the change in height through the lock is small, maintaining the forward volume of flow into the canal every time the lock is opened can be a problem. This has been solved by building a wide lock with an unusual six-sided 'lozenge' shape. This increases the volume of the lock chamber and thus the amount of water that flows into the canal every time the lower lock gate is opened. However, the boat only just fitted in the lock chamber, and it was painfully slow to fill, so we wasted a deal of time getting through. It's a lovely spot though, the wide Cherwell flowing across the far lock gate, silhouetted by the trees beyond.

The river's flow was against us, but the water was deep, allowing the boat to get up a head of steam. At Baker's Lock we got back on the canal, leaving the river to meander on in the valley below.

We passed through Lower and Upper Heyford, climbing steadily all the while, eventually reaching Somerton Deep Lock. This is the 16th deepest lock in Britain with a 12-foot drop. Does not sound a lot, but it is when you are in the bottom on the boat on your own waiting for the crew to crack open a sluice.

Banbury was four hours away by boat. The approach is urban with railway, motorway, roundabouts and industrial premises all around. But the centre is interesting with the canal going right past Debenhams' front door, a lock right outside. The canal was congested by a boatyard and hire base nearby and we had to wait for access to the lock.

A couple of hours after Banbury, we passed through the village of Cropredy. This is a famous boating location. It features a folk music gathering in August each year centred around the group Fairport Convention. The village pub, The Red Lion, was habituated by canal restoration guru L T C Rolt and mentioned in his famous book 'Narrowboat'. And most famous of all was the Battle of Cropredy Bridge where 9,000 soldiers fought on 29th June 1644 during the first English civil war. In that engagement, Sir William Waller and the Parliamentarian army failed to capture King Charles I.

After Cropredy the canal leaves the valley of the River Cherwell and climbs up through nine locks around Claydon, then on towards the summit at Fenny Compton. When the canal was first built there was a 1,000-yard tunnel here, but in 1860 the top was removed to leave the long cutting we cruised through. It has passing places that were originally underground, allowing two narrowboats to glide by each other.

There then followed ten miles of lockless but twisty South Oxford Canal, where the landscape played tricks on our eyes. We appeared to have boats behind us, but in fact they were ahead. Church steeples jumped somewhat magically from our left to our right and back again. Eventually, however, we navigated the nine locks down towards Napton and back into the Wigrams Turn Marina.

Chapter 9

Etruria and the Caldon Canal May 2009

© Copyright Waterways Routes
Map 08

Another Black Prince marina, part of the Hanley Festival Park complex, was where Lindsay and I collected our narrowboat, home for the coming week. Hanley is a suburb of Stoke-on-Trent, a region famous for the potteries. We had seen some of Stoke during our Four Counties Ring adventure a few years earlier. The drive through Stoke on the way to the marina was a depressing sight, full of dereliction, run-down shops and residents who mostly looked down on their luck. There was a great deal of roadway construction going on, part of which was aimed at straightening the river, particularly at Causeley Brook, to improve its flow. Industrial waste and sewage has been a problem on the Trent ever since the dawn of the industrial age.

The marina is close to Etruria. It was named after the Italian district of Etruria, home of the Etruscan people, who were known for their artistic products. Etruria was the fourth and penultimate site for the Wedgwood pottery business and adjacent to the Trent and Mersey Canal.

Having done the Black Prince handover, we came out of the marina around 4pm, turned left (south) towards Stoke centre and then left again after about 800 yards onto the Caldon Canal. The first issue to confront us was the twin-chamber staircase lock at Bedford Street.

Bedford Street staircase locks
Two narrow chambers and three pairs of chevroned narrow gates.

We had met staircase locks before of course on the Llangollen Canal and at Watford on the Welford Arm of the Grand Union and so we should have known what we were doing. The difference this time was that it was late and there was no lock keeper on duty. Lock keepers are normally present to ensure there are no disasters – and there can be disasters at staircases.

Bedford Street staircase
Note the size of the bottom pair of mitred gates and the presence of
an overflow channel.

A well-publicised one was at Llangollen where incorrect operation led to water flooding the nearside café and pouring down the high street.

However, I knew what to do. The boat was going uphill. That meant having the top chamber full before we went into the bottom chamber. Top chamber full, Lindsay opened the bottom gate paddles to drain the water from the lowest chamber. She opened both gates, as this lock is of type 'narrow', allowing me to drive the boat in. She shut the gates behind me and then walked up to open the middle gate paddles so that the water level in the two chambers would equalise.

Once equalised, she opened the middle gates so I could enter the top chamber. Except I couldn't – there was a large wooden beam, about one foot square, across the lock. There was also another one at the far end. I could also see the far cill, which was not right.

We were both baffled. Who should we phone? Would CRT come out this late? Would I have to reverse out and would we be stuck overnight in the middle of a rough area?

At first, I could just see the top of the beam, but gradually more of it came into view. We were sinking! Then madam had a brainwave and realised what had happened. She had closed the bottom gates to let me in, but the lower gates paddles were still open. Water was leaving the chamber and we were going down with it.

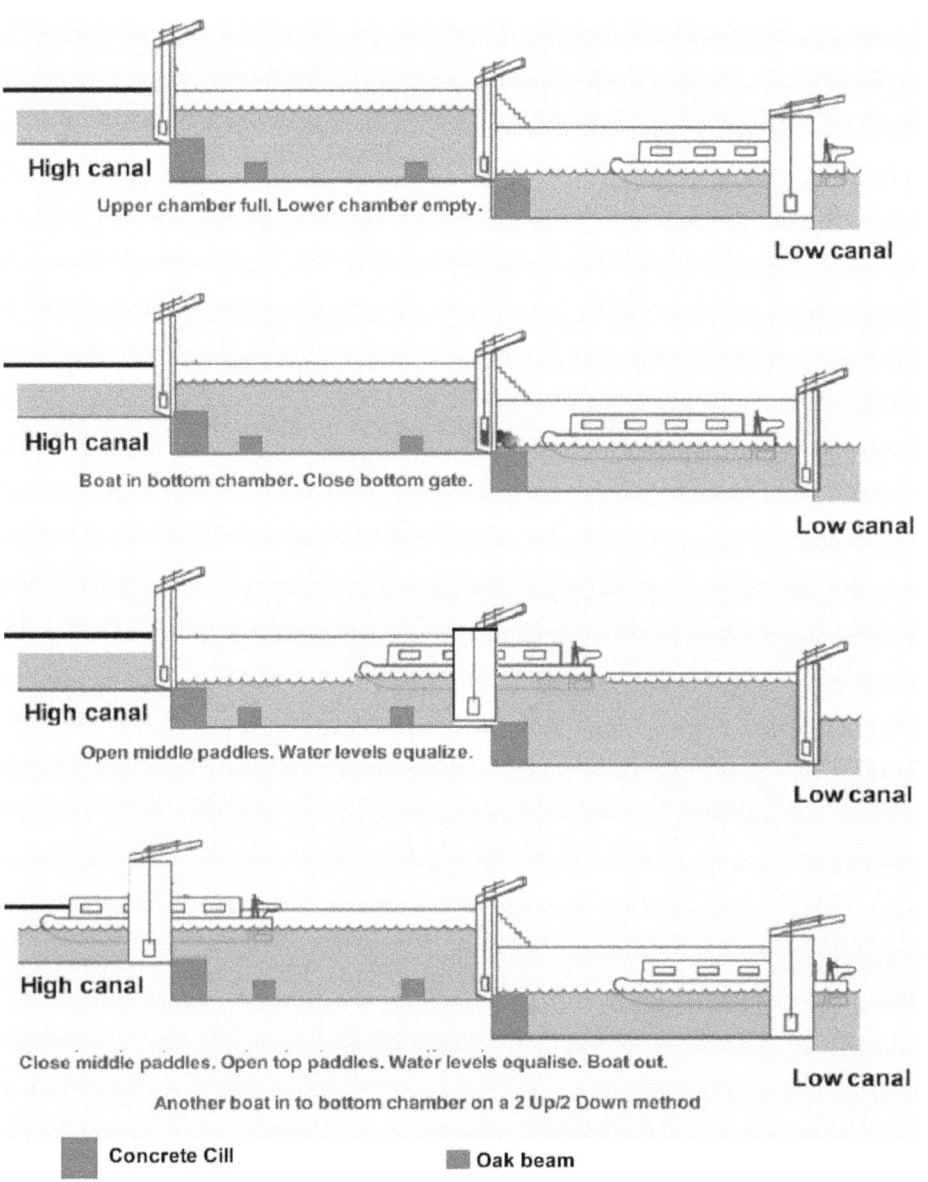

High canal
Upper chamber full. Lower chamber empty.
Low canal

High canal
Boat in bottom chamber. Close bottom gate.
Low canal

High canal
Open middle paddles. Water levels equalize.
Low canal

High canal
Close middle paddles. Open top paddles. Water levels equalise. Boat out.
Another boat in to bottom chamber on a 2 Up/2 Down method
Low canal

▨ Concrete Cill   ▨ Oak beam

How a two-chamber staircase lock works – going uphill

Based on an original work by Jennifer Petkus 2016

I realised I was then in a dangerous situation with the bow at risk of grounding on the cill. I moved the boat back, while Lindsay raced down the steps to shut the paddles behind me.

Recovery was swift – it was like our brains had emerged from a fog. She opened both top gate paddles to let water down from the canal above into the big central chamber. Gradually those timbers faded from view. While that was happening, she checked both central gate paddles were firmly shut – but gates still open of course because I could not get in until those beams had gone and the far cill had been covered at the very least. Finally, I moved the boat up to the top cill, allowing Lindsay to close both middle gates behind me. Then it was just a case of waiting for the top chamber to fill and equalise levels with the upper canal. And open top gates and hover around, waiting for her to get back on.

We didn't go far after that as we were both a bit shell-shocked. A simple mistake but one difficult to understand in the moment. If I had moved the boat a little sooner, it's possible it would have been suspended on those wooden beams – perhaps that's what they were there for. If I had been slower, we would have ended up in the lower chamber with the waterline level with the lower canal we had just come in from – so nobody was going to get flooded, but we were just a little shaken.

The boat stayed put on a lock-side bollard for a while, as we recovered our decorum. I had planned a pub meal at 'The Foxley Inn' in Milton that night, so we untied and moved on through Planet Lock, then past a number of disused pottery factories around Hanley and through Ivy House electric lift bridge. It was 7pm before the pub came into view.

It was shut, closed, kaput. What a shock that was. We had not encountered that before. Plan B came into force as it had on the Warwickshire Ring a few years earlier. Onion soup, beans and sausages from our reserve supplies. I took the boat around the corner onto public moorings, where we tied up for the night. What a day.

Phil and Liz and Dominique

We had a date the next day. Lindsay's brother, sister-in-law, husband and their daughter Dominique had flown in from the USA and were on their way to Llanrwst in North Wales to stay with Lindsay's sister. We had arranged to meet them at the Holly Bush pub alongside bridge 38 on the Froghall arm of the Caldon. I thought we could get that done in about three hours from Milton and arranged to meet at 1pm.

It didn't quite work out like that. Soon after we set off, I noticed the boat was sluggish. The wake from the propellor was coming out at a weird angle and the boat did not want to move, nor steer as usual. I sensed a visit down the weed hatch was pending.

Clearing the prop is a real pain in the butt. First, you have to find a spot to moor. You won't be able to go far – meaning stopping in inconvenient places, both for others and yourself. I found a bit of muddy bank, pulled in, allowing Lindsay to step off with centre line in hand. She held the boat while I walked up and down bashing in bow and stern mooring pins.

It's never a nice dry spot in these situations. I have to kneel down to batter those pins and always put the same knee on the ground. If it's wet, that knee ends up covered in a layer of mud, while the other remains pristine. Looks tramp-like later in the day when it all starts to dry out. And of course, at some point in the process, you will stand or kneel in that pile of dog shit you never saw.

I found a pair of red leggings wrapped around the prop. It took over an hour to unwrap them. I left them on the bank in the hope the owner, out walking her dog one day, would recognise them. Why she took those leggings off though will remain a mystery.

The Leek Arm

At Hazelhurst Junction we turned right before the bottom lock onto the Leek arm of the Caldon. This takes the canal on an aqueduct over the Froghall arm that then proceeds south through Cheddleton, following the valley of the River Churnet. I had planned to take our guests up the Leek arm because they had a long journey later that day, plus the Leek has no locks.

I moored the boat as quickly as possible, making sure it was secure. There were no public moorings there, so it was a return to mooring pin bashing and avoiding the dog shit. The latter would not do because we were about to enter the pub.

I suppose we were about an hour late. Lindsay and I walked down the path beside the aqueduct and then onto a rather cobbly towpath and into a warm and cosy Holly Bush pub.

James Brindley inspired turnover bridge 35

Allows horses going onto the Leek branch to cross over the main
Caldon Canal.

Phil, Liz and Dominique greeted us there. They didn't seem concerned
about the delay. We had a quick lunch and then out the door, turn right
and back to the boat.

However, only a few yards along that cobbled path, Lindsay disappeared
from view – she had gone splat, face down onto the towpath. We were
all a bit shocked but soon rushed to gather her back up. She wasn't hurt,
a grazed knee was all the damage, but it did show how accidents can
occur anywhere out of nowhere.

Once we had climbed back up to the top of the aqueduct, our guests could
see the boat. They were Americans and had never seen anything like that.
'Avril' our Black Prince beauty was nearly full length at 70 feet but of
course only 6 foot 10 inches wide. She had a 'cruiser' type stern, onto
which we all clambered and then went down one-by-one into the lounge
area via the boat's very steep, short set of steps. A guided tour followed,
past the galley, bedroom 1, bathroom1, bedroom 2, bathroom 2 and
finally out onto the foredeck.

That over, I pulled the mooring pins and we set off towards Leek. Liz was very nervous. She asked, "Should we be wearing life jackets?" I said, "If you fall off, Liz, just stand up and wait." I had moored the boat, quite inadvertently, on some private spaces before the aqueduct. Having overcome the wonder of a narrowboat, Liz was struck dumb by the concept of an aqueduct. Anika slipped gracefully over the canal below, she now some 50 feet above.

Black Prince narrowboat 'Anika' moored for the night

Leek – So Good We Did It Twice

Our trip to Leek and back only took a couple of hours and, quite understandably, Lindsay and I were pre-occupied in ensuring our guests were safe and having an enjoyable, indeed unique, waterways experience. (Actually, Phil and Liz had already visited the Florida Everglades, where they journeyed on one of those small, fast hovercraft. But they remained gracious enough about our humble boat and waterway – huge and very slow, the antithesis of alligator hunting on the Everglades.) Once we had returned to the pub and bade them goodbye, we vowed to explore the Leek arm on our own, after we had been to Froghall. The description of the Leek that follows is based on that second visit.

The journey to Leek was only an hour, but it's one of the most picturesque on the entire canal network, rivalled only by patches of the Mon and Brec and the Llangollen. It's twisty and turny, narrow in places and wide in other places. It cuts through a fabulous belt of woodland, populated by tall trees up on the hillside to the left and others plunging down to the right into the valley of the River Churnet. It's a ghostly, quiet, meandry waterway, still clear water creating a spooky illusion of travelling uphill – impossible of course. It invokes something chilling and prehistoric. I quite expected to see flocks of Compsognathus scampering around in the dirt between the slender trunks. Birds, dinosaurs of course, fluttered around in those dark woods – we saw jays and heard woodpeckers, their flashes of colour, chit-chatterings, twitterings and hammerings echoing through the canopy.

In the distance over my right shoulder, I could see the top of the water tower of what was once Cheddleton lunatic asylum. Staffordshire built a number of these institutions after Parliament passed the County Asylum Lunacy Act in 1845. Counties became legally obliged to provide asylum for their lunatics. This Act, following the work of John Conolly and Lord Shaftsbury, saw lunatics being treated as patients and not prisoners. However, asylums soon became overcrowded and rapid expansion took place. The Victorians built nearly 100 of those institutions between 1845 and 1890. In the 20th century, following new treatments and drugs, they began to be closed or converted into general hospitals. With the passing of the Mental Health Act in 1983, their fate was sealed.

Grade II listed octagonal water tower at the site of Cheddleton lunatic asylum

Entrance to the Leek Tunnel

At the end of the Leek arm is a tiny tunnel just 130 yards long. Anika squeezed through without difficulty and then continued about half a mile to a winding hole just before the terminus, where there is an unnavigable aqueduct. I turned the boat around to retrace our steps and then moored for tea and doughnuts.

Beautiful Leek arm of the Caldon Canal – looking back towards Hazelhurst Junction

Froghall Arm – A Bit of History

The Caldon Canal was opened in 1779 to bring limestone to the potteries from quarries at Cauldon Low, near Froghall. It had three narrow locks at Hazelhurst, but not in the same location as they are now. Problems with the canal line and increasing demand gave rise to continual changes and disruption over the years. In 1801 an extension was opened to transport coal to Leek. That had the three locks being replaced by a three-chamber staircase at Hazelhurst Wood near Denford.

In 1811 a 13-mile extension was built to Uttoxeter. It was not a success. It closed in 1845. It was replaced in 1849 by a railway, some of the track using the former canal bed. This was also the fate of some of the original canal near Endon.

A further rebuild near Hazelhurst was completed by 1841. This included abandoning the staircase, creating three new single locks on a new cut (reusing part of the original 1779 route) and building an aqueduct. Hazelhurst Aqueduct is now a Grade II listed building which takes the Leek arm over the original canal.

The Caldon's raison-d'etre was destroyed by competition from the railway. By 1960 it was little used and became unnavigable. However, in 1974, the Caldon was reopened as a leisure waterway following restoration by the Caldon Canal Society.

The canal drops down through the three locks at Hazelhurst Junction, passes through Deep Hayes Country Park and then plunges down into the valley of the River Churnet, where it sticks like glue all the way to Froghall. On the way it passes through Cheddleton, where the river's waters once powered a flint mill and supplied a brewery. There were also silk and paper mills and limekilns there.

After Cheddleton locks, the canal becomes a little narrower and begins to feel isolated. Anika glided calmly around and through bluebell-filled woodland, only for us to be awakened by the grumbling and clattering of an old diesel locomotive pulling a train of ancient rolling-stock. It disappeared as fast as it came but left a parting gift of a cloud of dense diesel fumes that drifted ominously our way.

The railway and canal keep close quarters around Cheddleton, only to wander apart until they meet again downstream near Consall Station. The canal follows the Churnet to Oakmeadow Ford Lock, where it merges with the river. Before then there are spectacular views over the river's flat flood plains, both sides, with dense woodlands and hints of blue in the far distance. The river section was delightful when Lindsay and I were there – calm waters, almost no flow, dappled sunlight through the trees and scores of native ducks and Canada geese all doing what waterfowl do.

At Consall Forge, the canal and river part company, the river plunging over the weir down the valley to Froghall. The railway passes over the canal at this point, meaning the river and railway have changed sides – they were both to our left on the way down to Consall Forge but were now both to our right. After Flint Mill Lock the canal has been squeezed down into a new narrow concrete channel at a point where there have been several breaches. Lindsay was driving the boat at this point, trying to enhance her tiller skills. We met a couple, out walking their snappy little dog, who tried to tell us we were going too fast. A bit rich seeing that they had overtaken us on the towpath. They were unpleasant, I was in a bad mood, and an angry confrontation ensued. He was a retired ocean liner captain, of course he was, who knew all about oceans. I stepped off the counter, got up close and told him to clear off – which he did.

As we neared Froghall we saw the cable factory of Thomas Bolton and Sons. This is still an important industrial site, having been built in 1892 to produce high-conductivity copper for trans-Atlantic telegraph cables and electrical generators. In 1975 it became part of BICC Industrial Products. In 1984 mergers of the copper and aluminium businesses of BICC and Johnson and Firth Brown formed Thomas Bolton and Johnson, as it is called today.

Consall Forge Station – canal and river now merged

Our journey would end at the winding hole in front of Froghall Tunnel. Anika had too big a hull profile to allow her into the tunnel. A pity, because Froghall Wharf Basin is beyond. It marks the end of the now derelict route of the Uttoxeter Canal. The guide books say it's a nice place to be.

We made it back to Etruria without any mishaps. That included a safe and efficient passage through that notorious two-chamber staircase lock at Bedford Street.

Chapter 10

Alvechurch to Stratford September 2009

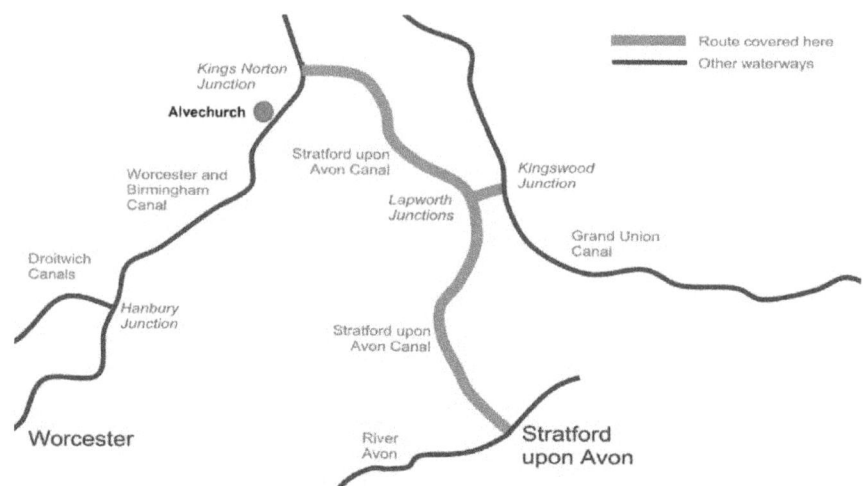

© Copyright Waterway Routes
Map 09

The past four years had seen us cruise the canal network using Black Prince narrowboats – between 62 feet and 70 feet long with two bathrooms and up to six sleeping areas. I decided to look at what else was out there and stumbled across ABC narrowboats based at Alvechurch.

Alvechurch is a substantial village in the Bromsgrove district of northeast Worcestershire in the valley of the River Arrow. It is 11 miles south of Birmingham, five miles north of Redditch and six miles east of Bromsgrove. From a boating viewpoint it's on the Worcester and Birmingham Canal. Head south from Alvechurch and you will meet the Tardebigge flight of locks – the longest flight in the UK, comprising 30 narrow locks over a two-and-a-quarter-mile stretch. Once past those the canal goes through Stoke Prior, a famous canal village, and then on to Worcester and the River Severn. We were to meet that river a decade later.

The boats from ABC had a number of key advantages. We discovered we could hire a 60-foot narrowboat with two bedrooms and two bathrooms (with showers and loos), a well-specified galley with fridge, cooker, twin sinks, fresh and filtered water and all the utensils ever needed. The galley was located at the stern of the boat so that a crew of two could keep in close contact during a voyage. Black Prince boats had the galley at the front or middle.

However, the crunch factor was that ABC boats had 230-volt mains electrical power. That meant a toaster, coffee maker, microwave and easy charging of phones. It meant not having to stick your head inside the gas oven when the igniter failed – as they always did. The only downside was keeping the engine running during periods of mains usage. But we did that anyway, never shutting off the engine until bedtime. We never went back to Black Prince, nice though their boats were, well-built and of good quality. (I understand that Black Prince do now fit inverters in most current craft.)

Lindsay and I came out of ABC's Alvechurch marina and turned left – north towards Birmingham. It was late afternoon. The handover at the marina had taken a while, so we were later than expected. We sailed under the M42 and past the two summit reservoirs that feed the canal, then on towards the Wast Hill Tunnel. This is 2,500 or so metres long, completed by 1800 and wide enough for two narrowboats to pass inside. Like the Harecastle Tunnel, it's a dark, dank, smelly hellhole with a big old bend in the middle. That meant we could not see an exit for nearly an hour. We were underground for nearly two hours in total.

It was gloomy when we emerged. Still heading for Birmingham, we were looking to turn right at Kings Norton Junction, a famous boating location, just before the famous Bourneville chocolate factory. Now looking for somewhere to moor and get a meal, our destination was the Horseshoe pub, but there was another tunnel, Bradwood, to navigate first, although only 260 metres long. After another hour, the pub came into view. We pulled in, bashed in some mooring pins, secured the boat and walked down the towpath, looking forward to steak and ale pie.

It was closed – up for sale. It's quite astonishing over all the years we had been boating how often that situation has caught us out. We had no choice but to return to the boat and use the microwave to heat up the couple of ready meals we had hoped to keep in reserve. At least that was better than French onion soup and baked beans.

The next morning, after the regulation full English breakfast, we set off down the North Stratford Canal towards Stratford-upon-Avon – Shakespeare's home town. After about 20 minutes we crossed the first of four aqueducts, at Major's Green, which carries the canal over the River Cole, and then met the electrified lift bridge. I waited on the boat while Lindsay trotted off to stop the road traffic and get the bridge lifted. She knew what to do, having had all those experiences on the Llangollen and Oxford canals.

After three hours or so lock-free, we found ourselves at the head of the Lapworth flight of locks. There were now going to be 50 narrow locks, all downhill, over the next three days before reaching Stratford. It was just Lindsay and me on board – it was going to be tough.

The series of locks which make up Lapworth Lock Flight on the Stratford-upon-Avon Canal are some of the most interesting to be found on the English waterways. The canal's locks are very similar to those we met on the Oxford Canal, i.e., they are narrow and only one narrowboat at a time can go through. Navigating Lapworth locks would therefore take some time – particularly the 6 to 14 sequence and shortly after that the 15 to 19 sequence, all of which are right on top of each other. In between each lock there are small pounds of water available for narrowboats needing to wait their turn – these mini-reservoirs are necessary for providing an immediate water source to the locks. The whole area is very picturesque, easy to wander around and also home to quite a lot of wildlife.

Kingswood Junction

Around halfway down the flight, there is the canal junction at Kingswood, where the Stratford Canal meets the Grand Union. We investigated this several years ago on our journey around the Warwickshire Ring. The locks all have the same characteristic ironwork and same structure as most locks on the South Oxford Canal – that is a single top gate and a pair of chevroned lower gates. An unusual feature of the Stratford-upon-Avon Canal is its split bridges, designed in the days of horse-drawn boats to let the horse cross over the canal without being unhitched from the narrowboat. Many of these bridges survive in their original form, and on some of the bridge stanchions, you can still see the deep grooves worn into the ironwork by boat tow ropes over many years.

Working lock 36

Note the closeness of the locks and the split bridges where a horse's ropes would have been threaded through. Notice the single top gate.

Chevroned lower gates at lock 32

A Flotilla of Aqueducts then on to Shakespeare's Country

Many barrel-roofed cottages can be seen on the canal side between Stratford and Lapworth. The one shown below is alongside an old section of canal reopened in 1995 to provide a route between the Stratford and Grand Union canals, which makes more efficient use of water resources than the previously used link.

Barrel-roofed cottage alongside the Lapworth flight of locks

Between bridges 32 and 33, there are seven lock chambers in quick succession – all very close with a short pound between each.

On our journey down that section, we met a young family coming up on a full-length 72-foot narrowboat which itself was towing a 70-foot 'butty'. A butty is a narrowboat without an engine. While their powered boat was in the lock, the butty was in the interconnecting pound, and we had to squeeze around it. It looked impossible to do, but after a great deal of pushing and shoving and a lot of mutual cooperation, we just got past. I could not avoid giving the butty a few minor scrapes here and there, but the owner was pretty sanguine about it – that young man in charge of both boats and his happy family impressed me greatly.

There are three more aqueducts on the Stratford Canal – the first of them at Yarningale Common and the shortest in *England*. The next is at Wootton Wawen, built in 1813. It crosses the busy A34 and has been hit by juggernauts many times but still survives. Finally is the Edstone Aqueduct, at 475 feet, the longest in *England*. Shades of the Pontcysyllte Aqueduct in north Wales but nowhere near as grand, nor so high, but nevertheless interesting to drive the boat across. Note the footpath handrail on the left, level with the bottom of the trough.

Edstone Aqueduct – longest in England

The 11 locks of the Wilmcote flight came next. These were a joyful sight, although hard work for Lindsay. She would fill the next lock then wander down a wide and well-manicured towpath. I would exit each lock, tie up and walk back to close the gates the boat had just come through. I walked on then to open the next gate, then back to the boat before motoring into the next lock. It was a well-practised drill which saved a great deal of time.

Locks 7 and 8 of the Wilmcote flight

Note the very short pound between each. Stratford-upon-Avon is in the far distance.

© Copyright Roger Kidd

Bancroft Basin, Stratford-upon-Avon

This was our ultimate destination – a jewel in Stratford-upon-Avon's crown. Stratford Basin opened on 24th June 1816, restoration being undertaken from 1961 to 1964, which led to the reopening of the Stratford/Birmingham Canal by Her Majesty the Queen Mother on 11th June.

We arrived at Bancroft Basin early because I knew mooring spaces are limited and manoeuvring in the basin, especially in windy conditions, can be tricky. The entrance is around a tight bend where the canal is very narrow then under a low concrete bridge. As it happened there was plenty of room. I showed off a bit by getting into the middle and then executing a perfect 360-degree standing turn – an old geezer reading his paper on the back of his boat grinned and said, "It won't go like that the next time you do it, son!" So true.

Moored in Bancroft Basin

We managed to moor right under Shakespeare's statue, had lunch and then set off for a bit of a tour. Jennie had told us how best to spend an afternoon in Stratford, so we began with a tour bus. This took us around the town and stopped halfway at Anne Hathaway's cottage, where we spent a few hours in the house and grounds and then in the tearoom. Anne Hathaway was William Shakespeare's wife, of course, and the cottage is where she grew up. It is, in fact, a spacious 12-roomed farmhouse, with several bedrooms set in extensive gardens. It was originally built in the 15th century and extended in the 17th century. It was known as Hewlands Farm in Shakespeare's day and had more than 90 acres of land attached. As in many houses of the period, it has multiple chimneys to spread the heat evenly throughout the house during winter. The largest chimney was used for cooking. It also has visible timber framing, a trademark of Tudor-style architecture.

For the evening I had arranged to have dinner at the Royal Shakespeare Theatre restaurant. We had an hour or so to spare, so we wandered down the banks of the River Avon and into the Holy Trinity Church. It's a wonderful building which houses the Shakespeare funerary monument. This is a memorial to William Shakespeare located inside the church in which Shakespeare was baptised and where he was buried in the chancel two days after his death. Anne Hathaway is buried in the grounds of the church.

After dinner we watched 'Julius Caesar' performed at the theatre. After the play, which was gripping, we came out into a warm moonlit night. There were scores of people of all ages sitting around the basin and on the grassy slopes, some with feet dangling in the water, some stargazing, others chatting in small groups and a few listening to music. Quite magical. What a place.

Anne Hathaway's cottage – the home of Shakespeare's wife

Back Towards Kingswood Junction

Our friends Sandra and Steve came to meet us at Bancroft Basin, spending a day with us on the boat travelling back towards Kingswood. They came with us last year, seemingly enjoying doing all the hard work while Lindsay and I put up our feet. Not really. Steve liked driving the boat, was very good at it and so spent most of the time at the tiller on those days. Sandra has been a good friend to Lindsay for a very long time – we first met her when she was in her early 20s and have always thought a lot of her. She did drive the boat on occasions but never really felt confident – but that's OK.

We had arranged for our guests to arrive in time for breakfast. Lindsay was out around town very early to hunt down some big mushrooms. We had a full English breakfast on the boat, cooked on its very well-equipped galley, then I washed up and soon we got under way. I manoeuvred out of the basin and let Steve take over.

From now on until we got back to Alvechurch, the boat would be travelling uphill. As you will see from the image below, these narrow locks have a single big gate at the high-water end and a pair of chevroned half-width gates at the low-water end.

The half-gates are easy to move but often get opened by the wind before you have had a chance to fill the lock and pin them back. Single-handed, that situation is a real pain – it's best to moor up and wait until the next day when it's most likely the wind will have dropped or at least changed direction.

The boat fairly flew up the Wilmcote flight, with Sandra and Lindsay doing their lock-wheeling trick. That's actually quite neat because even if a boat comes the other way, it will naturally leave each lock set in your favour. The only problem occurs if another boat comes out ahead of you, thereby unsetting all the locks ahead that the crew had lovingly prepared.

We don't always stop for lunch on these adventures. It can be difficult to stick to a day's plan when there are always issues of some kind or other. So we will often have lunch on the move with either Lindsay or me being at the tiller or down in the galley making a sandwich and a drink. That is why these 'reverse layout' boats are so nice – it's always possible to communicate when your crew/partner are just a couple of metres away, albeit at the bottom of a staircase.

However, when we had guests with us, we always made a point of mooring up and having a decent lunch. Not a cooked meal but a pretty comprehensive cold one. And plenty of time for chatting and storytelling. I always built that into the schedule.

When Sandra and Steve came with us, we always had an evening meal with them at a convenient pub where we could moor the boat for the night. On this trip, we got to the Fleur de Lys at Lowsonford and tied up for the night. After eating there our lovely friends got a taxi back to Stratford Station and a train home.

The next day dawned, and it was on towards Kingswood Junction. Lindsay and I were alternating between driving the boat and managing the locks – of which there were many. Just before lock 19 there is a large pound. I had left her on the boat and walked up to the lock. I had tied the boat to a bollard outside the previous lock and she had to walk back to shut the big gate and make sure its paddles were closed. In the meantime, I had got to lock 19 and became engrossed in conversation with a boat trader who sold coal to other narrowboat owners along the canal. I was supposed to be preparing lock 19 for Lindsay's arrival, but it was a windy day and I suspected she would not be able to get away from the bank let alone handle the boat in such strong crosswinds. Suddenly, there she was, giving me one of those looks!

I set to and emptied the lock, then opened one of the chevroned gates and pushed it back into its indent in the wall. That left the other gate in the middle of the lock. Now with narrow locks it's tempting to step over from the top of one unopened gate to the bank the other side. However, it is dangerous – one false move, a twitch, a blink out of place, and it would be a long drop into the abyss below, maybe cracking your head on the way down. It's tempting because the alternative is a long walk down the length of the lock and back up the other side to shut the remaining gate. And in windy conditions, especially so if one or other of the gates is being blown open. That's why working wide locks is so much more effort since there is no prospect of a stepover unless you are doing it on stilts or carry a ladder.

What a great week it had been. The reverse layout boat had been a great success, the destination wonderful and the countryside between just serene.

Chapter 11
Bristol Floating Harbour September 2010

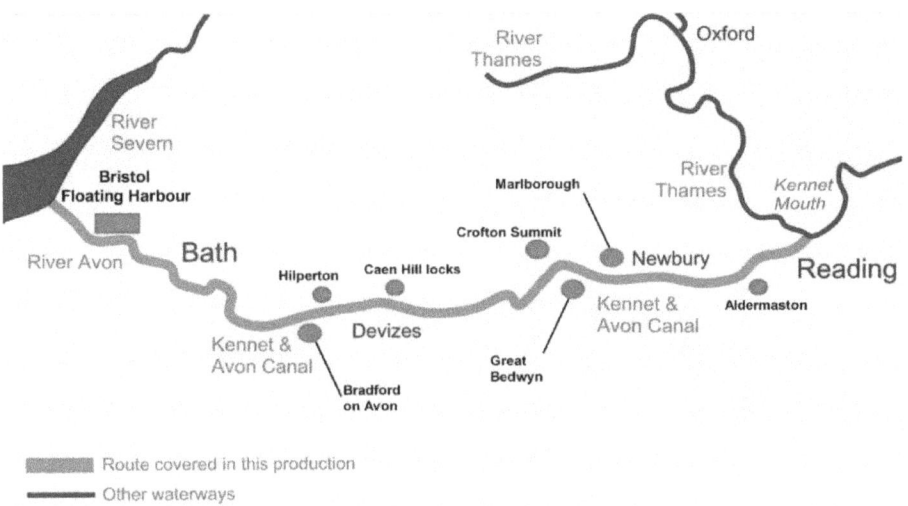

Kennet and Avon Canal

Map based upon 'Waterway Routes' © Copyrighted image

Map 10

This was to be another of those magnificent weeks in our boating machine.

We began from ABC's Hilperton marina on the Kennet and Avon Canal, just west of Devizes. The boat was 'Sabine's Gull', a 60-foot narrowboat with a reverse layout as last year. She had two bedrooms, two bathrooms with showers, a well-equipped galley at the stern and a dining area/lounge just in front of that. The boat had a 3kW inverter, meaning we had 230-volt mains power throughout for toaster, coffee machine, microwave and fridge.

Sabine's Gull

Sabine's gull, also known as the fork-tailed gull, is a small gull. Its generic placement is disputed. Some authors treat it as the sole species in the genus Xema as Xema sabini. Others retain it in the genus Larus as Larus sabini.

Nick and Dinny met us at the marina at the appointed time, we did the handover and after tea, coffee and jam doughnuts, got going about 4pm. That was a bit late by normal standards, so we were soon looking for a mooring space. I didn't want to go through Bradford-on-Avon Lock that evening so was a bit apprehensive.

Preparation

I had been apprehensive about this trip for quite a while. There were a number of reasons.

Firstly, I had acquired a troublesome injury to my right knee. I have had two operations on that knee over the years. The issue is pain over and around the patella (kneecap) tendon. Now, a narrowboat holiday is of course an activity holiday and it's hard to be genuinely active with a dodgy knee. There's likely to be little chance for a rest, especially once it was back to just Lindsay and me on the boat.

Secondly, this was going to be our first lengthy trip on a major river. We had been on the Thames of course but only a short section lasting just a few hours. The Bristol Avon from Bath down to Bristol was going to be a completely different kettle of fish. It has big barge locks up to 75 feet long and 16 feet wide, some of which are notoriously turbulent. I was still unsure of the best way to handle the boat in these. It has tall weirs with strong flows that draw a boat away from the lock channels and towards the weir. I was at that time very unsure of the relationship between river locks and their weirs.

And finally, the Avon is tidal on the way down to Bristol around each spring tide (i.e., twice each lunar month of 29.5 solar days) – and you guessed it, this was going to be one of those times when the weir at Bristol could be overtopped, resulting in high water all the way up to Keynsham. In those conditions a boat's speed over the ground can become deceptively high and the ability to steer can be lost.

Prior to setting off, Lindsay and I drove down to Bristol for a bit of a reccy. I had my knee in a brace, so having to keep it bent in order to drive did not help at all. We took a boat trip around the harbour, checking out mooring places, water points and the like, then, back in the car, followed the path of the river upstream as far as we could, trying to identify where I could moor the boat overnight on the way back to the marina.

Bradford on Avon

We got to Bradford-on-Avon around 6pm and started to look for a mooring place. The wharf area adjacent to the lock is a boating haven with two hire bases and a range of shops and hostelries. It was bound to be busy. I guessed we were too late to get into the public mooring slots so cruised slowly past a long line of boats moored on the towpath side using their mooring pins. No space, but we then spotted a gap between two boats big enough for us to nose in and then pull over the stern using a rope. There was a man reading his paper on the bow of a private boat behind. He watched what we were doing for quite a while. Nick, now standing on the towpath, had the rope in hand and was gradually pulling the stern towards the bank. Then, with about a metre to go, all movement stopped. We had not seen an underwater obstruction, specifically a part of the bankside concrete coping, which had fallen away. There was no choice other than for Nick to climb on at the bow then back out and reverse the boat back up the canal and moor like the others a long way from the wharf.

Ah, reversing[7]. Difficult at the best of times because a narrowboat cannot be steered in reverse. There is a mild steering effect, if you are going back fast enough, by pointing the tiller swan-neck in the direction you want the stern to go. But that's no good at a crawling speed. I had learnt the basics of reversing by accident when we were on the Warwickshire Ring. And I got a good demonstration from one of the Hilperton Marina handover team when he had to reverse about a quarter-mile before he could turn the boat around. In essence, you turn by executing a series of small forward-backward movements, turning the boat while still going backwards but with the engine powering forward. It's possible to turn a 60-foot boat in not much more than its overall length if you get it right.

And so, going backwards past the boat behind, I said to the paper-reading man, "You could have told us about that obstruction." "I could have," he said, with more than a flash of anger.

It's rare to meet that kind of attitude on the waterways. But a lot of private boaters, 'curtain twitchers' as we hirers call them, have a deep resentment of hire-boaters.

---

[7] The reversing process is as follows: Assume the boat is in mid-channel. Stand in front of the tiller arm, facing backwards. On most narrowboats the engine/gearbox controller (Morse Lever) will then be on your right. Make sure your right hand can reach the Morse lever.

Get the boat going backwards at about 2-3 miles per hour. Keep a firm hold of the tiller arm because it will want to bang hard left or right. Point the swan-neck in the direction you want the stern to go. When the stern deviates from the path you want, quickly put the boat into forward gear using a good amount of throttle and move the tiller over in the direction you want the stern to go. The idea is to use just enough forward power to position the stern but not so much that the boat stops travelling backwards. It takes a bit of practice.

With the stern now in the correct position, recover your firm grip on the tiller, bringing it back to the centre, and use the Morse lever to get the boat going backwards once more. You will not have to worry about what the bow might be doing because it will faithfully follow the stern. A good idea to look around now and again though in case there is a substantial cross-wind.

The four of us found a good restaurant that night, right on the quayside. In fact, one of the best fillet steaks I have ever had was served up. Afterward we thought we would walk into town, around ten minutes away. But at halfway we turned back because my knee was giving me a lot of pain. I said I was still wearing the knee brace and had been protecting, guarding, that knee when going up and down the steep stairs from the stern into the galley. Dinny then came up with a remarkable suggestion along the lines of 'take the brace off, *use* **the knee** – stop guarding it. And do a quad stretch every day'. Guess what? As soon as I started going up and down those galley steps 20 times a day, my knee improved. So much so that within a couple of days, I forgot all about it. (I have used that advice every day since and have never had to revert to that brace.)

The next morning, after mandatory bacon and eggs on the boat, I manoeuvred Sabine's Gull down towards the lock. It was chaos there, I have to say, with four boats waiting for the lock to fill. I think I was the only experienced captain because there was a cacophony of engine roaring, forward, reverse, and sometimes sideways going on. It was windy, which didn't help of course. I signalled that the first two boats should go into the lock together while I kept us under control and in centre channel.

Nick and Dinny were lock side and supervised the refilling of the lock and opening of the double gates. This is a big lock. My compatriot was a bit nervous, but I kept our boat steady while he managed to squeeze around and into the lock. I then neatly slotted in beside him. I must have been a calming influence – he thanked me for taking control of a sticky situation. But of course, six years earlier, it could well have been me wanting assistance. I was happy to help.

The John Rennie Aqueducts

After Bradford Lock, the canal runs alongside the River Avon for a couple of miles and then turns right through 90 degrees to cross the Avon via the Avoncliff Aqueduct. This was built by John Rennie and chief engineer John Thomas, between 1797 and 1801.

Although we had only just left Bradford-on-Avon, Nick was keen to stop here to take a look at a historic pub that predates the canal by hundreds of years. It's the Cross Guns. One of the oldest buildings in Avoncliff, the twin-gabled central section of the Cross Guns is believed to date back to the 1490s, the central inglenook fireplace being of the same style as those found at Hampton Court. With the construction of the east wing in the early 1600s, this Tudor residence became an inn known as The Carpenter's Arms. It provided respite for travellers and drovers using the ford across the river at Avoncliff. It was later used by quarrymen, millworkers and travellers.

At the turn of the 18th century, the Kennet and Avon Canal arrived. The additional trade this generated for the pub necessitated the construction of the western extension in which the snug was housed. Here, customers would have enjoyed smoking their clay pipes, playing cards, drinking ales and whiskies, partaking of snuff and sharing tales that stretched the length of the canal!

Avoncliff Aqueduct from the Bradford-on-Avon side

We parked the boat and wandered down to the Cross Keys. It's an impressive building, snuggled closely beside the aqueduct. Then back up the incline and over a picket fence and into the tearoom that sits on the opposite side of the aqueduct. It was a modest affair. Nick, with his management hat squared firmly on his head, declared "It will never work – too small, not enough custom and too many overheads." I have repeated "It will never work" to him many times since. He always takes it in good spirit. The teashop is still there – thriving apparently. It's now called 'No 10 Tea Gardens' and was a finalist in Bath 2019 Awards.

After tea and home-made cakes, back on the boat and westward towards Bath. The canal follows the path of the River Avon, changing sides over the second Rennie masterpiece – the Dundas Aqueduct. This magnificent structure was designed by Rennie and Thomas between 1797 and 1801 and completed in 1805. It is a Grade I listed building and was the first canal structure to be designated as a Scheduled Ancient Monument in 1951. Over many years leaks have developed and it was closed in 1954. For a while in the 1960s and 1970s, the canal was dry, and it was possible to walk along the bed on each side of the river, as well as through the aqueduct itself. The aqueduct was relined with polythene and concrete and restored, reopening in 1984.

Dundas Aqueduct across the Wiltshire River Avon

The Kennet and Avon Canal is one of the most popular in the country. Progress along much of its length is necessarily at a snail's pace on account of a plethora of residential craft, mostly beaten-up old tubs, moored bow to stern all the way to Bath. These boats are supposed to move every few days but never do as far as I can see. Canal and River Trust do ensure they are licensed, but that's just about it. No one checks how their owners empty their sewage tanks or cassettes – a lot of it is dumped on farmers' land or into the canal at night, I suspect.

Into Bath and onto the River Avon

From Dundas it's around four boating hours to Bath. That's about six miles, given all the linear residential moorings along the route – all of which have to be passed at tickover speed. One of the sights to see, we didn't, but if there's time, is the Claverton Pumping Station. When the canal was first built, Claverton lifted water up into the canal from the Avon below. It used a gigantic waterwheel, still in working condition today, and water-powered rocking-beam pumps. However, day to day operation is now done by modern electrically powered pumps which move over one million gallons of water each day.

We next had to deal with a set of six locks that would take us downhill and onto the River Avon. The view from top lock number 13 was really special, providing panoramic views over this beautiful stone-built city. All was going well until we met lock 10, Wash House, where there was a queue because the pound beyond had drained of water.

I walked down to peer over the balance beams. All I could see down below was an extensive muddy ditch containing a distinctive main channel bereft of water and a side channel moving off to the left, also drained. This was the first time I had met this situation. I had never considered how it might happen. I had always thought there would be water to float the boat but was clearly wrong. Luckily, the crew in the lead boat knew what to do. First, they disappeared down to lock 8/9 (Bath Deep Lock) for a while. When they re-appeared, about 20 minutes later, they opened the paddles at both ends of lock 10 to let water flow through and down into the pound below. They explained that the previous crew had not shut the upper paddles of the Bath Deep Lock, nor fully closed its lower paddles, thereby allowing water to drain out of the canal. They had rectified that and, following their return, the next pound began to fill – quite quickly actually, which surprised me. We met the same situation many years later, again on the Kennet and Avon, at Wootton rivers. However, I called out the Canal and Rivers Trust to check the far lock since by then had understood that a leak and subsequent drainage could be caused by a whole host of things, faulty gates or paddles, damaged culverts, vandalism and so on, as well as boater negligence.

Bath Deep Lock – it's a very long way down. Look at the height of that gate!

About an hour's delay was the consequence, which did concern me because I didn't want to be on the Avon too late in the day – it would be dark by 8pm. But with four of us in the crew, me driving, we fairly flew down the next few locks until we got to number 8/9 – Bath Deep. It's called 8/9 because there were originally two locks at that location, combined into one when the canal was restored in 1976. A road constructed while the canal was in a state of disrepair passes over the original site of the lower lock. The new chamber has a depth of 19 feet 5 inches, making it Britain's second deepest canal lock. There is one on the Rochdale Canal that is a bit deeper, but boaters are not allowed to operate it themselves – a CRT lock keeper is always present. However, I assure you, Bath Deep is plenty deep enough when you are down there on your own, just you and the boat in the lock, looking skyward on a gloomy day. It could have been a bit like the legendary black hole of Calcutta.

Then through lock 7 and onto the River Avon. It's wide and deep so life jackets all round. We needed to go westward, destination Bristol, some 15 miles distant. To our right, the river would lead us up into Bath centre, where navigation stops at Pulteney Weir. If there's time on the way back,

Lindsay and I intended to take the boat there and have a look around the town.

The boat responded well to the deep water of the Avon, fairly flying along with very little wake. I was on the lookout for Weston Lock, where there was a pub with a meal awaiting. But I had no idea where its associated weir would be, what it would look like or what the lock channel down the side of that weir would look like. The river seemed to go and on. I knew the upcoming weir was a big one (i.e., big drop), but I had no idea how it would be marked.

Eventually, in the distance, I saw a big sky low on the horizon bracketed at one end by tower blocks and at the other by tall trees. There appeared to be some kind of steel work/cranes in the far distance. I knew something was up and began to slow the boat. It was late now and gloomy and at the back end of a 60-foot narrowboat was having trouble seeing clearly. But then, hanging on a tree, I saw a tiny blue and white sign pointing to the right, saying 'Lock'. It was directing us to the right, off the river, up a narrow, overgrown stream – at least that's what it looked like. I had drifted past by now and had to stop the boat and reverse. *Is that really it?* I remember thinking.

Weston Lock sluice gate and weir

© Copyright Google Earth

Well, it was. We had come off a river perhaps 400 yards wide and were now going cautiously up a channel overgrown on both sides perhaps six yards wide. A pair of lock gates came into view about 100 yards ahead and I could see the mooring bollards. Now, it's frowned upon to moor overnight at a lock without a lock keeper, but we had no choice. Nick jumped off with the bow rope, which he tied to the bollard furthest away from the gates. Dinny banged in a stern mooring pin, then attached the stern rope to secure the boat. We all then scrambled up a steep bank and trotted off down to the Locksbrook Inn for dinner.

In September 2020, Weston Lock weir, or more correctly Weston Lock sluice gate, was opened by mistake. The barrier is there to alleviate flooding. When the river is in spate, it is raised to let the flood waters escape downstream. In normal river conditions, it remains closed and acts as a weir. On that September day the barrier spontaneously raised itself in what the Environment Agency subsequently described as a software failure.

The immediate consequence was that the river level between Weston Lock and Pulteney Weir, the stretch we had just navigated, quickly dropped by more than two metres. Some 40 boats were moored on that section. Prompt action by their owners allowed some boats to move out into deeper water. However, several were caught on the steeply shelved sides and rolled over, taking on water. A few sank. A few were damaged beyond repair.

Bristol Floating Harbour

The next morning saw us start another day which would end, all being well, in Bristol Floating Harbour[8]. There has been a harbour in Bristol since time began. However, the River Avon, on which the harbour is situated, was always a hindrance to shipping and hence trade because with each tide it became crowded with boats wanting to enter or leave. And neap (especially low) tides would often beach ships, causing them damage. In the late 1700s, ship owners began a project to make the harbour non-tidal by damming the river – allowing ships that were in harbour to stay afloat 24/7. Hence a 'Floating Harbour'.

Its 80 acres of basin and wharfage opened in 1809. It had a consistent water depth whatever the state of the tides, where boats and ships could be sure they would always be able to manoeuvre. There is a lock at each end of the basin; the largest is a sea lock which exits into the River Avon, providing access to and from the Bristol Channel. The smallest is behind the weir, which maintains a navigable depth back up the Avon to Bath.

---

[8] In the mid 1700's there was no proper harbour in Bristol. Ships would visit the town via the tidal River Avon. Its 12-metre tidal range would often leave vessels stranded in the mud until they refloated 12 hours later. The solution was to create a 70-acre pound situated between a lock at Hotwells and one at Netham. Construction began in 1804, using chief engineer William Jessop, and was completed in 1809. They called it a 'floating harbour' because it has a constant water level whereas the old version most certainly did not.

On spring tides (especially high) that weir is often overtopped, but the adjacent lock stops any increase in depth in the harbour.

The four of us quickly navigated Weston Lock. The next eight miles or so went through wide, flat countryside. The locks were wide and long and a little daunting, but we were going downhill towards Bristol and lock turbulence was not an issue. At Keynsham, spelt K E Y N S H A M for those old enough to remember Horace Batchelor at Radio Luxembourg in the 1950s, the River Chew joins the Avon, increasing the semi-tidal flow down to Bristol.

Keynsham has an interesting history for chocolate lovers. The Fry & Sons chocolate business merged with Cadbury in 1919 and moved to Keynsham in 1935. Cadburys built the factory on a 228-acre site with social facilities which included playing fields and recreational sports grounds. Called Somerdale after a national competition in 1923, Keynsham Cadbury was the home of Fry's Chocolate Cream, the Double Decker, Cadbury's Dairy Milk and Mini Eggs, Cadbury's Fudge, Chomp and Crunchie. The factory was closed in 2011 and all production transferred to the Bournville site.

Once we were through Keynsham Lock, we were on deeper semi-tidal waters, allowing the boat to glide along smoothly with little wake and minimal pressure on the tiller. Nick and I took turns to drive the boat while Lindsay and Dinny sat on the bow and chatted. Neither of them wanted to be at the tiller for long periods – Nick and I were happy to do that.

The terrain started to switch from woodland and flat flood plain to woodland and gorge. At Hanham we had to phone the lock keeper at Netham and announce our pending arrival. This was in case the lock had been closed by a spring tide. In fact, it was open, and we would be there in about an hour.

Just outside Netham Lock is the weir that maintains navigation back up the Avon to Bath. I moored up at Netham Lock to go and check in with the lock keeper, let him know how long we were staying in the harbour and pay the licence fee. Then off down the long feeder channel that leads into the harbour proper. At the end is a sharp right-hand turn and then under the railway bridge that carries the railway lines to Bristol's Temple Meads station.

Temple Meads is the oldest and largest railway station in Bristol, the other being Bristol Parkway. It was opened on 31st August 1840 as the terminus of the Great Western Railway from London Paddington – 116 miles distant. That railway was the first to be designed by the Isambard Kingdom Brunel. It has a special meaning for me because that was where my maternal grandfather, Arch, would collect me as I emerged from the train guard's van after my solo journeys from Paddington. That was in the summers between 1954 and 1959. Arch and I would then take one of those big green double-decker buses on the tortuous route back to Berkeley for the summer holidays. After 1959, my father would hire a car and drive us all to Berkeley, via Burford on the A40 – a dangerous three-lane trunk road. It was always a hellish trip and only a week or so – not a month on my own with my grandparents.

Another straight section follows, then a left-hand bend. On the hill above are the ruins of St Peter's Church in Castle Park.

The foundations of St Peter's can be traced back to 1106 when it was endowed on Tewkesbury Abbey with a 12th-century lower tower, the rest of the church being built in the 15th century. Excavations in 1975 suggest that this was the site of Bristol's first church; the 12th-century city wall runs under the west end of the present church. It was bombed during the Bristol Blitz of 24th–25th November 1940 and ruined. It is maintained as a monument to the civilian war dead of Bristol.

Floating Harbour Proper

From St Peter's Church there are some two miles of flat calm waterway before reaching the end of the harbour. The sea lock then gives ships access to the tidal River Avon and thence on to Avonmouth and the Bristol Channel.

Cruising down that waterway is a glorious sight. Multi-coloured houses high up on the right-hand bank, Bristol commerce on the left-hand bank. Boats, ships, of all sizes and heritages, moored on both sides.

The Matthew of Bristol, pictured below, is a replica of the 15th-century caravel that John Cabot sailed from Bristol to Newfoundland in 1497. In 1997 she sailed across the Atlantic once more to mark the 500th anniversary of the historic voyage. (Text from Wikipedia.)

Brunel's iron steamship The Great Britain was an awesome sight when seen from water level as we drifted slowly past.

Replica of The Matthew

Brunel's iron steamship, the SS Great Britain

On the deck of SS Great Britain

**Dinny and Nick pointing west towards the sea lock and
Avonmouth**

Moored at the western end and looking east

Twin-masted schooner

The four of us moored overnight at the western end of the harbour. In the morning we took the boat back to where the SS Great Britain has a permanent berth and spent a few hours wandering around Brunel's masterpiece. I was particularly struck by the reconstructed engine room – took me back to my Woolwich Ferry days, although on a somewhat grander scale.

After lunch, I moved the boat back under Temple Meads bridge so Nick and Dinny could alight and catch their train back home. Lindsay and I then began our journey home – it had been a few days to remember all right.

Back Towards Bath

I was aware that on our way back to Bath, we would be on the semi-tidal River Avon for a while but going uphill this time. Going uphill in big locks, where there is only one boat being lifted, could be problematic and so it proved. At Saltford, the lock is adjacent to the Jolly Sailor pub. We were in full view of those sitting sipping their pints in the pub's beer garden. On the way down, see picture earlier, we had Nick and Dinny for company. This time, Lindsay was on her own and I was on the boat. She emptied the lock as usual then opened one bottom gate, allowing me to guide the boat in. Once inside, it was pea on a drum time – the lock is huge and wide. I positioned us against the right-hand wall, right under the noses of the drinkers. I could see up a dozen or so nostrils, all of which seemed to begin twitching in anticipation of a pending drama. Lindsay shut the bottom gate and wandered up to the top gate to open the sluice. I don't know whether the sluice was sticky or just plain vicious, but I was hit by a tidal wave of water, making the boat career first backward, then forwards as it bounced off the back gates. I immediately applied a lot of engine power to keep us near the middle, making a huge amount of noise and severely disturbing those drinkers. The boat then lurched sideways, taking me across the lock to collide with the left-hand wall. In a narrowboat without a bow thruster, there is no sideways control.

How they all laughed. With hindsight, it would have been better, at that lock, to put the central line around a bollard rather than just rely on the engine to balance the boat between top and bottom gates. At least we gave the drinkers a good show.

Having got off the tidal section of the river, we eventually came up to the far side of Weston Lock, where we had moored on the way down.

The downstream side of the weir near Weston Lock

This remotely controlled structure determines the water level in Bath city centre. It failed in 2020, resulting in 40 or more boats being rolled over or grounded or sunk or severely damaged.

The landing stage at Weston Lock is a puny affair. It's also on a bend just outside the lock.

[9]The lock cannot be seen once you are up on the landing stage. I moored the boat to a bollard using the central line, as is standard practice, then let Lindsay off so she could prepare the lock. I could not see her though so had no idea how long that would take. Suddenly, a wall of water came

---

[9] I've witnessed a number of dramas where a crew had not secured their boat below a lock. In one case the boat ended up stuck across the canal with their centre line in the water. In another, the centre line snapped, and the boat got away.

Some locks are known for their fierce outflow. In that situation just wind the bow line around a bollard and secure that with a boatman's hitch. That knot is so useful because no matter how hard it has been stretched, it will not slip and it will always untie with ease. And think about the helm and the lockside crew having access to a pair of walkie-talkie radios.

around the bend, swept under the legs of the landing stage and caught the bow of the boat – which of course was sticking out into the stream. In normal circumstances I would have called out (probably yelled) to Lindsay to close down the paddle and so slow the deluge. Or she would have noticed. But I could not see her. And she could not see me.

I was lucky. I had time to get back on board, otherwise the boat would have gone on its way back to Bristol – no-handed!

Drained River Avon at Bath in 2020

© Copyright BBC News

The central line snapped tight as the water tried its best to take the bow away into the central stream. It really was a crisis moment. I could hear the line moaning, vibrating, creaking, going to snap at any moment. The water was acting like a giant crowbar, levering the boat free from its jailers. As luck would have it, the boat was pivoting around its centre of mass, pushing the bow out but the stern in. I dragged the central line from around the bollard, walked smartly back along the landing stage and leaped onto the boat deck, freeing the boat and allowing it to drift backwards into the central stream. That gave me an engine and tiller with which I could regain control. Crisis over.

Now in mid-stream, I could see Lindsay up on top of the lock gates cranking open their paddles. All I had to do was hover around, waiting for the lock to empty and drive in.

Bath City Centre and Pulteney Weir

Good moorings coming up on the River Avon

Bath city centre just around the bend. Converted wharf and
warehouse buildings to the right.

It only took some five hours in all to arrive back in Bath once we had left
Bristol. That left us at the city outskirts in mid-afternoon, fitting the bill
perfectly, as I wanted to spend the next day as near the centre and
Pulteney Weir as possible. Mooring up early meant I could move the boat
up to the weir the next morning, with some certainty that a mooring place
would be available.

I tied the boat to the railings shown in the picture above, just in front of
the narrowboat already there. We planned to find a KFC restaurant in
Bath that night but had no idea where it might be. Help was at hand from
my new iPhone. Lindsay and I found the location, dropped a pin on it and
used Google Maps and GPS on the phone to guide us right to it. We
walked for about 30 minutes or so, going uphill right through the city
centre, admiring all the architecture and stonework and general civility

of the place. I did find it a difficult walk because my knee was still painfully wrapped inside a hefty compression bandage. Too soon for Dinny's 'use that knee' diktat to have had any effect. After fried chicken and a cold coke, we had a rather peaceful gentle stroll downhill back to the boat and a glistening, twinkly Avon.

After breakfast I drove the boat around the corner, past the entrance to the canal and on up a short stretch of the Avon until, first of all, Bath Abbey came into view and then that magnificent weir.

We found ourselves at the head of the queue, just downstream from the weir. The plan was to spend a day looking around some of the sights of Bath.

Entrance to the Kennet and Avon Canal

The plans to see Bath City were somewhat curtailed because rain was absolutely sheeting down. We got off the boat and walked over, rather through, Pulteney Bridge, past the row of shops inside that span the Avon far below. Lindsay and I got on a tour bus which took us out past the Jane Austen Centre, museum of the author's life and works, then to the Royal Crescent.

The Royal Crescent is a row of 30 terraced houses laid out in a sweeping crescent. Designed by the architect John Wood the Younger and built between 1767 and 1774, it is among the greatest examples of Georgian architecture to be found in the United Kingdom and is a Grade I listed building. Although some changes have been made to the various interiors over the years, the Georgian stone facade remains much as it was when first built. The 500-foot-long crescent has 114 Ionic columns on the first floor with an entablature in a Palladian style above. It was the first crescent of terraced houses to be built and an example of an illusion of countryside created by a building or garden within a city. Many notable people have either lived or stayed in the Royal Crescent since it was built over 240 years ago, and some are commemorated on special plaques attached to the relevant buildings. Of the crescent's 30 townhouses, ten are still full-size townhouses; 15 have been split into flats of various sizes; one is the No. 1 Royal Crescent Museum and the large central house at number 16 is the Royal Crescent Hotel & Spa.

Moored at the head of the queue in Bath. Pulteney Weir is to the left.

Mooring in this area is banned now.

Once off the bus back in the city centre, we visited the Roman Baths, then Bath Abbey (although we had been there some years earlier for a choral concert) and had a latish lunch in Henrietta Park overlooking the weir.

I have to say, with the sun now shining brightly in late September, that whole area was a magical place. We could hear the River Avon pouring over the weir, there was birdsong in the air and child-song too with families sitting on picnic blankets amongst the neatly trimmed parkland.

Pulteney Weir

Note the trip boat close to the weir.

Later while wandering though the crowds to look at an exhibition of gigantic images displaying the hot-spots of Bath, Lindsay and I were spotted by a camera crew. One man was carrying a large camera with a fat lens on his shoulder while his compatriot held a furry microphone on the end of a long stick. He poked the microphone in my face and said they were filming a piece for the BBC about the supposedly poor visitor facilities in Bath; you know, few hotels, no car parks, poor restaurants, lack of toilets, too many fast-food joints and so on. What did we think? "Haven't a clue," said I. "We came by boat." Lindsay later told me I then began a lengthy diatribe about boating; how wonderful, how challenging. That sort of threw them because it didn't fit with the angle they were wanting – 'It's outrageous that Bath has such poor facilities for visitors.' As I droned on, I could see the will to live drain from the sound engineer's face. One of my auctioneer customers told me weeks later that they had seen the piece on BBC local TV and how much it made them laugh.

Pulteney Bridge over the Bath Avon with the weir in the foreground

This image was taken mid-stream as we turned the boat around.

Late that afternoon Lindsay and I wandered back over Pulteney Bridge then down the footpath to the boat. That evening we were booked in at The Steakhouse and Grill restaurant – which looked splendid as darkness drew in. We clambered over the low railings, then across the path and into the restaurant. It was about 8pm, but the place was empty. That was a surprise. I immediately wondered what we were in for. Lindsay and I had a drink in the bar on the ground floor then upstairs to eat, right over by the window overlooking the river. We had an excellent meal, lavish attention from the waiters, wonderful decorative surroundings and a spectacular view over Bath. What was there not to like? Clearly something, because we sat in splendid isolation all evening.

The next morning, we had the company of Sandra and Steve, who had travelled by train to meet us. We all had breakfast together on the boat, something I always enjoyed, but it was made all the more special by the location of course.

Steve and I had a brief chat about how to turn the boat around. We decided to let the river do the work. Sandra untied the bow line and pushed us off. I slackened off the stern line a little, holding the boat still with a half-turn around a bollard. The river grabbed the bow, which gradually came around about 120 degrees. I gently let the stern line run through my fingers, leaving the boat facing downstream and in mid-stream. I coiled up the stern line while Steve powered us on towards the Kennet and Avon Canal entrance.

Over the next few hours, we made our way back along the canal towards Dundas Aqueduct. It proved shallow with many underwater obstacles – mainly bits of canal-side coping stones. Funny that, I never noticed them on the way down. There were a number of wide beam narrowboats moored up, their sterns sticking out into the canal. Steve carefully navigated his way around these. And plenty of semi-sunk wrecks, which Canals and Rivers Trust never take action about.

Sharp left turn onto Dundas Aqueduct on the way back to Hilperton Marina

We needed to take on water so proceeded to the water point at the corner of the aqueduct – top right-hand part of the image above. There was a boat filling up already, so we had to wait. Another boat came in behind us wanting to use the toilet pump-out machine. We had used one of these during the two-week Warwickshire Ring adventure – or rather a marina employee had done a pump-out for us. I was interested to watch someone else use it so observed them intently. It's an efficient process, I have to say. First insert a token in the machine. Then unscrew your boat's toilet tank cover and push in the machine hose. Then put the machine in 'Suck' mode. It does get smelly as the sewage is sucked out, especially if downwind as we were. Lindsay and Sandra didn't think much of that and trotted off to find the source of ice creams we had spotted. Having emptied his tank, the boat owner put the machine into 'Flush' mode, whence clear water is pumped back into the toilet tank. This disturbs the bit left at the bottom of the tank. Finally, the machine sucks all that out and then reverses to put some clear water plus 'blue' (sterilising/breakdown additive) back into the tank. Process over.

While I was watching the pump-out process going on, I was conscious of a narrowboat to our left going backwards and forwards. Steve and I were a bit mesmerised. It was a full-length boat, that is 72 feet, and it seemed he wanted to turn the bow to the left and proceed onto the aqueduct. But he never got back far enough or made enough space on his right-hand side to be able to make the turn. We watched for about 20 minutes, getting more and more frustrated for that steerer. Meanwhile, the pump-out boat had gone, we had attached ourselves to the water point, and the girls came back with ice cream. All was good with the world, water was trickling into the tank, the sun was out in a cloudless sky, there was a cool clear breeze, we slowly slurped on our cornets and that bloke just kept on going, backward, forward, backward...

Sandra and Lindsay had tracked down the ice cream shop at the entrance to the derelict Somerset Coal Canal. A short arm is still in water, used now as moorings for a private boating club.

The Somerset Coal Canal (originally known as the Somersetshire Coal Canal) is a narrow canal built around 1800. Prior to dereliction it had basins in the west at Paulton and Timsbury, an aqueduct at Dunkerton and went via Combe Hay, Midford and Monkton Combe back to Limpley Stoke, where it joined the Kennet and Avon at Dundas. The canal connected the Somerset coalfields to London via the Kennet and Avon

Canal. From Dundas, going west, the canal rose uphill. Water supply was always going to be a problem. The canal followed the line of the Cam Brook, a minor river in Somerset. The Cam source is near Hinton Blewitt, then flows east through Cameley, Temple Cloud, Camerton, Dunkerton and Combe Hay. It then joins the Wellow Brook at Midford to form Midford Brook before joining the River Avon adjacent to the Dundas Aqueduct.

The Cam Brook was an inadequate source of water above Camerton, plus the mills along it had water rights. The canal was therefore designed with 22 narrow locks in a single flight, near Combe Hay, raising the canal over 135 feet. A pumping engine was used to raise water from the Cam Brook below. This was the first canal to entirely depend on pumping. (Some text courtesy of 'Grace's Guide to British Industrial History'.)

We moored near Hilperton that night. Sandra and Steve drove home. Lindsay and I packed up the boat ready for a short trip back to the marina by 9am.

Somerset Coal Canal eastern portal at Dundas

Chapter 12

Aldermaston to Abingdon on the River Thames 2011

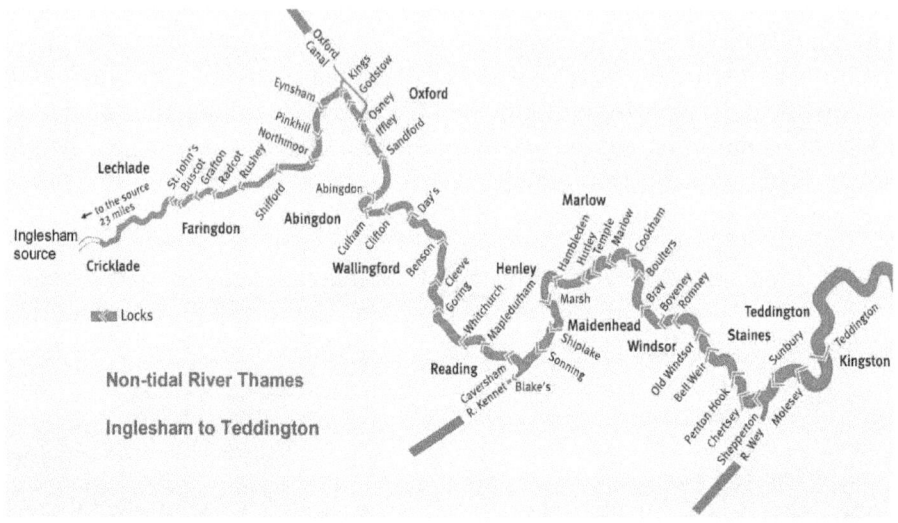

Non-tidal River Thames

Map based on an Environment Agency © Copyrighted image

Map 11

The following year we were back on the Kennet and Avon, beginning at Aldermaston, onto the Thames at Reading and then north as far as Abingdon and back. See maps 10 and 11.

Cousins Nick and Dinny met us for breakfast in a local hotel, since it was going to be an early start. We could have the boat from 10am. The boat was facing the wrong way, so the first job was to go westward under the lift bridge and into the basin in front of Aldermaston Lock. One of the marina staff volunteered to operate the electric bridge, stopping all road traffic while I drove the boat under, turned it 360 degrees and came back through. That should have been a straightforward operation, but I had not taken account of the strength of the wind. During the turn, which went well actually, the boat was pushed too near Aldermaston Lock gates – which are huge. It took a bit of toing and froing to rectify the situation, during which I heard an increasing cacophony of car horns and shouts of "How much longer, mate?" It's a truism that whenever the steerer gets in a difficult situation, mostly not their fault, a rent-a-crowd appears on cue as if by magic.

Now pointing eastward, I stopped to pick up the crew and we set off towards the River Thames. I had read that the trip down towards the river is not picturesque and the lock gear is in poor condition. There is a difficult stretch through Reading town centre, which is one-way controlled by traffic lights. And that stretch is on the River Kennet, not the canal, and can be fast flowing and turbulent.

Reconnaissance

Lindsay and I had made a reconnaissance visit a few weeks before to check out the hazards. We went first to look at Blake's Lock, the last on the River Kennet before meeting the Thames. It had a pair of quaint-looking wheels to raise or lower the paddles. There was no lock channel as such, the weir being just over the other side of a long, thin island. That fact did not register with me at all, as events later would confirm. We were looking for suitable mooring places of course, since mooring was not allowed through the town centre. The Fisherman's Cottage pub was right behind us, so I popped in to have a chat with the landlord. He suggested I moor the boat to the railings right outside. He assured me that was permissible, even though the crew and I would have to clamber over the ironwork along the river bank. And it would be fine to moor overnight there right in front of Blake's Lock – something frowned upon by waterways folk. Lindsay and I agreed that was a good plan, then set of to have a look at several of the small bridges over the Kennet that the boat would have to navigate through.

Those bridges were narrow, and all had limited headroom. I had read that in flood conditions the Kennet can be more than two feet higher than normal. That made me wonder whether it would then be possible to get through at all. Most of the abutments had considerable damage, presumably caused by collisions from out-of-control boats in fast-flowing water.

121

When going downstream on fast-flowing water, it's easy for the steerer to find themselves with an inability to steer. That's because a boat on a river flowing at say 5mph will need to maintain a minimum 2mph *through the water* if steering is to be maintained – leaving the boat going at 7mph or more over the ground. Too fast in most urban situations. When approaching an obstacle, the temptation would be to throttle back, killing off the speed through the water but also killing off the effectiveness of the tiller. Witness the bridge damage on the Kennet. In flood conditions on tidal rivers like the Trent, which decades ago carried extensive barge traffic, boat captains would often turn their craft through 180 degrees and go downstream backwards, with the tiller then at the front. It's a clever concept because the boat would go with the flow, making progress over the ground, but by driving the boat forwards into the water coming down, the stern could be positioned accurately, and the bows would follow. I would love to have tried that. Navigating through bridge arches would have been a cinch, though doubtless hair-raising but an exhilarating experience.

The River Thames uses a system of 'Stream Warning' boards to advise river traffic of navigation conditions. A 'Red Board' in front of a lock means river conditions are or will soon be dangerous. There is no such system on inland waterways. However, I had worked out a plan for going through Reading. One of the crew would be stationed at the bow, armed with the short pole, ready to fend-off against an abutment too close. On approaching each abutment, I would put the engine into a hard reverse, in effect stopping the boat over the ground. Then into hard ahead, giving me enough steering to control the bow through and under each bridge. It would require good judgement, but I thought it could be done. However, I didn't have a plan for a situation where the boat would not fit under a bridge at all.

In 2011 the only experience I had of River Thames locks and their procedures was that brief visit onto the river via Oxford, through Godstone Lock and back onto the South Oxford Canal via Duke's Cut. I was concerned about the mighty weirs at lock sites and worried that we might get swept over head first and sunk. I didn't know about lock channels, or cuts, and so undertook to visit a few sites on foot.

The Plough Inn at Long Wittenham sits on the southern bank of the main channel of the Thames, about half a mile from Clifton Weir. Boats heading downstream on the Thames would move right-to-left, keeping well away from a strong current flow over the top of the weir. The drop is normally around four feet but can be twice that in flood conditions.

I paid the pub a visit. It has a long garden dropping in defined stages to the River Thames. A bit like the terraced field systems from Stone Age agriculture. Each terrace is a direct result of gouging caused by extensive flooding of the river. It's quite a sight. At the very bottom is a landing stage, rickety to say the least and hardly likely to resist flood conditions were boats to be attached. I had a good look and decided we could tie up to the big trees at either end.

That landing stage looked suitable for two smallish narrowboats. But it being near to and under that weir made me nervous, especially if conditions worsened after we had left Aldermaston. I didn't fancy being woken by a raging torrent, lines pulled out, drifting backwards in the dark, past the lock and on towards Clifton Hampden Bridge. Standing on the landing stage, the weir was to the left – meaning the river flowed left to right. The flow looked to be about fast walking pace when I was there. The river is only about 40 metres wide at that point. The far bank is high, probably about ten metres above water level and very flat, indicating it is the edge of a Thames flood plain.

After completing that survey, the Plough Inn seemed a good bet for food and overnight mooring. At Clifton Lock, going upstream, we would need to keep left on the river channel as it bypassed the lock and head on until meeting the pub. Were we to continue upstream, we would of course come face to face with mighty Clifton Weir yawning above us.

That survey made things clear – in normal condition a boat would never bypass a lock channel because it would eventually meet a weir and go over or be rolled over by going under, were there no barriers of course!

Back at the Plough Inn, we would tie up pointing into the flow, towards the weir – the correct procedure when mooring in strong flow conditions because the curve of the bow would tend to push the boat inward towards the bank.

The next morning would see me having to turn the boat around with little space to manoeuvre. No problems there then.

Mooring in Reading

The four of us got safely down to County Lock in Reading and waited for the traffic light to go green. That was a filthy place to stay, even for the 15 minutes or so we were there. It's littered with drug paraphernalia, used condoms, rats, beer cans, fast-food wrappers and all the stuff associated with people who don't or can't care.

Then a gentle warble down through the middle of Reading, past Debenhams and under those little bridges.

River Kennet through Reading town centre

Mooring is not allowed in the town centre because of the unpredictable nature of the River Kennet.

© Copyright Canal and River Trust

The river's flow was modest, and the technique discussed earlier for avoiding those copious abutments worked well. We hit nothing at all.

As we approached Blake's Lock, it became apparent that mooring the boat in front of the lock and clambering over the railings just wasn't on. It had looked OK from the bankside outside the pub, but not from the water.

I then looked to my left, into the loop that comes around from Reading Prison, and spotted the Bell and the Dragon restaurant with its wonderful herringbone moorings. Neither Lindsay nor I had noticed it during our reconnaissance visit. That was *so* now the place to moor. I turned the boat towards the pub, neatly reversed into position and tied up.

However, that presented me with a problem. I had to tell the landlord of the Fisherman's Cottage pub that we could not make it. But we were less than 50 metres from him. Cousin Nick and I stood on the rear deck of the boat and concocted a plan. We would tell the landlord we had been delayed and were still at the marina in Aldermaston.

I got on the phone and began relaying the story, terribly apologetic. Just as I did, a police car came screaming round the prison bend, blues and twos going like the clappers. I was well into the story by then. "Hang on a minute," said the landlord. "There's a police car outside my pub and I can also hear one down the phone near you." "How amazing is that?" Nick had collapsed with laughter by now, listening to me change tack to blather on about life's chance events. "And you won't believe this," he said. "The tones are perfectly synchronised." I did believe him and got off the phone as quickly as I could. Nick couldn't speak for quite a while.

That night, laying in my bunk, I felt a bit ashamed at telling that lie. I should have told the landlord the situation and apologised. Ah well.

Dinny and Lindsay up on Blake's Lock, Reading, River Kennet

This is the last lock before meeting the River Thames – it has wheeled paddle gear like those on the upper Thames. Note life jackets ready for the river.

Towards Abingdon

The next morning the four of us had breakfast on the boat and then set off through Blake's Lock onto the Thames. We turned left at Tesco Corner and swept onto a wide, gently flowing river.

The original plan for that week on the water had been Oxford and back. It didn't work out like that because the timings in our Pearson's Guide book were badly wrong (since corrected). That had been the first time we had found any mistake. It meant going upstream against the flow was to take much longer than anticipated. In the end, destination Abingdon became the target.

We were now on a big wide river. Caversham Bridge looked much bigger from the water than it does in a car. The first obstacle to progress was to be Caversham Weir looming up in the distance.

Caversham Lock

Caversham is a good example of how huge the Thames weirs are and how disguised and narrow the approach to a lock can be. It was morning, the boat was heading due east into the sun, and trying to pick out the lock channel was tricky. I got closer to the weir than necessary and had to let the boat drift back with the current before making a sharp jink left into the approach to the lock.

Time to remember the strict protocol at Thames locks. Dinny and Lindsay were at the bow, while Nick and I were at the stern. I was driving the boat. As we approached the lock, its gates opened to let another narrowboat come out. I drove in slowly to the side of the lock that had the lock keeper's hut. Thames locks are huge – room enough for several 70-foot narrowboats and any number of fibreglass cabin cruisers, all in together. The lock keeper rules the roost. Going uphill, as we were, the aim is to have both bow and stern lines coiled up in hand ready to do a two-handed outward casting motion and so lasso a bollard high up on the lock side. It's a skill that has to be learned. The lock keeper will inevitably tut if he has to use his long-hooked pole to rescue a line dropped into the water. If a lasso fails, chances are the boat will have drifted away from the lock edge, making the next cast even more difficult. Most of us end up chucking the line at the lock keeper, who has to run after it before it drops back into the water. They don't like that, I can report. Having lassoed a bollard at each end, the bow and stern lines have to be held tight and the boat engine turned off.

I asked one lock keeper why this was – he said so he could hear you scream as you went down for the third time.

With all boats secure, the lock keeper will close the rear gates. On the Thames all locks below Lechlade are automated. The lock keeper just has to push a button on the control console and those huge steel gates shut like magic. Then he will walk to the top gate control panel, open the sluices and allow the lock to fill. That happens slowly with little or no turbulence. The boat rises gently in the lock, giving those on the bow and stern lines plenty of time to pull in their lines. Eventually the vertical movement ceases, the bollards are now below our feet rather than being above our heads and the boat is some six feet higher in the lock than when it came in. All that's left to do is to wait until the top gates have been opened, pull in the lines, start the engine, engage gear and then take our turn to sail out.

We cruised under Caversham Bridge, looking a lot bigger from the water than it does from bankside. Then through Pangbourne, on past Goring and Moulsford and finally on the approaches to Wallingford, where we moored for the night.

Nick in pensive mood

Wallingford Bridge is medieval, dating from 1100 AD, is stone-built, 900 feet long and has 19 arches. Our mooring spot was before the bridge on the right-hand bank, the latter quite high up and part of the Thames flood plain. There were no bollards – just hammered in mooring pins and three lines to secure the boat. The river had no flow to speak of, so we didn't have to worry about river level changes overnight. All four of us had a very good Italian meal just across the bridge and into Wallingford Town.

The next morning, we had a cooked breakfast as usual then pulled out the pins, wound in the lines and set off towards Benson, where Nick and Dinny would depart. The Le Boat marina was where they clambered off to get a taxi and then train home. It had been a joy to have them on board

Lindsay and I took the boat through Shillingford, then Little Wittenham to the south of Dorchester – not to be confused with Dorset's Dorchester. Then after lunch, past Burcot and under Clifton Hampden Bridge. It was here we had to watch out for Clifton Lock, make sure we bypass it and get into the weir channel. That's something not normally done, as discussed earlier, but I had completed the survey and knew what I was doing. However, it all looks so different from the water.

After a half-mile or so, we spotted the landing stage of the Plough Inn – coming up on our port side. No other boats there, since it was mid-afternoon. I made sure the boat came gently to rest then secured her using bow and stern lines by attaching to conveniently positioned trees. Next, tea and doughnuts and showers before eating in the pub that night. We were tired and gave no thought to that weir about half a mile further on.

In the morning, after a quiet night, I needed to turn the boat around before setting off back down the weir channel. This turned out to be far from straightforward because there was a strong northerly wind trying to take the boat up the river towards that weir.

We cast off both ends, setting the boat free. It immediately began to drift downstream with the flow. Then came the problem of turning around with a rapidly diminishing width of water. The river was wider upstream, past the landing stage, so I moved her up there and began the turn. Of course, while turning, the drift downstream continued and that proved tricky to judge. A turn manoeuvre in a restricted space involves many small backwards and forwards movements. I came close to running out of room at both ends as I shuffled the boat round. However, the real problem came with a bow swinging round and coming perilously close to taking out that rickety landing stage. I avoided that only at the last moment by a pretty brutal reverse of the engine, driving the stern into the bank, which as luck would have it was soft and compliant. Finally, straight and free and going in the wanted direction.

The fun was not quite over because the boat had to be turned once more in order to get into the lock channel. However, the river helped out by pushing the stern round once I had got the bow pointing at the lock.

Bright new day and full steam ahead on a deep, flowing River Thames. About two hours to reach, get into and then out of Culham Lock.

By this time Lindsay had become an adept steerer. She needed to be. We had come out of Culham Lock and were peacefully traversing its long lock channel on our way to Abingdon. At the end of that channel is a right turn away from the weir and then the straight section into Abingdon. The channel is heavily overgrown, so we could not be as far right as we normally would. Suddenly, just before the turn, out of the blue, a massive red bow appeared, moving fast towards us. It had a copious bow wave and was on our side of the river. Lindsay was to my right so had little time to react. But react she did, quickly shoving the tiller hard left and upping the power.

This of course initially put the stern into the path of the oncoming boat. However, in what seemed like an eternity, but probably within ten or so seconds, we were quickly moving over to the right, plunging into the vegetation and out of harm's way. A large red Dutch Barge, complete with threatening anchor, swept imperiously past at probably twice the speed limit, leaving us white-faced. I realised later what a good job Lindsay had done. She did not make the novice mistake, given the emergency, of moving the tiller the wrong way. Had she done so, the outcome would have been very different.

Abingdon Town

The river after Culham Lock was wide and smooth. It was a glorious sunny day, one of those days on the back of a boat when one felt life could not get any better. That thought was soon replaced of course by a feeling of impending doom, but on that day at least doom stayed away.

The town is on the port bank all the way up to Abingdon Bridge. And what a frontage it has. The only big issue was a lack of visitor moorings, which are before the bridge on a grassy bank on the starboard side.

Moored before Abingdon Bridge

Abingdon – River Thames waterfront

Entrance to the Wilts and Berks Canal

Back to Aldermaston

The return journey to Aldermaston was uneventful, apart from the last night. There is a pattern to hiring a narrowboat. Generally, you collect the boat at 3pm on a Friday say, run through the handover procedure with a boatyard staff member and then get under way at around 4.30pm. We usually hire in May and September where daylight lasts until about 7.30pm. So the first day is a short one and we cannot go too far. The same is true of the last day of a week's hire – the boat has to be back in the boatyard by 9am, handed back by 9.30am, making the last day very short. We usually try to get within a mile or two of the boatyard at the end of the penultimate day.

So there we were on a beautiful early October evening, sitting in the bow cockpit, tea and coffee in hand, wittering away. We were moored next to the towpath and secured by mooring pins at the bow and stern, hammered two feet into the ground. A few boats came past us going upstream towards Aldermaston, but none caused any issues with our mooring pins. It was going to be a quiet night.

We were below Padworth Lock just east of Aldermaston marina so would only have that lock to transit in the morning. Only one narrowboat came past us going downstream. It seemed in a hurry, but we thought nothing of it at the time. Towney Lock was built originally in 1718 and deepened in the 1970s. At nearly three metres, it is the deepest lock on the eastern Kennet and Avon from its summit at Crofton down to the Thames at Reading. It's also a nasty piece of work with vicious, badly maintained gate paddles.

Peaceful mooring just above Towney Lock, near Aldermaston

It was getting dark by 7.30pm. We went inside to prepare our final meal that week, after which we cleared up and set about packing our belongings and tidying the boat, ready for an early start the next day. We got to bed about 11pm, each into our own single bunk. The boat had two bedrooms so we each had a room to ourselves.

Lindsay said, "Does the boat have a list?" I hadn't noticed one, but that wouldn't be unusual – there's quite a lot I don't notice. I thought perhaps we had been using one toilet more than another, as that would list the boat over a period of a week. I told her not to worry about it – the boat was unlikely to come to harm with a little list.

I didn't sleep too well. I kept waking, turning and dozing over what must have been a few hours. My subconscious became aware that turning onto one side was easier than turning onto the other. I had a weird 'uphill' sensation that was trying to roll me out of my bunk but in my dozy state thought nothing of it. Then, at about 3am, in total darkness, I sat up wide-awake with a shocking realisation – the boat had a severe list, probably 30 degrees or more.

I yelled out to Lindsay in the next compartment. Get out of bed, get dressed (not easy at a 30-degree list), grab a torch and let's get outside. I really thought we were in the process of sinking or had already sunk (although canals are not THAT deep). However, my feet remained dry, so I knew the problem was not in the boat.

We clambered out into pitch-blackness and were met with a thunderous roar. The boat had indeed listed severely, with the ropes around the mooring pins stretched like piano strings. I shone a torch down towards the sound but could only see the lock gates. And then Lindsay let out a gasp – there was no water in the canal!

We walked down to the lock gates. The roaring was coming from the far gate of the pair. It had its gate paddle wide open, and water was thundering out into the next pound three metres below. The pound bounded by Padworth Lock and Towney Lock is one of the shortest on that eastern section. That open gate paddle had drained the pound, leaving us on the bottom with a crazy list.

So, back to the boat to pick up a windlass. I was not too happy clambering across a rather skinny walkway, having had balance issues earlier that year. So Lindsay volunteered, bravely, and walked gingerly across the top of the lock gates, windlass in hand. It was pitch black. I pointed a torch at her feet, but she had to feel the handholds because she could not see them. There was that deafening roar and the thought of a near four-metre drop to deal with. The air was saturated with spray, so her walk was hand-over-hand, slippery and risky.

Once on the far side, she was able to wind down the paddle. Silence descended. She came back over to the towpath side, and we then walked up to Padworth Lock to open both gate paddles and so refill the pound. We were there a couple of hours sipping tea and coffee from a thermos, still wittering away.

So what had happened? It's clear that the boat that passed us in a hurry earlier that evening was the culprit. When they got to Towney Lock, they would have seen it filled but didn't notice the top gate paddle was still open. They would have opened one or both gates to get in. There would have been no flow through the open paddle because the water level would have been the same both sides. Then having closed the top gates, they would have opened the lower gate paddle(s), emptied the lock and sailed away, *without closing the lower gates*. Not only that, but inexplicably,

135

they failed to notice the roar from the still-open paddle behind them. Or if they did, they put it down to a severe leak. They really were in a hurry.

An entire pound's worth of water had gone down below Towney in the period 7pm to 3am. Luckily, that pound is a long one where so much excess water would not have caused a flood. And in any case, the locks on the Kennet and Avon have spill-weirs to divert excess water over into the River Kennet alongside.

Canal breach at Middlewich in 2018

© Copyright Derby News

Not so fortunate were the crew of a narrowboat stuck in the breach at the Middlewich branch in 2018. A gate paddle left open caused an excessive flow in the pound below the gate. There was no spill-weir nearby, the canal overflowed at the point where an aqueduct begins, the embankment collapsed, and the result can be seen from the image above.

Chapter 13

Aldermaston to Hampton Court Palace on the River Thames 2012

Maps 10 and 11

In 2012 we hired again from ABC's base at Aldermaston, where our destination was Hampton Court, via Reading and the River Thames.

Getting to Reading on the Kennet and Avon is not a lot of fun. Many of the locks are in poor condition with heavy winding gear and leaking gates. This is a broad canal, so some gates are heavy and difficult to move. The local scenery is best described as scruffy, especially on the approach to Reading. The section from County Lock to Blake's Lock is one-way, controlled by a traffic light system. We had a long wait for a green light before we could proceed. The whole area there is not much more than a rubbish dump. Empty cans and bottles, fast-food packaging, drug paraphernalia and so on. I counted at least half a dozen rats before we got under way.

The one-way section goes through Reading town centre, down the middle of a pedestrian precinct. Department stores, coffee shops, cafés and boutiques – it's been done nicely, but boats are not allowed to moor. The River Kennet is deep and fast flowing at that point. Boaters heading for the Thames have to be aware that they are going with the flow, so could be going fast over the ground.

Very low bridges and high-water levels through Reading town centre in 2012

Several bridges have evidence of being poleaxed after crews failed to realise they had no steering. When we were there, the river was flowing fast. On the way into Blake's Lock, the last before the Thames, I failed to notice the proximity of the weir to our left. That would come back and haunt me on the way home.

After coming out of Blake's Lock, it's about half a mile before reaching the Thames proper. This time, we needed to turn right, pointing east, downstream on a wide and deep river. These narrowboats are a delight on deep water where they glide with little resistance. It's possible to far exceed the 6mph speed limit, especially when going with the flow.

It's then about an hour to Sonning. There are a couple of huge weirs at Sonning which take the Thames on a detour to the left, then around and back across the far face of Sonning Bridge. More of that later.

Henley-on-Thames and the Thin Man and His Dog

We tied up at Henley that night. It's where there is a large open space on the right-hand side, opposite Phyllis Court. It's Crown Estate – to whom we donated £5 via a bloke in a skiff. I asked for a receipt from Her Majesty but didn't get one.

We were there about 3pm, sitting inside having tea and doughnuts, when there was an almighty kerfuffle outside. A tall thin man was standing outside the boat, becoming somewhat agitated. We could see the middle of him from where we were sitting – the boat was 'reverse layout', you see, with the galley at the stern. He was yelling at Basil, a thin, very long dachshund. I got up on the counter (rear deck) to see what the fuss was about. The dog was chasing a duck, of which there were scores. Suddenly the duck shot between our boat and the one behind and disappeared under our rudder, followed by the dog. The owner had become apoplectic, running round in tiny circles wailing "Basil, Basil, Basil…"

Basil didn't seem to hear – he had his ears full of water after all. A minute or so went by. Basil didn't resurface. The duck did, but no sign of Basil. I thought that maybe he had become an actual sausage dog, squashed between the boats. Suddenly, the tall thin man fell to his knees, grasped the rudder with his right hand and plunged the top half of his body into the Thames. He'd seen a floppy Basil, eyes up, staring at him from a couple of feet under. He grabbed the dog and hauled him out. "Basil! Basil! What should I do?" came a plea for help from bystanders. "Grab him by his tail, hold him in the air and shake like hell," said I. Nothing. "Beat him in the chest with your other hand then," said I. I thought the dog was a goner but, out of the blue, he coughed out a great wadge of the river and began to breathe again.

We made the thin man a mug of tea and gave him a towel. Basil turned up his nose at a bowl of water.

Cookham Lock – just a little bit crowded

Windsor

We made an early start the next morning because we wanted to get to Windsor by mid-afternoon in order to find a mooring space. Windsor is a pretty crowded place and I'm talking about boats, not people. It's about eight hours on the river including a stop for lunch.

Good moorings on rings downstream from Boulter's Lock

We passed through Marlow. On the left-hand bank is a small marina and sailing club. In one of the riverside houses live Lindsay's cousins Virginia and Robert. We gave them a wave as we pootled on past. Then under William Tierney Clark's magnificent suspension bridge. Then Bourne End and Cookham, past Cliveden House up on the hillside and through Boulter's Lock. I paid attention to the next stretch because there were (rare) moorings here on rings if I could find them, on the right-hand side against a long length of stone wall. It was there we would be stopping on our way back from Hampton in the company of friends Steve and Sandra.

I spotted the rings – which should work well on the return trip. More of that later. Then on past Bray and a whole load of expensive houses and even more expensive restaurants. And finally, after a long loop around Dorney Lake, of rowing academy fame, and Windsor racecourse, the glorious sight of that castle hove into view.

Mooring on the Thames under Windsor Castle

Another payment was made to HM's coffers for the privilege of banging a couple of mooring pins into her hallowed turf. We walked to Windsor Town for dinner that night. The best bit was walking back to the boat under a black, black sky, peppered with innumerable points of twinkling light. And a slopping and slurping Thames, reflecting and gently wittering back to us.

Hampton Court Palace

The river makes a long loop around the castle grounds past Datchet on the left-hand bank. There are signs everywhere, 'No Mooring'. That is a pity because there would be miles of wonderful spots to stay. On the other hand, I doubt if HM wants to deal with scores of uncouth, newly rich, cruiser-owning pseudo-toffs, moored up with their budgie smugglers, their bikini-clad birds, with them (sic) always two decades younger, hoping for a glimpse of a royal.

Plane trees line the Thames riverbank behind Windsor Castle

The banks of the river are peppered with pristine rows of plane trees. Through the trees, in the hazy distance, Didcot Power Station. Made me a bit mumsy given my six years with the CEGB at the start of my engineering career.

A long stretch then past Old Windsor and on towards Runnymede up on the hill. There is free mooring there on the right-hand bank. There had been moorings prior to that, but all were reserved for private boating clubs of various sorts. I frequently looked back over my shoulder to see if we were about to be run down by the numerous French Brothers river buses that plough this section of the Thames. I couldn't help noticing all sorts of little inlets going hither and thither, none marked, and I wondered if they would cause us navigation problems on the way back. They did, as we shall see.

Runnymede hosts the Magna Carta Memorial erected in 1957 by the American Bar (Legal) Association. After the assassination of President Kennedy in November 1963, the British Government gave an acre of land at Runneymede to the USA in Kennedy's memory.

Then under the M25 at Egham, past Chertsey and into Shepperton Lock. It is a big one, with the fourth highest drop of all those on the Thames. It is the fifth lock from the estuary. Half a mile beyond, the River Wey joins the Thames. We sailed across Wey Junction and on through Desborough Cut, eliminating a loop and saving a few miles.

Leaving Shepperton, and those massive film studios behind, up came Walton-on-Thames, Sunbury and Molesey. The approach to Molesey Lock had me worried. There are few directions signs on that part of the river – or if there are, they were covered by vegetation long ago. I chose to go left at the long stretch that is Taggs Island. I began looking for the lock channel, but there was not one – just a huge weir straight ahead. I then saw a cutting opposite the Swiss House chalet and turned down there. Bliss, left at the end and lock in view.

Good moorings outside Hampton Court Palace on the River Thames

Note: The boat is pointing upstream with Hampton Court Palace bridge in the distance. Entrance to the River Mole is to the left. Today the Mole is only navigable for about 400 metres up to

Once out of the lock, Hampton Court Bridge was in the distance, with the palace itself just beyond the bridge on the left-hand bank. It had taken three days to get there. I turned the boat around – what a joy to do that on such a wide river – and tied up just underneath the palace garden gates.

Return to Aldermaston – Day One

Lindsay and I walked over Hampton Court Bridge and found a rather good Italian restaurant. I wasn't so enamoured with the waiter, who was the usual flirty Italian. Lindsay didn't seem to mind. The next morning Sandra and Steve joined us, and we set off upstream – destination, those moorings on rings at Boulter's Lock.

It was a dull, overcast day. Steve was going to drive the boat the whole day. Sandra is not too interested in being at the tiller, preferring to sit at the bow with her camera. Lindsay is usually up there with her. Just me and Steve at the stern. He is 25 years or so younger than me. He's a good boatsman, very calm when things go pear-shaped, as they always do.

On a wide river these narrowboats move well. However, there had been a great deal of rain in the previous weeks and there was a noticeable flow against us. We could see the water piling up against the abutments as we sailed under Hampton Bridge. Molesey Lock had its gates closed, making us tie up at the landing stage. Water flowing over the weir to our right looked alarming, so we knew something was up.

Eventually the lock gates opened, and we motored in. The boat was going to be going uphill all the way back to Aldermaston. While on the Thames we had to comply with lock keepers' instructions. That meant lassoing a bollard which might be six or even eight feet above our heads. Steve steered the boat in nicely on the keeper's side and brought it gently to a halt. I had already coiled up the stern line and was holding it in two hands with the free end trapped under my little finger. As a bollard came into view above, I did the approved casting outward and upward move with both arms, releasing the coil from both hands while crying out "Praise the Lord!" It didn't work. I missed the bollard and scrabbled to try again.

The ladies at the bow also failed miserably. Lindsay forgot to trap the end of the line. She got the rope around the bollard all right, but it slid off into the water. Then of course, the rocking movements on the boat made it start to drift away from lock side, but Steve, good man that he is, had already turned off the engine. The keeper wasn't a happy bunny. He retrieved the bow line with his long-hooked pole. I had already coiled up and was ready for another go. "Praise the Lord!" I yelled as if it was going to make any difference.

Another boat was on its way in by now, just as ours drifted out into its path. The captain, who must have been a Christian, stopped his boat sharpish without any comment. He just sort of wallowed there, allowing his crew to observe and learn.

We did make an utter bollocks of tying up at that lock. It didn't help that, when the ladies got onto their bollard, they immediately pulled in the bow. Now as everyone knows, a boat has a bow that curves gracefully to a point. If the bow line is pulled too tight, the stern is forced out away from the bank. That made my next casting impossible. The keeper had walked back to Steve and me by then, so I just threw the whole coil at him, using just one arm. It was an impressive effort, I have to say. It went right over his shoulder and the knobbly bit at the end hit him on the back of the head. If he was in a bad mood before, he went right off us at that.

Eventually all the boats came in and got tied up. The keeper shut the rear gates and opened the top sluices. We rose silently and majestically up past those damn bollards, determined to do better at the next lock.

And we did. From then on, praise the Lord, we lassoed our bollards and pulled our ropes like true boating professionals. Time raced by and after stopping for lunch, we had been going against the flow for some five hours and were passing Runnymede. It was getting very gloomy and had started to rain. Both Steve and I put on wet gear, me steering while he changed and vice versa. We passed around old Windsor and then Windsor itself, seeing the back of the castle on our left and then its glorious front when we came around the final bend and looked back over the stern. That bit is very Piccadilly Circus, what with all the motor launches, posh fibreglass cruisers, French Brothers river buses et al to avoid.

It was now 5pm. I knew we would have to be on our mooring by 7.30pm if there were to be any light left. Hired narrowboats are not allowed to move in the dark. It was mid-October after all. But we were now in a sheet of gloom and progress was slow. The rain had got down my neck and was starting to fill my boots. Steve, peering into the distance, stood there manfully gripping the tiller arm – trying to keep the boat just to the right of centre. He looked like a drowning rat. The temperature began to drop, and the ladies retired to the warm of the lounge. They did, however, put the kettle on, and two steaming mugs of tea kept us company on the rear desk.

An annoying niggle then began to appear. On the way down I had concerns over the number of unmarked inlets there were. Some of these would just be two ways around an island, but others could also lead to a weir and the prospect of having to reverse or turn around – not something to relish in front of a weir. Steve and I had to begin a game of chance in which we had to guess which path to take. Some of these inlets are wider than the river, so it became tricky. And of course, each time we slowed to make a decision, our end of journey time stretched out.

We got through Bray Lock at about 7pm. There was no lock keeper – he had gone home, meaning we had to operate the lock ourselves. That didn't mean heaving gates open and operating sluices; it just meant we had to operate the control consoles ourselves. Luckily Lindsay had some experience of doing just that, once before having been taken for an actual lock keeper. Once through Bray we could see the twinkling lights of Maidenhead to our right in the far distance. There was nothing else moving on the river. They were all tucked up in the warm. We were pushed on into the gloom and sheeting rain, getting wetter by the second. It was just us and the drone of the engine out on that huge river, with the dark descending and our cabin lights ascending skyward. There are few public moorings out there, so we had no real choice other than to push on.

Finally, we could see Maidenhead Bridge ahead in the gloom. Where were those damn moorings with rings I had spotted on the way down? It was now 8pm and almost dark. I turned on the headlight at the bow to warn oncoming craft that we were there, still going slowly upstream. The boat should not have been moving at all. Slowly the wall with the rings emerged on our left, but in the dark, it was impossible for Steve to see how close we were to the concrete embankment. There were boats moored there already and Boulter's Lock ahead – would we be able to find a space?

Lindsay and Sandra appeared at the foot of the steps into the cabin, and we had a quick discussion. Steve and I would park the boat in a gap that had appeared. The girls would get off and walk towards the lock to spot any better places to stop, then phone us if we should go on.

We waited in now darkness, listening to vehicles passing on the road above. I was really wet and took the opportunity to change my jeans for a dry pair. The phone rang, and Sandra told us there was a space further up. I pushed out the bow, then clambered back and Steve motored on, keeping to the left. We should have been on the right of course. Out of the mirk appeared another boat coming straight towards us – he was on the correct side of the river. His bow headlight was dazzling. Steve and I both thought *collision* and I pressed the horn button. Luckily, we were both moving very slowly. We edged carefully past each other. It was another narrowboat, and I shouted an apology that they accepted with a "That's OK, mate."

I saw Sandra and Lindsay waiting on the nearside concrete bank. Steve got us in, and we tied up on those mooring rings. What a day. Still not over though. When we have guests on board, we always moor up for lunch. Time for good food, conversation and a few laughs. At the end of those days, we all go to eat at a pub or restaurant. And that is what I had planned. I had booked a table at the very upmarket 'The Boathouse' restaurant on the island at Boulter's Lock, now just a few hundred yards ahead. But we were nearly two hours late and like drowned rats. What on earth would they and their customers think when a bunch of Romany travellers turned up at their door? Plus, Sandra and Steve had their day bags with them as they would get back home via taxi and train.

We needn't have worried – the staff were terrific, helping us get out of wet gear and offering towels. They made space for all our stuff – coats, umbrellas, bags, boots… They found us a good table overlooking the lock.

The ambiance and the food were first class. Just before 10pm the staff called a taxi for our lovely friends. Lindsay and I trudged off in the pouring rain back to a welcome, warm boat and collapsed into bed. The best laid plans…

Return to Aldermaston – Day Two

We awoke to bright sunshine, just downstream of Boulter's Lock. I was surprised at how close we had got the previous night. There had been heavy rain with flooding that week and the river was choppy to say the least.

It was now just Lindsay and me on the boat. We got through Boulter's without any issues, but the river looked angry.

As we proceeded upstream the locks were being 'red-boarded'. We found out subsequently that we had been lucky – we were very nearly the last boat through at each of the locks. On the section beneath Cliveden House, the engine was near 2,000 rpm, but we were making hardly any progress over the ground. We were overtaken by pensioners walking their dogs along the Thames path. Some of the lock landing stages were underwater with just the tips of their bollards showing.

The river looked menacing with fallen leaves racing by and copious whirlpools and eddies.

At Marsh Lock before Sonning, the river was rough with white-topped waves. Gongoozlers had gathered on the wooden walkways.

An angry Thames at Marsh Lock

After Shiplake Lock, on the approach to Sonning Bridge, we were shocked at how small the centre arch, the only navigable arch, looked. The river had risen so much in a week. Even more shocked by the flow from the weir stream coming from our right, straight across our bow. That flow was a river in its own right on top of the real river, with huge currents, eddies, whirlpools, white-topped waves and debris seemingly dancing down an angry Thames. As soon as our bow hit that cross-current, it dived to the left. I managed to contain that and turned into the cross-current, going parallel to the bridge and now head-on into that stream. The stream was so strong that the boat barely made any progress over the ground. As we crawled up parallel to the bridge, under considerable power, I realised we were too near and did a quick shimmy right and left, which still left us parallel to the bridge but at least a little further away. I was going to have to judge when to turn hard left out of the cross-current and into the centre arch. I let the bow get level with the arch to the right of the centre, pushed the Morse lever through 90 degrees for maximum power and pushed the tiller right and onto its end stop. The stern moved away quickly, the bow came round, and the boat powered across the stream. We both ducked as our bow slotted neatly through the centre arch. It seemed to take forever for those 62 feet to get all the way through – the cross-current gave us a final kicking as it took the stern away, the boat very nearly scraping the brickwork to our left. But we had got through the bridge into the lock channel and into calm waters – relieved but shaken.

Sonning Bridge during the Thames 2012 floods

Note: The waters look calm because their level had peaked when this image was taken, and the flow had stopped. The footbridge over the weir stream can just be seen in the far distance, only just above the river level.

Neither of us had realised just how much the river had risen at this point. And I'm guessing that a number of boats hit the brickwork of the bridge, especially lightweight cruiser types with wheel steering whose lack of inertia would not have helped resist the river's current.

Sonning Bridge in 2014 after the fitting of crash barriers

The footbridge in the far background now has its normal headroom. Note the watermarks on the bridge abutments.

Reliving our experiences, Lindsay admitted she had been very scared and had her heart in her mouth for several minutes. I was too busy, in the zone as it were, to be scared, but it came back to haunt me a while later.

We got through Sonning Lock by operating the consoles ourselves. It was getting dark, but we wanted to get back on the Kennet and Avon Canal and reach the Bel and the Dragon pub in Reading and their excellent herringbone customer moorings. We should have moored on the river for the night, but in these circumstances the temptation, especially in a hired boat, is always to push on in the hope it will be all right. It wasn't going to be all right.

A drunken bystander, who somewhat surprisingly knew what he was doing, helped us through Blake's Lock. Almost immediately we needed to make a right turn out of the lock channel towards the pub. This just happens to be on the junction of the River Kennet, its back channel and the weir stream – the weir I had ignored on the way down. The Kennet was in near flood, as we realised the next day when we saw that County Lock was close to being overtopped.

At that point I did not realise I was going to have to turn into the weir stream. I did not realise the weir was so close. As I turned towards the pub moorings, the boat started to crab to the right and began to spin. I was going sideways onto the weir in near darkness. Lindsay was with me at the stern. She was very quiet. I slammed the engine into reverse and, once going backwards, slammed it into forward gear, allowing me to get the stern over to the left.

However, I needed to reverse onto a pontoon and, now in forward gear and drifting head-on towards the weir, tried to get the stern further over to the left. The bow was still rotating to the right and the boat glanced the bank amidships. It was now dark, but we had a bit of luck. In reverse and using some power, we came off the bank and shot backward into the side channel just enough to get the stern into one of the herringbone slots. However, those slots are only 40 feet long and the boat was 62 feet. The bow again got caught by the current and I thought for a moment the boat would jam on or lever those pontoons apart. But in reverse the boat came back slowly into the herringbone. Lindsay and I looked at each other in the shadows of the pub's lighting. We didn't say a word – just tied up and went inside.

Blake's Lock Weir from the Bel and Dragon in Reading

The weir is just to the right of the barge. Blake's Lock Cut goes past
the three-storey building on the right.

A number of gongoozlers had had a whale of a time observing the fun
from the tower block upon high. I thought I heard both cheers and jeers.
Lindsay and I had a fillet steak and a bottle of wine in the Bel that night
and then slept peacefully in our bunks. What a day.

Return to Aldermaston – Day Three

County Lock and Weir at Reading

Note the height of the River Kennet – almost no drop at the lock. On our return the weir had been overtopped.

On boating days, I am usually awake first then take Lindsay her coffee in bed and then go outside with my tea and sit on the stern rail. It's glorious if it's sunny, often with low-level mist hovering above the water. Not so that day. The roar of water, thundering over the weir just 40 or so metres away, coming fast around the pontoon we were attached to, was deafening. I wondered how the hell I was going to get the boat out. As soon as the bow sneaked out into that flow, it would be gathered up and shoved unceremoniously left towards the weir. The River Kennet was angry, boiling with rage – it wanted to smash me and crew into that weir, chuck us over and suck us under, never to be seen again.

Breakfast over and with Lindsay on the bow acting as lookout, I untied, engaged forward gear and moved smartly into the stream. As predicted, the bow got swept to the left while the rest of the boat did its best to lever the pontoons apart. As soon as the stern was free, I engaged reverse. The river had turned the boat anticlockwise and gave me a chance to power backward directly into the flow. It worked well. Within a couple of minutes or so, the boat had gone backwards up into the main river channel that goes past the prison. Then smartly into forward gear, lots of power and full left tiller got us out of the main flow and nudging into the channel for Blake's Lock. Lindsay indicated no other craft were coming our way and so hard left tiller once more, a bit of toing and froing and we had turned right and were pointing homeward.

It was a gentle cruise up to the traffic light that controls the one-way system through Reading. The river splits into two a bit further on, most going around the prison loop and some straight on towards Blake's. It dives left of course before the lock, joins up with its compatriot coming from the prison and thunders over the weir. I nosed the boat in towards the landing stage at the light, ready to hop off and press the button. But I could not get the bow anywhere near that landing – the flow was too strong. I tried all sorts, but nothing worked.

Meanwhile, I hadn't realised there was another boat behind ours. That had been moored overnight alongside the prison and had come out behind us. He went straight past, ignoring the traffic light, still on red. He shouted, "I'll prepare the lock and wait." We were not amused.

Lindsay managed eventually to throw a line around a bollard and haul in the bow. I powered the stern over, secured it with a line, hopped off and pushed the button. The light took an age before going green.

We motored up the river, past that glorious town centre, under the little bridges, now with even littler headroom, and on towards County Lock. The river was still wild. I had to use a lot of power against the flow. I went into the lock quite fast, somewhat to the alarm of the couple waiting in there with their boat. Didn't hit them though – their boat, not the couple, although I was pretty seething inside. When I got off to help wind and push, she saw we had a hire boat – they were a privateer. She said to me, in a rather snooty manner, "Have you much experience of boating?" "About 1,000 hours at the tiller," I said. She didn't reply.

Chapter 14

Hilperton Marina to Crofton on the Kennet and Avon Canal 2013

Map 10

Lindsay and I live in Weyhill, about 20 miles from Newbury and the same from Devizes. Both towns are steeped in canal history. Devizes is most famous for the Caen Hill flights of 29 broad locks in three groups that lift the Kennet and Avon Canal over 237 feet up over the Marlborough Downs.

We hired from ABC again that year. One of their 62-foot, two-bedroom and two-bathroom, reverse layout narrowboats. Their marina at Hilperton was the start. We collected the boat around 2.30pm and got out of the marina as usual about 4.30pm after going through all the handover and safety stuff. Hilperton is close to Trowbridge in Wiltshire, meaning we were going to sail east towards Devizes and up Caen Hill first of all. We moored close to the marina late that afternoon, having our customary tea, coffee and doughnuts once we had packed away all our gear and foodstuffs we brought along. These boats have fridges and microwaves (not to mention toasters, gas oven, gas hob, etc.), so along with us came a few ready meals for when we couldn't find a pub or didn't want to cook on board.

Sandra and Steve joined us at Semington the next morning. I had had difficulty finding a mooring the previous evening. There are 48-hour public moorings just before the first lock in the Semington pair. I didn't want to go past the lock, but when I got there, I could not find a space. All the moorings were occupied by privateer boats, there were big gaps between them, and all were of the scruffy, semi-derelict, traveller type – all probably camping there some while. I had to reverse nearly half a mile, well past the designated public spaces, until I managed to find a grassy bank, dog-shit and weed-free enough for me to bang in the mooring pins. I was observed by quite a few unkempt weed-smoking individuals, who smirked at the sight of a hire-boater having to go backwards.

Just before the first Semington Lock is the entrance to the currently closed Wilts and Berks Canal. There are plans to restore all 70 miles in due course, but it is going to be a slow process. I'm a member of the canal restoration society and have helped them with a number of projects, including the acquisition of the Peterborough Arms pub near Lacock in Wiltshire. The canal will eventually be in water all the way to Abingdon on the River Thames.

All the locks on the Kennet and Avon are broad and long. They were designed to take Thames barges originally. A crew of four should make light work of them and by late evening we planned to be in Devizes with all 36 locks behind us. In ideal circumstances it's best to share a double-width lock with another boat, but there were none around. So a single boat in a broad lock was going to be the pattern all day.

After Semington there are three swing bridges. These are unique to the Kennet and Avon. Each has a mooring pad before and after and a chain and pin arrangement keeping them closed. A windlass is used to release the chain so the bridge can be pushed open. It's surprisingly easy for such a big structure.

Then five locks in the Seend flight. All the locks today were going uphill. There's nothing special to watch out for, other than going in too fast and hitting the top gate. Even that's not too bad because behind each pair of top gates is a wall of water. We tried to only open one of the bottom gate pair because doing that saves so much work overall. It's how the commercial bargees used to do it. However, the Canal and River Trust encourage opening both gates in order to avoid damage to the infrastructure. We didn't do that. Steve and I could get the boat in through one gate without hitting it or the lock wall and then manage to stop the boat before the far end.

We found ourselves at Caen Hill Marina. We moored outside and had an early lunch because it's not advisable to stop once the ascent of Caen Hill has begun. See note 14 on page 298.

At the bottom of the Caen Hill flight of locks below Devizes

We had hatched a plan for the next six hours or so. I would start off driving the boat into and out of each lock. Sandra and Steve would open and close top and bottom gates and fill each lock. Lindsay would go ahead to do some 'lock-wheeling'. This was a technique used by commercial bargees in the canals' heydays. It's based on a peculiar fact that a crew member can go ahead and prepare any number of locks in sequence. By 'prepare' I mean empty each lock ahead if going uphill and fill each lock ahead if going downhill. In times past, a bike was used to get from lock to lock. Now, provided no other boat comes out ahead of yours, those locks will remain in the prepared state until you get to them. If another boat comes down a flight and passes you going up, or goes up a flight and passes you going down, they will automatically leave the lock in your prepared state.

When I began boating on the canal network, the concept of lock-wheeling took a long time to get my head around. Intuition initially says if you can empty all those locks ahead, why can't you open all the gates ahead as well? The answer is that there is always some water left in each lock, otherwise a boat would not be able to float over the concrete cill at the lower end of each lock. And some water remaining means there would be some water pressure to keep the gates closed. If the gates leaked and all water drained out, you would see a concrete staircase going uphill that no boat would ever be able to climb.

So we made a start on Caen Hill. Empty the bottom lock, open one gate, sail in, close the bottom gate, fill the lock initially by opening one paddle and then both. When full, open one top gate, sail out into the short pound between each lock, shut the top gate, leaving the lock full. That's it. Repeat 29 times. Steve and I changed over every six locks or so while Lindsay went three locks ahead on average. Her lock-wheeling meant we never had to wait to empty a lock – the next one was already empty, and Sandra could just go walk up to it and open the bottom gate.

It took us about five hours in total. We celebrated by an evening walk down Devizes high street and enjoyed a good Italian meal. Sandra and Steve then went home, happy they had successfully dealt with one of the most iconic sets of locks on the UK canal network.

Crofton Pumping Station

We had arranged to meet friends Debbie and partner Jan for lunch at Pewsey. The canal guide we were using said it would take about three hours. I did not know it was an early version for the Kennet and Avon Canal and the timing had been revised to five hours. We got to Pewsey eventually at 2pm and luckily the pub there, nowadays derelict, kept open so the four of us could have lunch. Very pleasant it was too, although I felt a bit of an idiot having deprived them of a short trip on the boat.

The canal at Pewsey is a disgrace. There is a sanitary station at the western end right near the Waterfront pub – too near actually if the wind is from the west. The visitor moorings there have a 48-hour limit, but that whole section, probably a mile, is populated by private liveaboard boats, mostly semi-derelict, who constantly move up to the sanitary station, do their stuff and move back onto the public mooring places.

There is never any room for true visitors like us who hire or others who have their own continuous cruise boats. It's a shame because Pewsey is a delightful village with plenty of local history – Wolf Hall, Jane Seymour's (Henry VIII's Queen of England) family home is nearby, although not now the original building.

Lindsay assisting a maximum size broad-beam barge at Crofton Top Lock

From Pewsey the canal continues uphill through the Wootton Rivers flight of locks and through the Bruce Tunnel in Savernake Forest. And that is the summit of the entire Kennet and Avon. From the summit it's all downhill to the Thames in the east and to the River Severn in the west. The summit is 460 feet above sea level. Water is fed downhill in both directions via the pumping station at Crofton and the lakes at Wilton Water close by.

Crofton is actually below the summit. Not a problem towards the east, but in modern times a pipeline feeds the canal to the west, now with electrically powered pumps. Crofton has been restored and is open and in steam every bank holiday. It houses two original Boulton and Watt Cornish beam engines and a pair of hand-stoked Lancashire boilers that provide the steam generation capacity.

**Crofton Pumping Station behind Crofton Top Lock, where a
traction engine fair was in progress**

We met an interesting Australian couple at Crofton. They commissioned the building of a broad-beam boat from Colecraft, one of the best UK narrowboat builders. A year later they flew to the UK and collected it from the manufacturer's base in Southam, Warwickshire. We met them as they were halfway round a tour of the UK broad canal network. On completion of their tour, they planned to sell the boat before returning home.

There are seven locks in the Crofton flight, all the broad type of course. The technique adopted for these locks, going downhill now, was fill the lock and open one top gate. Motor in, taking care not to hit the bottom gates at the far end. And you really don't want to do that because some of these locks have big drops and, going downhill, there is no tall wall of water to act as a buffer should you hit the infrastructure. Close the top gate and open one paddle on a bottom gate. The steerer must be alert to make sure the stern of the boat is kept forward of the white painted cill mark behind them on the lock edge. There is no turbulence going downhill. Once the crew are happy the boat is lowering freely, the second paddle can be opened. It's just a matter of then opening one of the lower

161

gates and motoring out. Then of course closing that gate, making sure both paddles are closed before leaving for the next lock.

Handling wide locks with a crew of four is easy. The steerer can stay on board, leaving the three other members to deal with the walking, winding, pushing and heaving. It's a lot more effort with just two on the boat – so a help if the steerer can get off when required. That might mean shinning up and down a slimy ladder with a windlass in one hand. Lindsay and I dealt with the Crofton flight pretty well, she and I taking it in turns to drive the boat in and out, the other handling the lock infrastructure.

We took the boat up to Great Bedwyn, where there is a 70-foot winding hole. It was a calm day. I turned around without clouting anyone else and, after lunch, set off back towards Devizes.

Back to Devizes

Iconic image at Burbage Wharf

Getting back to Devizes was straightforward. Our aim was to get a mooring on rings that night at the wonderfully named Honeystreet

162

Wharf, just beyond Pewsey. The next day would then be an easy cruise to Devizes, where we were due to pick up a crew of four, all Bourne Valley Riding Club friends – Lindsay is their chairman.

Between Wootton Rivers and Pewsey at the 'Long Pound', there is a nature reserve. Neither of us had expected that to extend over the canal where we had to push through a mile or so of reeds. While in amongst them I wondered what would happen if we met a broad-beam boat coming the other way. In theory, on the Kennet and Avon, two broad-beams can pass each other, but the image below illustrates the problem.

Ploughing through reeds on the Kennet and Avon east of Pewsey in 2013

We didn't, but I gather those reeds do not foul the propellor. It would have been necessary for both boats to push into the reed bed each side and, well, mow them down.

Honeystreet Wharf

Honeystreet wharf has been around for more than 200 years. It started life as a barge building centre, a timber trading wharf, and centuries later now hosts a new and busy café and narrowboat holiday hire business. The canal arrived in Honeystreet in 1810, prompting Victorian entrepreneur Samuel Robbins to begin to build his wharf and timber yard.

Over the years the buildings on the wharf were added to, caught fire, fell down and were replaced. The iconic chimney was built after one of the fires, to act as the equivalent of an extractor fan removing fumes from the sawmill's engine house and reducing the fire risk.

The mainstay of Honeystreet business was timber – importing, drying, sawing, selling and building barges out of it to transport it. And the sawmill is still there today.

The Barge Inn, on the opposite side of the canal to the sawmill, was once known as the George Inn. It was roughly halfway along the canal and served as a bakehouse, slaughterhouse and shop for provisions for those living and working on the waterway.

We arrived at Honeystreet in good time to grab one of the last pair of mooring rings outside the Barge Inn – now a popular spot for music, food, drink and camping. The pub is in the middle of the crop circle region of Wiltshire.

The Barge has had a chequered recent history. A decade or so ago, it was bought by an eclectic band of bohemian narrowboaters who managed to obtain a grant to operate the pub as a community asset. It didn't work and went bust. But it's now in new ownership, still bohemian, but looking good – at least when we were there.

The next morning, we had breakfast at the pub then a leisurely cruise back to Devizes. It was a quiet Saturday evening and we managed to moor at Devizes Wharf, on rings, ready to be joined by a new and inexperienced crew for our trip down Caen Hill. It was to be another of those very rare, fabulous days!

Down Caen Hill

I met our very good friends Dave and wife Di, plus Andy and wife Jemma, early on Sunday morning. They are two couples Lindsay and I originally met via the Bourne Valley Riding Club (BVRC), where Lindsay has been chairman for the past 20 years and more. They are a generation below us, early 40s, who have decided to encompass life without children. Both the girls are competent horse riders and ardent supporters of the BVRC. Neither of the boys ride – horses that is – but both are, or have been, petrolheads on two wheels and four.

It was a glorious autumn day in Devizes. Sun shining, gentle breeze wafting through the trees. I had the boat moored on rings right on the old wharf. It is a lovely spot. I watched both their cars arrive, park and decamp their crews, ready for the day's adventure.

Neither of the couples had been on board a narrowboat before. My first job was a safety briefing, during which Dave said something like "Bloody hell, Pete, didn't know we were having a lecture and then a written test," having noticed my clipboard and pencil nearby. I explained how wide, downhill locks worked plus safety at locks. Walking everywhere – no running. Then a quick tour inside the boat, leaving behind a plethora of gasps and wonderment as we shimmied along those 62 feet from stern to bow.

In spite of living in the area all their lives, neither couple had been to see the national wonder that is the 29-lock flight from Caen Hill to Foxhangers. That's the norm though – Lindsay and I live near Winchester and have rarely been there. We've been to the hospital many times and passed the prison once or twice but exploring England's finest and first Norman cathedral – er, nope.

I explained how we would deal with the locks as a team. I would drive the boat while Lindsay would organise the manning of the windlasses and the heaving of the gates. I didn't want to let any of our visitors drive the boat because I knew from experience that it would slow us down, plus encourage the gongoozlers, of which there were many.

We used lock 50 as a training exercise. I moored the boat at the landing stage so that the crew could all decamp lock side. The lock was empty, giving Lindsay a chance to explain the machinery and the operation of the paddles. From that lock it is not possible to see the awesome sight that is the endless collection of black and white balance beams stretching away down to infinity. They had that joy to come.

At the top of Caen Hill, ready for the journey down

Adjacent to lock 47 is a small but perfectly formed café. It was a beautiful sunny day and Jemma suggested she go and get bacon butties for the whole crew. We had done two locks by then and they were beginning to get the hang of it. Taking advantage of the café was a good idea because we were not going to be able to stop for lunch for three hours or so. Although each lock has a substantial side-pond below where it might be possible to stop, access to these is prevented by a bund stretched across each entrance.

A few more locks went by. There were no boats ahead of us, so the crew began a lock-wheeling. With me alone on the boat, Lindsay, Di and Jemma went ahead to prepare the next lock. That meant making sure the lower paddles were down and then lifting the top paddles to fill the lock. It was a calm day, enabling the boat to just wallow between locks, waiting for the girls to open one top gate. Andy and Dave closed the gate behind once the boat was clear. And so on.

Jemma appeared with bacon, tea and coffee. Cannot recall now how it all got distributed to where it was needed – but it did.

Going down

Looking up – Dave looking back

Dave and me putting the world to rights

Jemma

Andy

Di working hard

Dave

The guide books suggest it takes about seven hours to get from Devizes to Foxhangers at the bottom of Caen Hill. With a crew of five we fairly flew down – a well-oiled human machine. We moored for lunch at Sells Green opposite the Three Magpies pub. It was around 3pm when we tied up the boat and retired inside for something to eat. It had taken about five hours.

Lindsay and I make a point of preparing a sit-down lunch whenever we have guests on board. Nothing cooked – it would not be practical to do that on the move. But a comprehensive cold meal nevertheless. It was a bit of a squeeze getting us all around the table in the galley. The boat was from ABC once more, again with the galley at the rear that we had found worked so well on previous trips.

Lunch was ham, salami, turkey, cheese, mini Melton pork pies, gammon and egg gala pie, hard-boiled eggs, little silver pickled onions, mayonnaise, salad cream (for the connoisseur), Branston brown pickle and not to be forgotten yellow piccalilli. My God, I love that stuff. As did Andy and Dave. Plus, wholemeal bread rolls, soft white bread[10], French sticks, crisps and on and on. There was a fridge on board, which meant we could bring M&S pre-packed continental salads in individual portions, including salad dressing, saving so much preparation time.

There was no alcohol but, even so, lunch turned into a memorable feast of storytelling, mostly around horsey exploits. I do remember telling one tale about the shower on one of the first narrowboats Lindsay and I had hired for a week. I'm quite a big bloke and didn't fit too well in that shower. It had a plastic front curtain which stuck to the body like glue. There was a single mixer control lever, but it was impossible to operate front-on since that meant my backside poking out of the enclosure. However, the height of the lever was such that it just fitted into my butt crease if I faced out. I found I could adjust the flow and temperature by doing a little dance, moving my hips up and down while simultaneously clenching and releasing my butt cheeks. I enjoyed doing that and was exceptionally clean by the end of the week.

We got moving again around 4pm. There were two more short flights of locks, one at Seend and the final one at Semington. I had arranged for us to all to have dinner together at the Somerset Arms pub in Semington Village, a few hundred yards down the lane from the canal. That meant being able to moor the boat after the last lock where there were 24-hour visitor moorings. As usual though, I could see a few gaps but not enough space. The whole lot was occupied by a ragbag of gypsy or Romany

---

[10] Why soft white bread you may ask? I hadn't thought any adults liked that stuff, but I was wrong. When Nick Hamer, Lindsay's brother-in-law, had been on the boat years earlier, he made a point of asking if we were going to have soft white bread for lunch. He had lived in Belgium as a child where apparently English soft-white is rather revered.

occupied craft, clearly living there and not visitors. I can say that with some confidence because Lindsay and I had passed that way six days earlier. I remembered a number of those boats and their sneering occupants when I had reversed back up the canal.

However, Andy was on the bow and spotted a gap. It meant getting on the towpath and moving one boat back a bit and another forward. Doing that can often cause friction. Nevertheless, military man that he is, Major Andy was willing to give it a go.

I nosed our boat into the gap. Andy leapt cat-like onto the bank, bow line in his teeth, then proceeded to adjust the lines of the other craft. As luck would have it, neither boat was occupied. He made enough room for us to be pulled in sideways – job done.

That day, a glorious day, with great friends, ended with a good pub meal, lots more chat and me drinking far too much scrumpy. The crew called a taxi to get them back to Devizes. That would take about ten minutes. Our journey had taken about ten hours overall – I would not have had it any other way.

The next morning saw Lindsay and me packing up and moving the boat about an hour down the canal to Hilperton Marina.

Chapter 15

Aldermaston to Great Bedwyn on the Kennet and Avon Canal 2014

Map 10

This trip would complete our exploration of the entire length of the Kennet and Avon Canal from Reading in the east down to Bristol in the west.

One of Britain's inland waterway wonders, which connects the River Severn with the River Thames. Construction began in 1794 and was completed by 1810. The name 'canal' is a bit of a misnomer because the waterway is actually made up of two navigable rivers joined by numerous sections of canal. The rivers are the Gloucestershire Avon and the Berkshire Kennet. There are 104 locks over a distance of 87 miles. The high point is at Crofton near Marlborough.

The week began at Aldermaston Wharf, again using a hired ABC narrowboat. We had the same crew for day one as we had the year before when going down Caen Hill. Andy, Jemma, Dave and Di met Lindsay and me at 10am and we set off westward.

This time I let Dave and Andy have a session steering the boat. They both turned out to be naturals. Jemma and Di were not keen though – happy to chew the cud in the bow with Lindsay.

We were heading for Newbury, a town with a considerable canal history. That would be around eight hours away for us, including a stop for lunch, but only about 40 minutes by car. How we take that for granted now. The first hour of so got us past the lift bridge and the huge Aldermaston Lock and on through mostly wooded terrain to Frouds Bridge Marina.

At Frouds Bridge the canal turns into river for about a mile and a half up to Woolhampton. It's a nice section where the river, the railway and the A34 run parallel, encompassing some 250 years of transport history. On the left, just before the lock, is the wonderful Rowbarge Inn – a spectacular place for eating, drinking and staying overnight. Lindsay and

I often meet cousins Robert and Virginia for lunch there, sitting outside in the sun if we can in the extensive grounds.

The Kennet can often come in hard from the left, immediately before Woolhampton Lock. It's a bit of a brute with a drop of nearly nine feet, but the paddle gear is well maintained and easy to operate. It's sometimes necessary to moor up, walk up to the lock, make sure it's empty and open the gates; notice I said gates. In flood conditions the Kennet will push the bow to the right, giving no chance of a recovery. Inexperienced boaters will end up hitting the lock sidewall and be pinned onto the offside vegetation. Both gates wide open allows experienced crews to power their way in and then stop before hitting the top gates.

The canal is climbing uphill of course at this point, all the way to the summit at Crofton. It is canal from here to Colthrop Lock. Then river to Monkey Marsh Lock.

Monkey Marsh Lock was built between 1718 and 1723 under the supervision of the engineer John Hore of Newbury. It is one of only two remaining working examples of turf-sided locks on the Kennet and Avon, the other being Garston, from more than a dozen originally. They were quick to construct. Their copious leakage was compensated for by ample supplies from the Kennet. Monkey Marsh Lock is listed as an Ancient Monument by English Heritage.

Moored by the CRT Café in Newbury

After Monkey Marsh Lock comes the longest straight pound on the canal – so-called 'Long Cut'. Then three more miles and four more locks, all operated beautifully by our fully trained and experienced crew, then moored up for the night in Newbury. The whole day was a joy – but very different from excitement of the Caen Hill descent the year before. We said goodbye to Andy, Jemma, Di and Dave, who had been wonderful company.

The next day saw Lindsay and me setting off westward towards Kintbury. The canal rises all the way to Crofton of course and so we were faced with handling large double locks on our own. We took it in turns to steer the boat and push the balance beams. It's a quiet, heavily wooded section, taking some seven hours by boat. On the way we met the last horse-drawn barge still operating on the canal network. Their tow rope had to pass right across the top of our narrowboat, which thankfully was mostly clear of clutter.

The balance beams on some locks were high off the ground. These had a steel step attached which in theory made it easier to get from one side to the other across the top gates. I made the mistake of jumping off one balance beam, the jolt injuring my back. I would pay for that stupid manoeuvre via a lot of pain and ibuprofen over the next four days.

We moored at Kintbury that night in a quiet wooded spot opposite the Dundas Arms Inn. It's named after one of the founders of the Kennet and Avon Canal. Lindsay and I had booked a table for that Sunday evening. We arrived to be told the booking had been cancelled because they had an exceptionally busy Saturday and had run out of supplies! We limped disappointed back to the boat to raid our emergency stock of frozen lasagne.

To Great Bedwyn

A stroke of good fortune occurred the following day. We were joined by our good friends Steve and Sandra for the trip to Great Bedwyn. Good fortune because I was seriously inhibited by back pain, having jumped off that balance beam. Steve took over driving the boat while Lindsay and Sandra operated the locks.

Kennet Boat Company's horse-drawn barge

I sat quietly and very still on the rail across the stern of the boat while the crew got on with the journey westward. Every two hours I downed a pile of either ibuprofen or paracetamol in an attempt to minimise the pain. We got through Hungerford Lock pretty quickly because a boat came out just as we appeared around the corner. Then on to Hungerford Marsh Lock, which has a swing bridge across the middle of the chamber. The swing bridge is a still used relic of times past when it hosted a cart track to Freeman's Marsh, commoner's land, and the River Dun.

We had lunch at Froxfield. One of our usual sit-down types when there are guests aboard. Quite often Lindsay and I will not stop for lunch if we are alone on board, preferring to keep going when we need to keep to a schedule. One of us will make tea or coffee and a sandwich in the galley area just below the steps down into the boat. That's why a reverse layout of these boats is so pleasant.

On past Little Bedwyn and then Great Bedwyn and immediately a problem. I was now driving the boat to give Steve a rest. We had planned to meet cousin Dee and her friend Mike that night. Mike lives in Great Bedwyn. We had a date at The Three Tuns in the High Street. After Burnt Mill Lock the boat had to be turned around for the return journey the next day. There are visitor moorings after the lock, all the way down to the winding hole just before the next lock at Bedwyn Church.

Hungerford Marsh Lock from 1976
Note the swing bridge across the chamber and the choppy state of the water.

© Copyright Dr Neil Clifton / Hungerford Marsh Lock No 73 and Swing Bridge

However, all the moorings were taken. I took the boat slowly down the line, checking for gaps, but there were no spaces. Then of course I reached the winding hole.

At this point the boat was facing west with the towpath on the left. On the other side of the canal, next to the winding hole were private moorings and a sequence of small wooden stages used by a local fishing club. As bad luck would have it, a man toying with his enormous rod were perched on the stage closest to the winding hole.

It was a windy afternoon. Bright sun but with a howling gale in our faces coming from the west, right up the canal. You can guess what was about to happen and it did.

I made a mistake in judging the conditions and attempted an open water turn within the space that was the winding hole. However, I had not taken the boat far enough down the canal. As soon as the boat had got to about 45 degrees, it got hit by the wind and began to rotate quite quickly and drift sideways back up the canal. Steve was with me on the back and began to look nervous. It became evident that the bow was never going to make even 90 degrees without demolishing the stage that the fisherman was on. He saw what was coming, dropped his rod, kneeled down and prepared to fend-off. No chance actually. A 15-ton narrowboat caught by the wind is a monster. Steve grabbed my sleeve and pointed to the apex of the winding hole on his left – no words were exchanged, but I knew what he meant. I abandoned the turn and got the boat moving forward again. We were now right across on the non-towpath side. The stern narrowly missed the fisherman, but I was close enough to see his bulging eyes and purple face. I've learned to lip-read 'f*** off' and its associated 'f***ing idiot' from some distance these days. I headed for the centre point of the winding hole, did a rapid turn to the right and buried the bow deep into its sandy bank.

Well, then, of course, executed a classic winding hole manoeuvre, turning the boat through 120 degrees or so with the bow still buried in the sand, followed by a powered reverse to complete the turn. Steve looked a happy man. The fisherman was still purple.

There was still the problem of where to moor overnight. I began driving the boat slowly back up the line already tied up for the night. Suddenly, a lady's head appeared from the side of a pram hood on a boat about 50 yards ahead. As we drifted slowly past, she shouted "Looking for somewhere to stop?" "Yes," we said, "any ideas?" "Well, you can tie up alongside us if you like." I was a bit gobsmacked because I had never had such an offer before. "We will need to climb over your boat to get to the pub. Will that be all right with you?" "Of course," she said, "but I've just done my washing, so you will have to push through my wet knickers." Never had an offer like that either. Her smalls were pegged to a washing line inside the pram hood, you see.

There was a bit of reversing and toing and froing before both bow and stern lines were hooked up to her boat. She was most helpful. I said, "It's likely we won't be back from the pub until ten-ish or so – are you happy about that?" She was.

The four of us had tea and cake and a reminisce, then made our way across the canal and past the railway station to The Three Tuns Inn, where we met Lindsay's cousin Deidre and Mike. When done, Lindsay and I said goodbye to Sandra and Steve, who would drive home, then made our way back to our boat via those now nearly dry knickers.

Back to Aldermaston

I was conscious that we needed to make a prompt getaway the next morning. I hadn't checked what time our companions wanted to leave. We had a quick breakfast, tidied the boat, untied bow and stern and drifted free. Our friend popped her head out the pram hood to say goodbye – how kind she had been.

It was just Lindsay and me on the boat now. We would be travelling downhill all the way back to Aldermaston. I set off towards Burnt Mill Lock to find another boat about to enter. Both gates were open and one of the crew beckoned us on to join them in the lock.

Sharing a lock is good practice wherever possible. It saves water plus a considerable amount of leatherware in not having to walk around all sides of each lock and back and forth over bridges. Not to mention effort in cranking winding gear and heaving on balance beams. The downside of course is sharing can become awkward if you don't like the other crew or they don't like you. Who goes first, are they in a hurry, how are jobs shared, are they communicative, are they more or less experienced, how do they use ropes in locks, if at all, are all issues that can cause friction.

It turned out that the crew with whom we would be sharing the lock were a husband-and-wife couple about the same age as Lindsay and me. For some reason the four of us clicked straight away – funny how that happens. I drove the boat into the lock alongside theirs and stopped before the end – always a good move. I didn't touch their boat, nor did I touch the infrastructure, so John, the guy on the tiller, saw I was not a beginner.

Nor was he. Theirs was a private boat that John and Sue, his wife, had commissioned after he retired. It turned out he was a mariner, a sea-captain with life-long experience of both military and commercial sea-going craft.

We quickly established a routine at each lock. We would take it in turns to exit the lock, the lead boat going ahead to drop off their crew, who would prepare the lock ready for both boats to enter. As luck would have it, another boat had come up past us and no other boat had got in ahead of us, meaning each lock was already filled and ready for us to go right in.

And go right in we did. Charge in in fact. The teamwork was a sight to behold. We hardly had time to chat before the crew had got cranking and both boats had begun their speedy descent.

John and I and Lindsay and Sue rotated the tasks of steering and cranking and pushing. In no time at all, it seemed we had gone through Hungerford, Kintbury and Newbury, then Ham Lock, Bull's Lock, Widmead Lock, Monkey Marsh Lock, Colthrop Lock, Midgham Lock and Heale's Lock.

Finally, we approached Woolhampton Lock, where John and Sue were going to stop overnight at the adjacent Rowbarge Inn.

We moored up at Woolhampton, not just to bid farewell to our new friends but to check out the passage through the lock. There had been heavy rain in the area over the past few days. The River Kennet comes in from the right just in front of the lower lock gates. It hits the far wall there and then turns right through 90 degrees before thundering under an electric swing bridge some 100 metres ahead. It was essential we had a plan to deal with this scenario – and we did.

We followed the approved procedure, which went like this: I would take the boat down into the lock and open the lower gates. We needed to be the only vessel in the lock. The boat would stay within the safety of the tall lock walls, observing the Kennet thunder past, going right to left. Meanwhile Lindsay, carrying a two-way radio, would be positioned at the swing bridge, stop the traffic, close the barriers and open the bridge. Once fully opened, she would call 'clear to proceed' on the radio. That was the signal for me to apply a lot of power, engage forward gear, plus hard left rudder (keeping the bow to the right) to get the boat out into the stream.

We gathered speed pretty quickly, albeit with a lot of scraping along the lock wall. I had positioned the boat with the stern against the left-hand wall and the bow against the right-hand wall – viz. diagonally across the lock. As soon as the bow got into the current, it dived left of course, but the hard left rudder resisted that.

We shot out of the lock like a rat up a drainpipe. Then past the little kink in the channel before the swing bridge and out onto mooring bollards on the other side. I tied up and walked back to help Lindsay close the bridge and the lock gates.

After a very late lunch break, we motored on down to the Aldermaston Marina – only an hour. The boat was due back the next morning at 9am. We thought it best to go through Aldermaston Lock and the lift bridge that evening rather than try to do that the next day during an early rush-hour. Plus, the boatyard wanted the boat returned pointing west. I could have gone through the lift bridge backwards, reversing past the marina to find a mooring. In the end we took the boat through Padworth Lock, turned around in the winding hole there, then back through Padworth and back up to the marina. Then pack up, ready for a quiet evening, and off by 9am the next day.

Chapter 16
Monmouthshire and Brecon Canal May 2015
Single-Handed

Map 03

Beacon Boats' stunning boathouse in Llanfoist, Abergavenny, in 2015

Beacon Boats have since moved to a new custom designed boathouse and marina at Llangattock.

I had always wanted to spend time driving a narrowboat single-handed. That is, cruising inland waterways alone – just the boat, the water and me. I had read a lot about the techniques required, most notably from Colin Edmondson's 'Going it Alone' notebook published in 2003.

So, in May 2015, I booked a week alone on one of Beacon Boats' craft. I checked, of course, that they would permit me to go single-handed. It would mean a return to the Mon and Brec Canal, for Lindsay and I had explored it together many years earlier. The difficulties experienced then were still fresh in my mind. Right in the middle at Llangynidr are the only locks, a close grouped flight of five.

The first issue was parking. Beacon Boats is in a stunning location in a valley surrounded by tall trees. The road up to the parking and unloading area is narrow and very steep. The business had acquired a new car a few months earlier – it was a long, wide Mercedes C Class Estate and automatic. There was only one remaining parking slot. I had to reverse uphill into that. As I backed up rather gingerly, I did think the front of the car was going to fall over the edge, then the whole lot roll down into the canal. I parked at a crazy angle with the bonnet way below the boot and looked to apply the handbrake. No handbrake. The car had no handbrake. I knew that of course but had never had a need for one until then. The car said put me into 'Park' and you will be OK, mate. I obeyed its instructions and got out. It didn't roll away, but would it still be there when I returned in a week's time?

I grabbed a trolley and proceeded to get my weeks' worth of stuff from the car and into the boat. That's significantly harder without one's partner to help. In the process I met Alasdair, the owner of the boatyard and builder of most of their craft. He looked me up and down, asked about narrowboat experience, threw out a few tricky questions and chewed the cud a bit before letting me keep my stuff on his boat. I was the first hirer going single-handed, you see. He was protecting his assets.

The boat was a cracker, I have to say. It was wider than a normal narrowboat because the Mon and Brec, although a narrow canal, has locks designed for boats up to 9 feet 2 inches wide, about 2 feet 2 inches wider than mainland narrow locks. She was called 'Kingfisher', about 48 feet long, had a beam of 7 foot 6 inches and a canopy over the entire length of the bow in an area usually covered with a timber and canvas 'Cratch' on traditional narrowboats. She had a semi-trad stern with storage space and seating.

Kingfisher had a bow thruster*, a king-sized double bed at the front, a walk-through bathroom with a huge double shower, an impressive lounge area and galley at the stern.

There were going to be half a dozen boats going out that day. I was to be the first. Alasdair did the handover, giving me a grilling as we went through the boat. Finally, he said I could set off, but he would remain on board for a while.

The other boats were moored herringbone fashion. The first task was to move out and turn left around all those other bows pointing the wrong way. The width there is limited, and Alasdair was watching me carefully. Now, on an unfamiliar boat, it takes a while to get used to how the controls feel. I put Kingfisher into forward gear and tried to move the throttle gently forward. It didn't, it jumped forward, causing Alasdair to say, "Go easy, go easy." I was going easy, I really was. Anyway, I got the bow around the others sticking out into the channel and, with big right tiller and lots of power, got the stern to move away and into the canal proper. We had begun to move left up the canal, north, as required.

I had expected Alasdair to stay on board for a while, but he asked me to move the boat to the towpath side so he could get off. A bit of a relief to be honest. I was now on my own and looking forward to the adventure to come.

Beacon Boats' wonderful 'Kingfisher'

48 feet long by 7-foot 6-inch beam narrowboat on a tea break at
Gilwern Wharf. The boat is pointing north towards Brecon.

I didn't want to travel far that first evening – it was 4pm before I got moving. I moored at Gilwern and walked down the road to buy fish and chips. I had intended to cook on board, but the whole day, travel, parking, etc. had been a big stress, so blazing up the gas hob would have to wait.

The next day dawned. It was strangely quiet on board. Of course, Lindsay was not there, but she doesn't usually make a lot of noise. No, it felt emotionally cold and a bit empty. I expected I would soon get used to it. I intended to get through the five locks at Llangynidr before nightfall. The canal guide books said that they were about three hours distant. However, I knew from past experience that this section of the canal is both twisty and exceptionally shallow.

From Gilwern to Llangattock was straightforward, apart from the spectacular scenery. The canal follows a 115-metre contour line all the way from Sebastopol near Cwmbran in the south to the Llangynidr locks, a distance of over 25 miles. Quite extraordinary, I have to say.

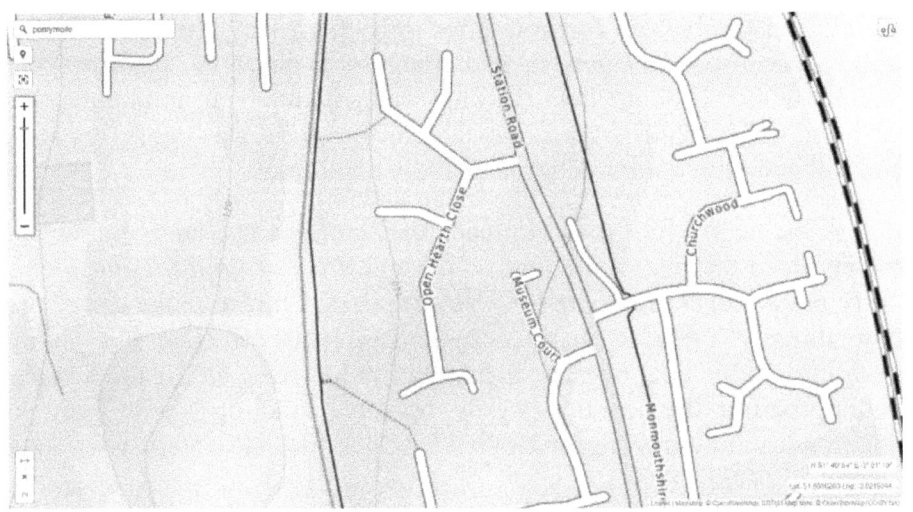

Canal on the 115-metre contour at Sebastopol, Cwmbran
© Copyright elevationmap.net

Canal still on the 115-metre contour at Llangynidr, towards Brecon, over 25 miles from Cwmbran.
© Copyright elevationmap.net

However, it's not at all joyful for the boater. In the 200 years or so the canal has been in existence, there has been heave and subsidence along the route. In places it's very obvious that water levels are close to the top of the towpath and in other places close to the bottom of the canal. There seems to have been a dearth of dredging, meaning the boat was almost literally on the bottom for mile after mile. Increasing engine power is useless because water gets sucked from the front of the boat, making matters worse. It didn't help that this was a heavy boat, unlike the one we hired in May 2007 from Cambian Cruisers. That was light, very rock and roll actually, but far better in shallow conditions.

It took me nearly four hours to reach the first lock at Llangynidr. I had remembered the rule of the road – '*Always drive around the outside of every bend, never cut a corner.*' Nevertheless, I had to make use of the bow thruster[11] on too many occasions. It was effective but highly irritating on this boat because it first had to be 'selected', using a push-button, before the joystick would operate. Fiddling about with an unnecessary button while single-handed on a difficult waterway is not a great deal of fun.

And of course, I could not go for four hours without having a pee. I didn't want to tie up and use the loo, so I stopped the boat in a bridge hole, letting it wallow there, while I went down to the bathroom at the front of the boat and did my thing. I could have just hung out over the side, err, as it were, but thought that a bit uncouth, not to mention illegal.

First Uphill Lock Single-Handed

---

[11] All Beacon Park boats have a bow thruster. These devices allow the steerer to move the bow right or left via a joystick at the stern. In essence they consist of an impellor fitted in a below-waterline tube at the bow that runs from one side of the boat to the other. The impellor can be electrically or hydraulically operated. If electrical, a DC motor is attached to the impellor. One or two 12-volt traction batteries fitted in a waterproof compartment below the bow decking drive the motor. If it's a hydraulic thruster, a hydraulic motor is attached to the impellor driven by a pump on the engine.

Both types are effective, providing a sideways force at the bow of around 70kg. However, overuse of the electrical type will quickly drain the batteries. Hydraulic bow thrusters can be used for long periods but are significantly more costly to install and maintain.

Kingfisher had an electrical bow thruster. I could understand why from our first visit to the Mon and Brec – it is a very shallow canal. They will not always get you out of all the jams, but will certainly help with a few.

The first lock heading north is a few yards beyond bridge number 132. The five locks ahead were all going uphill, and each had to be left empty with their lower gate paddles open. This arrangement is adopted on some canal where there are issues with canal infrastructure or water supply lower down the canal line. Leaving lower gate paddles open prevents the lock refilling should the lower gates close via the effect of strong winds, for example, or user forgetfulness. It prevents pressure building up on the sides of the lock chamber. It's a pain in the bum if you are time restricted because you will have to fill and then empty each lock as you go. Worse, if the previous boater had been going in the same direction but had not emptied the lock, it would be: empty, drive in, fill and empty again and like that all the way up the flight. Best then to complete one lock, moor up, put the kettle on and wait for someone else to pass on by.

I could see the lock was indeed open, allowing me to sail right in. I was able to stop the boat right next to a slippery-looking lock ladder. I had put on a life jacket that morning because I was going to be handling locks on my own. That meant it was tricky to stuff the windlass in my belt. Did that though and now with the centre line held in my left hand, pinched tight by my little finger and thumb, I used both hands to climb the ladder onto the lock side. (Those lock ladders are slippery and always covered in green slime.) Some boaters clench the rope in their teeth, but that doesn't work if you have dentures – I don't, but a lot do. I pulled the boat forward and wound the rope around a bollard, using the non-slip boatman's hitch. (That's a good knot. It cannot slip no matter how hard it's being stressed, and it can be undone quickly however tight.)

With the boat secure, I could walk back and close both mitred lower gates, ensuring their gate paddles were also closed. Then walk back up to the single top gate and carefully open one ground paddle so the lock could begin to fill. (If a paddle is opened too quickly, especially single-handed, the boat could be pushed forward and hit the top gate hard. So, 'single-handed slowly does it' is a golden rule.) Some single-handed boaters leave the boat with the engine running and forward gear engaged. This keeps the bow on the top gate as it rises in the lock. I didn't want to do that since I was in no hurry, plus there is always the danger of the bow getting snagged on the gate as the water rises.

Next, with the boat alongside, I could open the top gate. The boat had drifted to the far side of the lock, but I had the centre line to pull it in and could get aboard. That's another golden rule – take the centre line with you at all times. Make sure it can't snag or fall back into the water. I could have chosen to pull the boat out of the lock at that point – but I got on and drove it to a free bollard and walked back to close the top gate. Finally, back to the mitred bottom gates, open both paddles and wait for the lock to empty. Then open the first one and walk all around to open the second one. (On most narrow locks it's possible to step over from one gate to the other but at the risk of a devastating fall. However, the Mon and Brec is wider than other narrow locks and stepover cannot be done.)

So there it is. One uphill lock completed and four more to go. Reading that description emphasises how much more of an effort single-handed boating is than doing it all with a crew. As for single-handed on broad canals, well, getting anywhere would take forever and you'd be so knackered at the end of a day that you'd need the next one to recover.

Talybont on Usk

It took three hours to get through the next four locks, but that was with a stop for lunch. And what a glorious spot that is. I can't think of a more delightful section anywhere on the canal network that I've been through.

The Ashford Tunnel was next, short and dry for a change but a tight squeeze in places. It was late afternoon before I got to Talybont, where a couple of boaters on the towpath helped to pull the boat into a tight gap in the public moorings there. That evening I could have gone to the pub but decided to cook on board.

Electric lift bridge at Talybont

Pencelli

The next morning was an early start. I needed to get through the electric lift bridge at Talybont before its 8am curfew. I had never operated an electric lift bridge on my own before, but I knew the ropes. Moor close to the bridge. From the towpath side, walk over the bridge and close the gates across the road. Walk back over to the control unit, insert the BW (British Waterways) key and initiate the close sequence. That operates the red flashing lights on the roadway and an alarm warning motorists of road closure. The bridge starts to rise. That's the time to walk swiftly back to the boat, cast off and wait for the bridge deck to reach maximum height. Then drive the boat through, moor up again and walk briskly back to the bridge to incur the wrath of angry motorists. Finally, initiate the close sequence, wait for the bridge to close, remove the BW key and then pin back the gates over the roadway. Back to the boat for tea and a slug of Valium.

I intended to go on to Pencelli, where I would turn the boat around and head back south. Lindsay would be joining me for the rest of the trip. I had wanted to complete an entire week single-handed, but cooking and eating on my own the previous evening had not been a lot of fun. So I had wimped out, phoned her and persuaded her to join me.

The trip to Pencelli was only about three miles, but there were going to be three lift bridges on the way. These were all manual, operated by using a canal windlass and a lot of cranking. They were all hinged on and operated from the canal offside for the convenience of farmers, who would be the most likely users. That's not a problem for a crewed narrowboat. If the bridge is open, just sail under and through the gap. If the bridge is closed, simply moor before the bridge and drop off a crew member who walks across to crank it open. Drive the boat through and under the raised trackway, moor up and wait for the crew to lower the bridge, walk back over and back to the boat via the towpath. Collect crew and away.

However, there is a problem for a single-handed boater should they come across a closed bridge. Mooring is fine. Walking over the bridge to open it is fine. But they are then stuck on the offside without any access to their boat.

There are a couple of standard solutions to this tricky problem. One, if possible, wait for another boat to come by and let them open the bridge. Even if they are single-handed, there will be a minimum of two crew to get both boats through. The first boat could tow the other or, on a broad canal, both boats could be strapped together side by side. In my case, there would in all probability be a long wait. So waiting was not viable.

The second solution goes as follows: drive the boat up to the bridge and put its bow gently onto the superstructure. Disengage the engine. Push your windlass into your belt. Get up to the bow, hold the bow line and clamber off the boat onto the bridge, taking the bow line with you. If you are lucky, there will be a concrete pad to use. If not, or if that cannot be reached, there will be no choice but to scale the handrail and heave yourself onto the bridge deck. Now use the windlass to wind the bridge open. Use the rope to pull the boat up to the bridge and get back on board and drive it through. In all this, bear in mind that you will be operating on the offside of the canal. There will certainly be obstructive vegetation and no bollards or convenient mooring space. Once through, taking the stern line with you, get off the boat by using the gangplank or back-up to the bridge infrastructure and clamber onto the hinged part of the raised deck. Use the windlass to close the bridge. Pull the boat to you using the stern line and get back on board.

I set off at 7.30am. It was cold and, like an idiot, I forgot to wear something warm. By 8am I had got past the electric lift bridge without any hassle. I wasn't looking forward to those three manual lift bridges if I am honest. One unexpected reason was that apart from unusually high sides at the bow, the boat had a castellated canopy that made getting off at the front an almost impossible task. The canal was following the 115-metre contour all right, steep hillside to the left and steeper fall down the valley into the River Usk to the right. The canal was heavily overgrown on the offside, making it narrow and claustrophobic. The boat was consistently pushing through reeds and weeds, so much so that I never knew for certain where the banks were. The towpath side, if you can call it that, was not much better. Nevertheless, it was an oxymoronic experience that cold morning, carefree and anxious, to be driving that big lump of metal up a narrow watery way, clinging so valiantly to the side of that mountain.

Bridge 148 came into view through the trees and shrubs. My heart was thumping. I had been using the bow thruster a bit and was concerned about how much battery life was left. Would I be able to use it to get the bow near enough to get off? And then, getting off meant lying flat along the gunwale so as to avoid the canopy castellations and then rolling out – like from bed after one too many.

It was open. Yes, one of those rare days when it all went right. It was a tight squeeze for sure, but we just got under. And praise the Lord, the next two were open as well!

I turned the boat around at the winding hole at Pencelli Castle, just before bridge 155, and headed back. There then followed one of those optical illusions that occur on canals from time to time. It felt like the boat was going downhill all the way back to Talybont. I hadn't been aware of going uphill on the way out.

First Downhill Lock Single-Handed

The boat and I were now heading south. I was due to meet Lindsay at the Country Craft hire base, just after the fourth downhill lock at Llangynidr. She planned to leave her car at Beacon Boats and then taxi from there to meet me. As is always the case on 'there and back' canal trips, I hardly recognised anything I had seen on the way up, apart from the tunnel. I moored the boat on a bollard before the lock and then set off to check the surroundings. It's a beautiful location. Really. The lock was empty with lower gate paddles open as directed. There was no sign of a boat coming up, so I was free to begin the downhill procedure. The top gate was leaking quiet badly, I have to say, meaning there was already a substantial flow of water through the chamber.

One key thing to remember at locks: you have control. If things start to go pear-shaped, drop the paddles and assess the situation. Work out a plan.

I walked down to close both paddles on the mitred lower gates and the gates themselves. Then back up to open both ground paddles either side of the single top gate. The lock filled in no time. I was free then to open the top gate, walk back to the boat and drive it in. The boat was now in the lock and level with the lock sides. Easy to step off with the centre line in hand. I tend to loop the end of the centre line around a bollard if I'm having to let go of it, as I was when I went back to close the top gate behind the boat.

Going downhill is a no-turbulence situation. It's not like coming up where, if you let in too much water too fast, the boat can get banged around, especially in a broad lock. No, the issue going down is to make sure that the stern of the boat stays well forward of the concrete cill under that top gate. I always liked going into a downhill lock. There's always the fear of crashing into the far gates and then tumbling over the top. Never happened though.

Time then to let the water out of the lock while keeping an eye on that stern. There have been many techniques used by single-handed boaters over the century and a half that there has been commercial traffic on Britain's inland waterways. Colin Edmondson's 'Going it Alone' book is an excellent guide but too detailed, too complicated, I felt, for the occasional holiday boater like me just wanting to experience single-handed boating for a few days or a week or so.

I thought about it and chose to do the following. Prior to setting off I had asked the boatyard to fit a longer than normal central line to Kingfisher. With the boat in the lock and ready to go down, I took the central line with me up to the lower gates, now at the front of the boat of course. Then with the bow a couple of feet back, I wrapped the central line one turn around the balance beam. No knots, just free to be pulled back while applying some frictional resistance. Then opened one paddle, letting the boat sink in the lock. The boat was going to drop about ten feet, making the roof about five feet below my feet. But since the roof had started off about five feet above my feet, the central line was initially going to go slack and then pull back a little. I opened the second paddle and let the whole process complete itself. It worked a treat. Gentle, quiet, no fuss.

The lock was empty, the lower gate paddles were fully open and the boat roof now five feet below my feet. All I had to do was gather up the central line, shin down the lock-side ladder and step carefully onto the gunwale. I drove the boat out. No need to tie up and walk back to shut gates because they had to be left open.

I went through three more locks before mooring at Country Craft to wait for Lindsay to arrive. She took a bit longer than I expected because she got lost on the way up the hill past Beacon Boats. She ended up on the top of a nearby mountain and scared herself witless. But eventually her taxi pulled into the yard. I was pleased to see her. I had enjoyed the single-handed adventure but disliked being on board on my own.

Sheer Effort in Going Single-Handed

What did I feel about my single-handed experience? Challenging, enjoyable, risky and lonely are adjectives that come quickly to mind. The big ones though are greatly extended journey times and the sheer effort of it all. On broad canals there is a great deal of walking right around each lock. The 'walk right around' activity can occur four times per lock depending upon where you are and on which canal. On narrow locks this can be shortened to 'step over to the other side' if you are brave enough. On some broad locks there is a footbridge across the lock, making the journey a bit shorter. However, on a flight such as 'Wootton Rivers' on the Kennet and Avon, there is no shortcut – each lock is adjacent to, but not too near, a bridge supporting a roadway that has gated access to each lock. So working through each Wootton Rivers lock means walking some 500 yards over often rough ground, including getting to and from the landing stages. Not to mention opening and closing two gates, plus four paddles up and down.

For those wanting to set out single-handed I recommend getting a copy of Colin Edmondson's excellent treatise on the subject – see Acknowledgements.

On Towards Cwmbran

We tied up at the visitor moorings that night and walked down to the Coach and Horses pub for an evening meal. The next day saw us work speedily through two remaining locks then heading for Llanellen overnight.

The canal section from the last lock at Llangynidr and Gilwern is exceptionally shallow and meandry. It was impossible to maintain a pace more than one or two miles per hour. Any faster saw the water ahead being visibly sucked from the canal and forced under the boat by its propellor, resulting in the boat's bottom scouring through canal mud. In places the water level was up to two feet below the canal towpath. It didn't help that Kingfisher was obviously a heavy boat with a deep draft.

The section down to Gilwern was entirely different. The water level was in some places lapping over the towpath, allowing the boat to glide sweetly through that magnificent terrain. It would be impossible to increase the water level in shallow areas because that would result in the canal overflowing its banks.

The section from Llanellen, where there are mooring rings (always a joy to behold), to Pontymoile Basin is almost impossible to do justice in words. Matched only by the Caldon Canal, it's twisty and almost prehistoric in places. The way it sticks to the mountainsides, the way it creates those uphill and downhill illusions as the vegetation cover and light changes, is nothing short of jaw-dropping. Just as on the Caldon, I swear I saw a family of dromaeosaur flitting in and out of those fern-covered woodlands.

Pontymoile Basin is the site of the junction with the now in-filled three-mile Monmouthshire Canal to Pontnewynydd, originally having 11 locks and completed in 1812. It was an unsuccessful commercial venture killed off by railway technology. It's now little more than a place to turn around. Bridge 51 carries the A472 over the Mon and Brec at this point. And that's where our journey south temporarily ended. Stuck fast, under the A472.

I initially thought there was debris wound around the propellor. I tried to unwind it by attempting a violent reverse back the way we had come, but it didn't help. There was no point in using either the short or long poles because we were already marooned in the centre and deepest part of the canal. I got down the weed hatch, with Lindsay looking worried, only to find nothing. I then realised the boat was on the bottom. The only solution was to try and bow-haul Kingfisher. Lindsay put the boat into forward gear at a tickover while I got the bow line over my shoulder and heaved like hell.

The boat began to move. Foot by foot she came out from under the bridge and began to float once more. But I could not get her near the canal side to get on board. Out came the gangplank and on I clambered.

We crawled into Griffithstown – a stark reminder that this was now industrial South Wales. The canal was shallow, not much more than a muddy brook really, full of weed and a great deal of household detritus. We plodded slowly past a long line of Victorian houses, their back gardens open and accessible via rows of broken-down, kicked-down or just plain rotten fencing. The boat would stop when I tried to move any quicker than tickover.

We managed to make it to the 'Open Hearth' pub (its name a reference to steel making) in Sebastopol, about two miles from the canal terminus as it now stands. But I could not get the boat near enough to the towpath to consider mooring for the night. Even the gangplank would not span the gap.

We had no provisions left on board for an evening meal. Lindsay and I decided we would have to risk wading through filthy oily water to get to the pub. Then as luck would have it, a couple walking their dog suggested a solution. There was a small landing stage sticking out into the canal from the pub's front door. It was not intended to host narrowboats as it was a flimsy fisherman's affair. The bystanders suggested I park the boat alongside the stage and secure it using bow and stern ropes and mooring pins hammered into the bank either side of the structure. That way, there would be no damage caused and it would mean we could alight and walk over to the pub. Clever. The boat would be blocking the canal of course, but it was now nearing 7pm and no one else was likely to come by. Actually, I got the feeling that no narrowboats had been that way for a while given the look on some locals' faces as they walked on past us up the towpath. (That's right, the pedestrians were overtaking us.)

It was a rough area all right, but the crowd in the pub were a friendly lot. We signed a visitor book kept for adventurers like us who had made it that far. Then enjoyed a nice meal.

On returning to the boat, I was concerned at the risk of overnight vandalism. The local yoof might have seen a flash boat in a rough area as a target for a bit of hostile fun. In the event we hit the sack and had a peaceful night. In the morning we both got in that shower – it had been a very sweaty day yesterday. As I untied the ropes and pulled the pins, I had a quiet look around. The canal was shallow but also narrow. There was no room for two boats to pass without either or both getting stuck.

I drove gingerly up to the winding hole before bridge 47 and very slowly turned the boat around. Lindsay took over and headed north for a delightful journey home, once she had got us under that A472.

Update – Dredging the Southern Section

Autumn 2019 was the date set for dredging the southern end of the Mon and Brec Canal. The local council expected to remove some 7,000 tons of silt along with bikes, shopping trolleys, plastics and loads more rubbish. Narrowboats would once again be able to navigate the four miles between bridge 57 and Five Locks at Cwmbran, the southern terminus.

But then came Covid. It's now 2024 and I cannot confirm that the dredging was done. However, the canal is in water down to Cwmbran and narrowboats can reach the town, albeit slowly.

Chapter 17
Guildford to Teddington Lock on the River Thames 2015

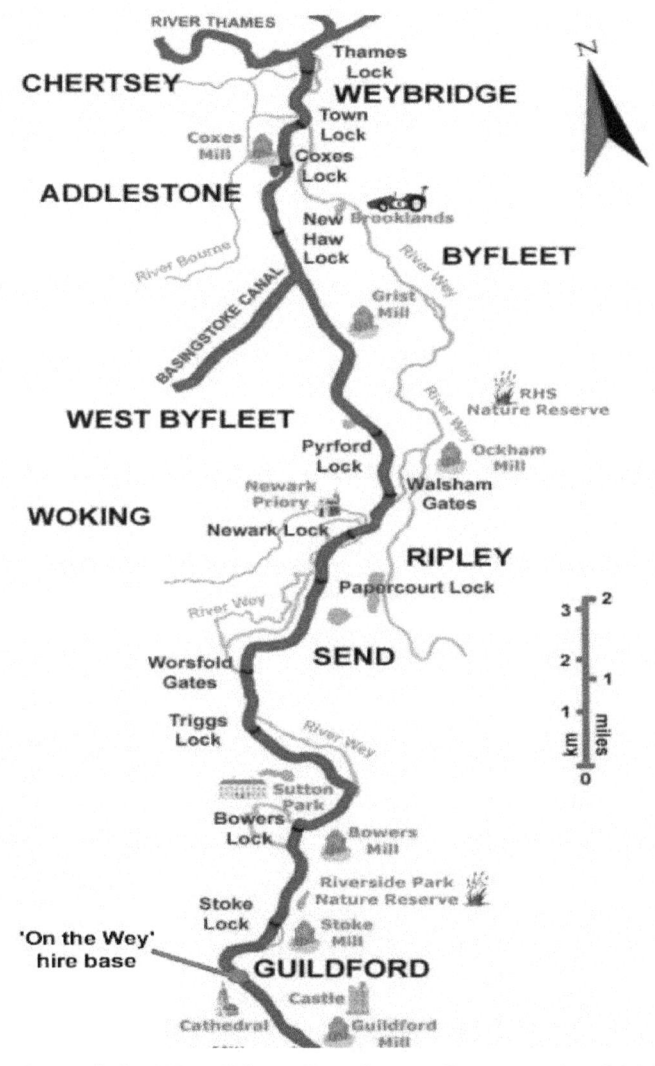

Map 12

In 2015 we hired a narrowboat from 'On the Wey' in Guildford. The plan was to explore the River Wey Navigation up to Shepperton and then go down the Thames to Teddington Lock, where we would moor for the night before turning back.

For that trip our boat was 'Stepping Stones', the very same one hired the previous year by Timothy West and Prunella Scales for one episode of 'Great Canal Journeys'.

Stepping Stones was not built for the hire industry. She was originally ordered by a private boater but then put up for sale and thence acquired by 'On the Wey'. She was based on a Jonathan Wilson/Tim Tyler shell and how different that felt on the water. She steered and glided as silkily as Silky the Silkworm in his silky pyjamas.

'Stepping Stones' was beautifully built but a 4-foot-6-inch-wide double bed at the stern and spiral steps down into the cabin meant getting in and out was a problem. Rumour had it that Timothy West's sound engineer was permanently grumpy because his equipment kept catching on the furniture.

Collecting Friends at Guildford

We had wanted to start our trip by going south to Godalming, the current southern limit of navigation. However, Stepping Stones was not a guaranteed fit through Broadford Bridge downstream of Godalming and we would have to use the winding hole before that.

Lindsay and I collected the boat from On the Wey's small two-berth boatyard just before the Rowbarge pub in Guildford. Having got formalities completed, the owners Julie and Ray walked up to Stoke Lock while I drove the boat there. She was unusually responsive to the throttle and tiller, taking me a bit by surprise. Julie watched as we went through the lock, downhill of course initially and through the other side. Ray took over, turned the boat around and then explained the National Trust's required procedure for going through the Wey locks in an uphill direction.

The 'Wey Navigation' is essentially the River Wey in places and canal in between those places. Somewhat like the Kennet and Avon, a mixture of river and canal. And just like the River Kennet, the River Wey can be unpredictable after prolonged heavy rain.

The locks on the Wey are broad. Each lock has a pair of mitred gates at each end of the chamber. Adjacent to each lower gate hinge and embedded in concrete, there is a yellow corkscrewed steel stake about a foot high. After entering the lock and closing the lower gates, the steerer has to back up and throw a stern line up and around that stake, sort of lasso fashion, and then tie the boat tight into the 'V' between the chamber wall and the gate. Only then can one upper gate paddle be gingerly opened, followed by the other once the deluge has stabilised. The issue here is that there are no ground paddles – they are all gate mounted. The yellow stake is used to keep the boat as far back as possible, preventing turbulence sending it forward for an inevitable and violent crash. It's a neat solution because as the turbulence dies down, the boat rises up. The rope allows the boat to come forward, just a little, thereby removing any risk of getting the stern stuck in or under that lower gate 'V'.

Of course, all the locks were going to be downhill initially as we headed for the Thames. Having had a demonstration of how to go uphill, I promptly forgot about it until the procedure was required. Actually no. I forgot about it and received a stern reminder from the lock keepers at Thames Lock before the journey home.

We said goodbye to the boat's owners and set off south towards Guildford town centre, where I had booked a table at The Weyside pub, a pleasant two-storey building with a riverside terrace, just upstream from Millmead Lock. I had been concerned that there were no specific public mooring places shown in any of the guide books. However, after going through the lock, the pub came into view on the left-hand side of a sweeping right-hand bend, just before Guildford Rowing Club boathouse. I found a spot on the left after the clubhouse under a row of trees. I bashed in the mooring pins. Then up the little track beside the boathouse and into the pub.

Our friends Andy and Jemma had planned to join us the next morning for a trip downstream to Pyrford, where the boat would stop overnight. They had been with us on that wonderful day in September 2013 when we went down Caen Hill on the Kennet and Avon. However, we had heard a few days before that Di Symes, also on the Caen Hill trip and Jemma's best friend, had just been diagnosed with an aggressive brain tumour. She was not expected to live more than a few months.

I didn't know if they would want to come along now. But they did turn up at the pub at 9.30 as arranged and I walked them down the path to the boat. Jemma was in bits, eyes red and puffy and she very emotional. We all gave her plenty of hugs while just sitting quietly on the back of the boat, sipping tea and coffee.

Andy suggested we make a move, saying it would take Jemma's mind off her friend. We were now a bit behind schedule and so I abandoned the idea of going upstream to Godalming. The boat was still pointing that way of course, but none of the maps showed a winding hole within reach. Where would I turn around 62 feet of Stepping Stones?

Surrounded by rowers from Guildford Rowing Club

It was a Sunday and, all of a sudden, the river was full of canoes, kayaks and rowing boats replete with professional-looking but very young crews. Guildford Rowing Club had opened its clubhouse doors; it was juniors' day and their boats had poured down the slipway into the river. Even so, Andy and I pulled the mooring pins, gently pushed out the bow and moved the boat away from the towpath. As luck would have it, the clubhouse was on one apex of an S-bend, and we were heading for the other. That made the river wider than normal and just around the bend I decided we should try to turn the boat. Andy went up to the bow to do the best he could to let all these boats know what we intended. We were literally surrounded. None of the crews paid our 15 tons the slightest attention and neither did their instructors, who were zipping around on their little powered launches. And of course, most of those boats had their crews facing backwards and so had no idea where they were in relation to us.

I decided to turn just past the S-bend. It looked like the boat would fit, but I was not sure. Andy gesticulated to the junior crews and their instructors. I'm sure they just thought he was some mad man waving his arms and shouting. As the boat reached 90 degrees, the bow gave the bank a good swipe, gouging a foot or so of mud and soil into the river. Andy jumped off, rope in hand, and began to pull the boat round. At this point we were blocking the river. I'd stopped the engine so I could yell at some juniors about to give us a broadside and them a head-on. Several instructors started to get shirty, "How dare you disrupt our training day," that sort of thing. Andy continued to pull on the bow rope and gradually Stepping Stones floated free. I restarted the engine after checking there were no little dears near the prop and brought the boat into the far bank. Andy joined me at the stern, took hold of the tiller, and we set off.

Towards Pyrford

Our destination that evening was the Anchor pub, a hidden gem on the banks of the Wey Navigation, adjacent to Pyrford Lock and a short distance from West Byfleet. Pyrford Village was built on land once owned by Westminster Abbey. It was not allowed a public house, so the Anchor was built just over the parish line in Wisley. (Background via Wikipedia.) The Anchor has extensive public moorings on bollards right next to its beer garden, where customers can sit quietly and watch boats and birds flutter by.

However, we had to get there. Andy drove the boat while Lindsay and Jemma sat up front and chewed things over. The first lock, Millmead in Guildford centre, was quickly upon us.

National Trust regulations require at least one rope to be used to hold a boat going downhill. I have rarely found it necessary to use ropes in locks, preferring to use the engine and gently-does-it-with-the-paddles to ensure a smooth ride. But with NT spies all around, we obeyed the rules.

That meant Andy driving, me up on the lock side with the central line looped once around a bollard and Lindsay and Jemma on gates and paddles. Jemma was an old hand, having been with us on Caen Hill. Stoke Lock followed quickly – it was the second time we had been through there – then a lovely stretch up to Bowers Lock.

Sitting on a tight bend that pushes the Wey Navigation back onto the course of the River Wey proper is Bowers Lock. The lock, originally opened in 1653, nestles amongst mature trees near the site of Bowers Mill. The mill only survives today by the mill house which has been converted into a private residence. The building now called Bowers Mill is not the original but had been constructed specifically by the Duke of Sutherland as a laundry to serve Sutton Place, which he had then owned. The mill had made paper, flour then linseed but had closed by 1910, with the mill building demolished in 1947.

Bowers Lock is on a river section that sits on a 90-degree bend. Its recent claim to fame is being poleaxed by Stepping Stones in the hands of Timothy West. It is a tricky place, I have to say, there often being a strong crosswind across the lock when going north – as we were. The wind took our bow away coming out of the lock, resulting in us heading 180 degrees in the wrong direction. I had to reverse back in, set the boat up again with the bow pointing to the right and the stern against the left-hand chamber wall. That enabled us to power out, with hard left rudder, into that wind. The boat then made a 90-degree turn to the right as required.

We moored for lunch on the left-hand bank just after Bowers. Delightfully quiet spot, thoroughly rural, sunshine dappling through trees wafting in the breeze. We stayed there for about an hour, chatting away, with Jemma back to her old self.

Andy continued to drive the boat. We went through Triggs Lock and on towards Worsfold Gates, where the River Wey begins a series of meanders across an extensive area of water meadow. We were still heading north into a strong, gusty wind. Then Andy lost his hat. It landed behind us and floated just like a little model boat. He stopped Stepping Stones then gently backed her up towards the hat. However, rather strangely, the hat wanted to keep its distance from her stern. Andy and I held a conference. How valuable was the hat both in monetary and emotional terms? Well, let's just say he didn't want to lose it. We devised a plan. I had the boat hook to hand. I would hang off the stern via the tiller stem and snag the hat. Didn't work; the hat was always too far. I then tried the same trick using the short pole which was also to hand. Didn't work, because the pole was heavy, and its tip just sank. Meanwhile, Lindsay and Jemma up at the bow never noticed the boat had been stationary for over 15 minutes. Until they did, when a couple of worried faces appeared up there. looking back, seeing Andy and me chatting away, wondering what the heck we were up to. The river was wide at that point, allowing us to formulate a plan that did work. We captured the hat by reversing back past it, via keeping a wide berth, and then gently sneaking up with the hat drifting along our port side. Capturing was completed by the boat hook. Andy plonked it straight back on, river water pouring down his face and neck, in his ears and soaking his shirt. Nevertheless, he was overjoyed.

The remainder of the journey to the Anchor pub in Pyrford was most enjoyable and event free. Andy brought the boat in to the bank and found a mooring on bollards right outside the pub beer garden. As I was about to step off the counter, I was met by a young boy aged about eight years. I looked down on him, as he was blocking my exit, and he looked up at me and said, "Hello, Mister, do you live on that boat because you can't afford a house?"

From the corner of my eye I saw a young woman sitting alone at a table, clearly his mother, lower her head and hide her eyes, doubtless hoping the earth would swallow her up.

Lindsay and I said our goodbyes to our friends. I think the day had cheered Jemma just a little.

Weybridge

Lindsay and I had breakfast at the Anchor the next day and then sat outside next to Stepping Stones, waiting for friends Steve and Sandra to arrive. They were going to be accompanying us to Teddington. First, through Pyrford Lock, then under the M25 at Woodham where the Basingstoke Canal joins the Wey Navigation.

Under the M25 at Woodham Junction and the Basingstoke Canal to the left just ahead

Then on to Coxes Lock and its spectacular mill and mill stream. Coxes Lock was built between 1651 and 1653, as part of an important link to transport heavy goods between London and Guildford. Coxes Lock is the deepest unmanned lock on the Navigation with a rise of 8 feet 6 inches and is 1.5 miles from the Thames.

The mill buildings and land around them were donated to the National Trust in 1983 after flour production ceased. The entire seven-storey building was then renovated and given a postmodern outlook. The internal spaces were converted into flats for rent.

The onward into Town Lock on the outskirts of Weybridge. This lock is notorious for the difficult entry from and exit to the River Wey at Weybridge.

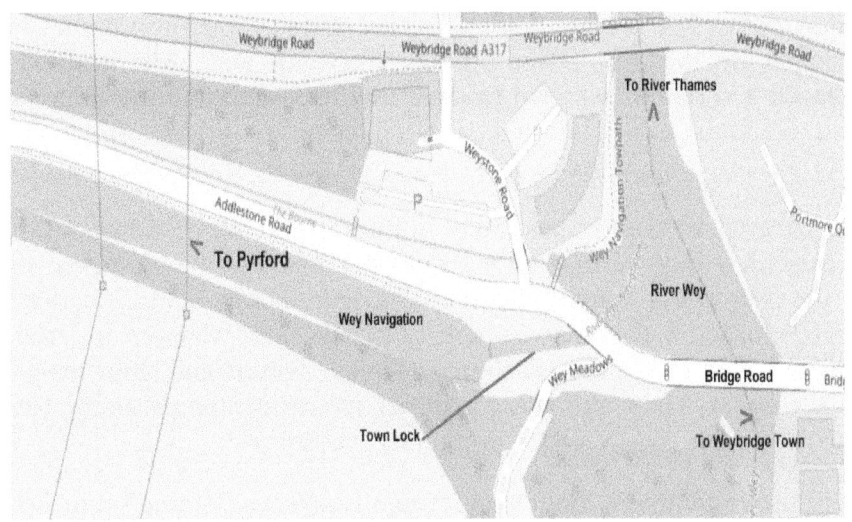

Town Lock, Weybridge

© Surrey Archaeological Society 2010–2020

The original bridge over the River Wey at Weybridge

A Grade II listed structure. The exit from Town Lock comes in from the right.

Happy days! The bridge, notable for its series of cast-iron arches, was designed by the Weybridge County Surveyor and built in 1865. It replaced a series of wooden bridges that had straddled the river there since medieval times, with the first reference to a bridge on the site in 1235. Prior to that, crossing was only achieved by wading across a ford.

The wide wharf pool immediately in front of the Wey Bridge was once an extremely busy terminus for barges unloading at the old town wharf on the Weybridge bank. The Wey Navigation saw a huge variety of cargoes loaded at the wharves here, or bypass it for wharves upstream in Byfleet, Guildford and Godalming. Timber, wheat and flour were the usual cargoes. The wharf was converted into residential use in the 1990s. (Text based on Wey Valley Community website.)

Steve drove Stepping Stones into Town Lock, with me up on lock side and Sandra and Lindsay operating the gates and paddles. Exit from the lock is via a long dark channel that leads out into the original extensive wharf pool in front (i.e., to the north) of the cast-iron Wey Bridge. Steve came out too fast and left himself no room to turn left. As it happens, the rest of us had a grandstand view of his difficulty, and irritated demeanour, as we watched up above from the lock. Lots of churning water, back and forth and full rudder in both directions before he got the boat under control and back where we could all get onboard. Steve's problems were compounded by a strong flow from the Thames under the bridge that kept pushing him against the bridge abutments. The picture above was taken with Stepping Stones backed up to the entrance to the lock channel, marked by the big black and white pole in the background.

Steve and me at Town Lock in front of the original Wey Bridge

We moored for lunch and then set off for a date with the lock keeper at Thames Lock. This is the only manned lock on the Wey Navigation and that is because the lock has a flood control role plus the lock is actually a two-chamber staircase.

Lock keeper's cottage at Thames Lock, the last downstream on the Wey Navigation

Teddington

Stepping Stones emerged from the Wey Navigation in early afternoon sunshine and set off on her journey eastward on the mighty River Thames. The Wey joins the Thames just east of Shepperton Lock. We took the Desborough Cut, opened in 1935, to save some time and cruised past Walton-on-Thames, Sunbury, Hampton and Hampton Court, where we had been a few years earlier. The locks this far east on the river are all huge but operate using the same protocol as those smaller further upstream. Basically, going downhill, snag a bollard at both ends of your boat, turn off the engine and wait for the lock keepers to do their stuff.

Hampton Court Bridge

The Thames is wide and awe inspiring at this point. There is a wide variety of river traffic, including sailing, rowing and canoeing craft, particularly on the section between Kingston Bridge and Hampton Court Bridge. There are river buses, large barges preceded by their tugs, fibreglass cruisers, narrowboats, powered yachts, hotel boats, restaurant boats and so on. The river was benign when we were there, but it was always necessary to keep looking over one's shoulder to see what might be coming up fast.

The three locks in Teddington are all manned throughout the year and mark the boundary between the tidal and non-tidal river. I had phoned the lock keepers before we set out to establish whether we could moor there overnight – but of more importance, whether I could turn the boat around. A rather incredulous lock keeper asked me how much space we needed. I said about 70 feet. There was a pause. Fine, she said; if it had been 400 feet, there might have been a problem.

Big boats at Teddington

Moored at Teddington Lock having turned and now pointing west

The huge weir complex at Teddington can be seen in the distance. 'Thames Venturer' pictured above was right behind us.

I turned around within the lock pool and moored up quite close behind the 'Thames Venturer', a training boat of some kind. She towered above our stern and had a huge rudder. I walked over to the centre lock complex and paid our mooring fee.

That was as far as we were going to go, since hire boats are not allowed onto the tidal section. And a VHF radio licence was also mandatory. So the four of us made tea, ordered our evening meal via the 'Just Eat' website and settled down for some gentle wittering.

The next morning, Lindsay and I were back on our own. Steve and Sandra had left us last night after a very good but sizeable Chinese meal delivered direct to the boat. We had inadvertently ordered double of everything.

No cooked breakfast then, just tidy the boat, on with our life jackets and prepare to get under way. Suddenly, there was a roar like an aircraft overhead and the boat jumped forward. There was an almighty crash in the cabin as loose china and vases went everywhere. What the hell! The boat was not moving, maybe drifting back a little.

I climbed the galley steps out onto the counter and looked around. We were still secure on our ropes. Nothing obvious. Then it happened again – I was nearly knocked over. Thames Venturer, behind us, was testing its engines. I was close to her stern. from where she towered skyward. Her gigantic prop was being rotated for a few seconds, sending a wall of water and a powerful shockwave under our boat. Stepping Stones leapt forward and then rebounded with her ropes acting as springs. I jumped off the boat and ran back to gesticulate to the captain. Did he know we were there? I thought he had moved back from where he was moored originally, but we would have felt that all right. He responded with a few friendly hand waves; he had already sent us some of the watery kind.

In hindsight, I had moored too close to his stern, giving him no room to manoeuvre. Basic mistake when on big waterways replete with big boats.

Back to the River Wey Navigation

We had hoped to moor outside Bentalls in Kingston upon Thames on the way upriver, but a problem with the boat's macerator toilet delayed us for a while. But we did tie up for lunch at The Albany pub on the south bank, just before Hampton Court. That did feel very special. We were the only boat right outside and we tied up on rings. Something about that clanking noise they make fills me with pleasure. I do like a bit of an audience and the concept of bringing a boat into a perfect landing in front of a crowd of boozy gongoozlers is simultaneously appealing and scary. I clambered off the boat and went inside to order a pint of cider and a light lunch for us both. We sat on the towpath, life jackets still on, and had our lunch. We were bathed in warm sunshine and just sat quietly overlooking that magnificent river, warbling and bubbling away to itself just below our feet.

At Walton-on-Thames we turned right towards Shepperton rather than go straight on through Desborough Cut as we had on the way down. We had plenty of time. It's a loop that adds about a mile to the journey and was, still is, the original course of the river. It was a tranquil detour that we both enjoyed.

Then straight on past the face of the mighty Shepperton Lock and into the central feeder channel leading to the River Wey. Thames Lock hove into view, the only manned lock on the Wey. It's a staircase with just two chambers. We had to wait outside the bottom chamber while the lock keepers finished their lunch. Nevertheless, it's a nice spot, dappled sunlight through a dense canopy of trees but a somewhat rickety landing stage with loose handrails not inspiring confidence. The keepers came round and opened the single bottom gate, allowing Stepping Stones to move around the corner to the upper lock chamber. Then, having equalised water levels, they opened the bottom pair and in we went. And I mean 'they' by the way – a husband-and-wife team.

It was at this point I was reminded in no uncertain terms of the procedure[12] for going uphill on the Wey. One keeper pointed out the yellow corkscrewed metal post near the 'V' of the nearside gate and asked me to lasso it using the stern line. I missed of course, so she kindly used her long hook to pass the stern line around the post. I was instructed to pull the boat back hard into the 'V' and tie the rope tight to a stern rail. I was concerned about this, but in fact the rudder and rope fender fitted neatly into the 'V'. The rope was not far off vertical, probably 30 degrees off, but I could see that, as the boat rose in the lock, the rope would become increasingly horizontal and let the boat drift away from the bottom gate.

The keeper opened one top gate paddle, followed smartly by the other. Stepping Stones was hit by a violent wall of water which pushed her hard back into the bottom gate, only for her to rebound but be held by that yellow post. The keepers could have opened the paddles one at a time but wanted to give us a lesson and I'm grateful they did that.

---

[12] The River Wey was purchased in 1912 by boatbuilder William Stevens. In 1964 his son gave it to the National Trust. Restoration began in 1973 after formation of the Wey and Arun Trust. To save money, all the wooden lock gates were replaced by steel, and ground paddles replaced by gate paddles. A similar process was followed on the Warwickshire River Avon.

One consequence was that boats going uphill towards the summit faced a torrent of virtually uncontrollable water at each lock, threatening to overwhelm their boats. To solve this, National Trust installed a system of 'yellow spikes' at the lower gate end of each lock and insisted that each boat be tied to that spike during the filling process. I can confirm that the deluges still happen but further confirm that the yellow spike procedure works very well.

217

The journey back to Guildford was problem-free apart from the approach and entrance to Town Lock in Weybridge – where we had all mocked Steve on the way out. Although he was not on board, he got his own back because I made a complete Horlicks of the turn into the channel that leads to the lock. It really looks impossible from the back end of a 62-foot boat. It's close beside the iron bridge and you have to do a 90-degree turn to the right and slot the boat up the channel behind two posts that stick out of the water. It does not help that the river current is continually pushing you sideways onto the bridge. I backed right out and made it at the second attempt. How Steve would have laughed.

Stepping Stones then slid smoothly all the way back to her owners in Guildford. What a great week on a fabulous craft.

Author's Note: An abridged version of this article was printed by 'Waterways World Magazine' in their February 2022 issue published on 31st December 2021. Our thanks to Julie and Ray White, owners of 'Stepping Stones' for permission to publish and all the friends mentioned.

Chapter 18
Wrenbury Mill to Llangollen 2016

Map 01

In 2016 we went back to the Llangollen Canal. We started from Wrenbury Mill Marina (ABC again), down to Hurleston, back past Wrenbury, on to Llangollen and back to Wrenbury. It was a joyful experience, so different from the first visit all those years ago where I remembered almost nothing, apart from that damn dog.

We had not been down to Hurleston on our first Llangollen visit. Lindsay never forgave me for not getting to Snugburys Ice Cream parlour there. Sisters Chris and Cheryl Snugbury started making ice cream over 30 years ago in their Cheshire farmhouse kitchen. More than 300,000 people now visit Snugburys each year, now run by the Snugbury daughters.

First, we had to get to Hurleston and then down the four locks there into the junction with the Shropshire Union Canal. There was a queue of boats waiting. The reason was that over the two centuries since construction, the four locks have become twisted and their chambers forced inward. Progress through each lock has to be supervised to ensure boats do not become jammed between the walls. The locks were attended by a team of knowledgeable volunteers – ours a nice young man who was partially deaf and with some physical disability. (He told us how his hearing had been transformed by cochlea implants.) He ensured we had our fenders in-board before we began the descent. The view over those Shropshire hills was a sight to remember.

I turned the boat around in the junction pond and then went straight back into the bottom lock for the ascent. Lindsay had kept the bottom gates open, meaning it had to be a quick spin through 360 degrees, which I'm pleased to say it was. A couple of gongoozlers cheered or jeered – I'm not sure which.

After coming out of the top lock, I drove the boat for a few hundred metres or so and then pulled over at the visitor moorings by bridge number three. A turnstile buried in the vegetation there marks the entrance to a footpath that would lead to Snugburys.

It was at this point I realised that the arthritis in Lindsay's hips were beginning to cause her a real problem. Several of the turnstiles were the kind where you have quite a big step up onto a horizontal board, then swing a leg over and straddle the top rail – before doing the reverse and stepping down. She found it difficult to step that high but more difficult to swing her leg over the top rail. I had to help her with both manoeuvres, and she became quite distressed. We didn't know how many of these obstacles we would have to tackle. The ground conditions were not good either, lots of cracks and deep ruts and holes. Plus, we were not sure of the route, increasing her anxiety. Nevertheless, she was determined to get her ice cream and we did eventually make it. Then sat quietly in the sun and slurped away. What a joyous place, I have to say. We got back to the boat via the A51, walking slowly along the grass verges.

We had made a date to meet Lindsay's sister Sue and George the morning after next and so we had to get a move on. We were well behind schedule; it was early afternoon and lunch had been a 99 with two scoops. Without further delay I untied the boat and set off back towards Wrenbury. The aim was to get somewhere near Grindley Brook before nightfall. There were five locks to get through and then the Wrenbury Lift Bridge. Luckily, the bridge had been opened for a bunch of lads on a couple of narrowboats ready to set sail from the ABC marina.

They very kindly let me go first, but I soon realised that was something of a mistake. Pretty soon, about 30 minutes or so, with them well-oiled by this time, we were a convoy of three fast-moving ABC narrowboats with us at the front. I pushed on as quickly as I could, well above 4mph, I'm sure, but I could not get rid of the boats behind. The only consolation, and a very considerate one, was that when we stopped for the first lock, Marbury, a flock of young lads poured forth to assist. After that we could pursue a more leisurely pace since navigation through each lock had the effect of enforcing a 15-minute gap between boats. The locks on the Llangollen are singles of course.

We were never going to get to Grindley Brook that night. We were forced to moor out in open country when we ran out of light. Lindsay and I had planned to eat at a canal-side pub but never got there. We ate on board, resorting to emergency supplies of onion soup, baked beans and toast. We had already microwaved other 'emergency' supplies.

The next morning it was up early and get going. Into the Grindley Brook staircase – that second chamber gate is mighty intimidating – then moor up at the top for a cooked breakfast. We got supplies in the shop, right there by the lock. I was up on the counter sipping my tea, Lindsay was in the galley juggling frying pans full of sausage, mushrooms, bacon, fried eggs and baked beans left over from the night before, when who did I see coming out of the lock? Our young friends on boat one from the day before. As they got nearer, I saw one of the lads at the bow lift his head and sniff the air. Fried bacon had drifted down the waterway, you see. It was possible to hear his stomach rumble as hunger spread over him and his mate. "Do you want to pull over for breakfast?" I yelled, feeling chivalrous but in danger of incurring Lindsay's wrath. For an instant they thought about it – but politely and with reluctance declined. Their need to push on was greater than ours. They sailed past with long faces and 'what have we done' expressions.

Having cleared up and washed up, we got moving again towards Whitchurch, where the canal performs a hairpin bend with a hand-cranked lift bridge at its apex. It was at this spot 11 years earlier, on our first visit to the Llangollen, that we came across a privately owned narrowboat stuck in the mud right on that corner. As we motored by, the owner asked if we could give him a tow off the mud. I was happy to do that even though I was a boating novice. I chucked over the stern line, gently took out the slack and gunned the engine. Nothing happened for a few seconds. Then slowly the pair of us moved on down the canal. Boy was the owner grateful, although slightly embarrassed that he had been rescued by a humble hire boat. Only years later did I discover that towing is prohibited by hire boats. And I could not have foreseen that, in 2017, Lindsay and I would benefit hugely from the generosity of another boat crew who would rescue us from a perilous predicament on the River Thames.

Lindsay took control of the boat then let me off, windlass in hand, so I could crank the lift bridge. My God, that requires some effort. Crank it up, let the boat pass, then crank it down. Then put the kettle on – no, not really. It was destination Ellesmere that night, specifically the Ellesmere arm of the canal where there are good moorings on rings.

We arrived there about 4pm to be met with a line of moored boats as far as the eye could see. I was hesitant to go into the arm because of the need to turn at the end and come back up should we not be able to find a space. However, down it we went, gently gliding past a solid line of boats. We were following another narrowboat, clearly looking to moor up, as were we. In the distance I spotted a space, as did they. Both boats got near and the one in front of us began to put his bow into the gap.

Their tillerman looked behind, stared at us for a while and then did a remarkable thing – he used his bow thruster to push their bow out again and beckoned for us to use the space! Lindsay and I were perplexed. Did he really mean that? Was he just going to the end, turn around and moor back in that space? I waited for him to come back up – there were no other boats behind us. As he came past, he stopped and said, "You can have that space – your need is greater than ours." We thanked him profusely and got tied up without further ado. The only explanation for their generous offer was that they took pity on a pair of grey-haired pensioners – I was 71 then, you see. That was the first time I realised how other people might see me – as an elderly old geezer doddering along the canal in a boat too big and barely under control. Sobering thought, I must say.

We walked into Ellesmere Town that evening. It was warm and calm, with an orange sun settling into the horizon to our left. We found a fish and chip shop and munched happily back to the boat – it had been a lovely day.

Up early again the next morning as we were going to meet Suzanne and her new friend George. Suzanne had been with us on the first visit to Llangollen, accompanied by husband Nick Hamer. Nick had very sadly died in 2010. George had come on the scene a year or two ago. I had met him a couple of times – he was pleasant enough but was a quiet man, not a talker, and I found him tough going. Perhaps he would open up a bit once on the boat. Sue told me he was a bit of an action man though, having a private pilot's licence and being a member of a boating club on Anglesey, despite being in his early 80s.

We had arranged to meet them at the Jack Mytton pub at Hindford. Another blast from the past, we had the pleasure of eating there during the first Llangollen visit. The landlord then was an irascible individual perfectly willing to show contempt for customers he didn't like, but the pub itself was warm, literally with a huge open hearth, and the food outstanding. However, the weather that morning was atrocious, making for slow progress. We arrived late of course to find Sue and George waiting on the towpath under windswept umbrellas. I pulled the boat in while they got aboard and then set off for the first New Marston lock. George stayed with me out on the counter in the lashing rain – much to his credit. I assumed he knew about boat handling at locks, but that proved a mistake. I brought the boat into the lock landing stage and came to a halt. I asked George to step off the counter holding the centre line while I set off, windlass in hand, towards the lock. Sue and Lindsay were still in the galley chatting away. I got about 50 yards along the towpath and for some reason looked back, only to find the boat halfway across the canal and George literally at the end of his tether.

I walked back to help and together we got the boat back under control. It was clear that George had no experience of handling a narrowboat. Nor much boat-handling experience in general, including how tiller steering works. But I was sure he would be a quick learner.

Looking over the edge of the Pontcysyllte Aqueduct, 126 feet above the River Dee

Sue and George stayed with us over the next few days. That meant another trip over the Chirk and Pontcysyllte aqueducts for Sue and Lindsay and me. Much had changed at the Llangollen end, where the banks are now encased in concrete and a fine towpath is in place. However, the canal is narrow and shallow and still has an eastward flow, meaning that the boat has to push a lot of water though that concrete channel, meaning progress is very slow – probably less than two miles per hour if that. Trying to go any quicker was pointless.

Nevertheless, slow progress did make me venture down the weed hatch on a couple of occasions. It brought back memories of the first time I had to do that at Audlem on the Shropshire Union and being assaulted by Bagins, Sue's unruly hound. On the one-way section, George went off on foot armed with a two-way radio, which proved a useful bit of kit. And we moored for the night in the new Llangollen Basin.

On the way back to Hindford, George was with me on the counter most of the time and I got to know him a little better. Like Sue's husband, Nick Hamer, George had served in the RAF. He was an engineering technician. Nick had been a flight engineering officer. George and I shared a military connection, and conversation became easier and more fluent. He told me he had been responsible for a pod of USA Thor missiles brought to Britain under Project Emily in 1959. George's missiles were based at RAF North Luffenham, near Oakham, Lincolnshire, one of four similar sites in Britain.

Thor missiles could be brought to operational readiness in 15 minutes after receiving an authorised and authenticated order to launch. Strict understandings about the operational control of the missile included an agreed British and US launch through a dual key system and a veto for each government. Although Thor deployment in Britain was an interim measure, their presence played an important part in the Cuban Missile Crisis of October 1962, the tensest period of the Cold War with the USSR, when 59 of the 60 missiles were made ready. (Paragraph © Copyright Historic England.) George told me of his responsibilities at that time and I gained much respect for him.

It was clear as we neared Hindford that George was itching to take over the tiller. Suzanne appeared suddenly up on the counter and more or less demanded such. I had to explain that we had a schedule to keep if we wanted to get the boat back on time. Which we did. In our early boating years, I experienced first-hand how giving the tiller to a trainee has a disastrous effect on timescales. I had not that much experience then myself but at least could keep the boat going ahead and around obstacles at a steady pace.

Delightful spot for lunch downstream of Grindley Brook

I did let George drive the boat through the New Marston pair of locks that are upstream of Hindhead. He managed the first lock, going downhill of course, quite well. However, on coming out he struggled to keep the boat going in a straight line and clearly had not been at the helm of a tiller-steered craft before. He found it difficult to cope with the dynamics of such a large craft in confined spaces. As did I of course during that initial training session in Stourport-on-Severn.

Progress was very slow, especially as we approached each bridge arch. I was glad to have made that decision earlier in the afternoon to resist Suzanne's demands.

George and I never fell out over his inexperience, and he enjoyed his time at the tiller. He was to come with us on a trip down the River Severn in a couple of years hence and vowed to gain more tiller time at his boat club on Anglesey.

I moored the boat outside the Jack Mytton pub, and we all decanted inside for a high-class meal. But what a disappointment. There was none of that homely atmosphere, no open fire, no irascible owner and no good food. The place had been converted into an upmarket burger-type establishment. It had been sold and refurbished in 2015 apparently, but at the time of writing has been closed for several years. We had our, admittedly good, burgers and then said goodbye to Sue and George.

We moored upstream of Grindley Brook that night and ate at the Horse and Jockey pub just a few hundred yards down the road. Next morning, down that staircase with the assistance of the lock keeper. Then the three locks below Grindley which are close together and on a tight curve. We had lost our crew of course, so it was just Lindsay and me from now on. For all our narrowboating history it had been me who drove the boat in and out of locks, who moored to drop off or pick up crew and who held the boat via the centre line while waiting a few minutes at locks. Lindsay was happy to be up on the lock sides, dealing with gates and paddles and happily chatting to other boaters. However, it was becoming apparent that her hip arthritis was causing her an increasing problem, so I was going to have to do more to help.

One way I could do that was to get off the boat once it was in a lock and assist with opening and closing of gates. Going eastward, the Llangollen narrow locks are all downhill. For the rest of the journey back to the boatyard, we worked the locks in a different way. She would fill each lock and open the single top gate to let me drive the boat in. I always liked doing that going downhill because it often felt like you were going to fall out over the far edge. I hopped off to close the rear gate. At the far end would be a pair of narrow mitred gates. Lindsay would open one paddle at a time, walking across the board-way on top of each lock, letting the boat settle down in the lock. I stayed on the boat so I could keep the rudder clear of the cill. I then used the boat gunwale ledge to get to and climb up the lock ladder, taking the centre line with me. I could then open, or help her open, both gates. I then pulled the boat out of the lock until its stern was just clear of the gates and, with the boat secure in the far walls of the chamber and the centre line secured on a lock post (or at the very least spread out along the grass), help her to shut both gates. I didn't mind stepping over carefully from an open gate to the other closed gate, rather than walk all the way round – usually over a canal bridge. Finally, I would pull the boat out of the lock and round to the landing stage, where we could both get aboard.

Now this sounds like a lot of effort, but it's often what's done by single-handed boaters. And it's surprisingly easy to bow-haul a narrowboat. Once you have got it moving, it tends to keep moving and is quite easy to manage from then on. And bow-hauling using the centre line is better than using the bow line because that gives you control of the boat in any conditions.

There were some delightful places to stop between locks on the way back to the boatyard, as the image above illustrates. For our final night we moored just before the Wrenbury Lift Bridge and ate at the Dusty Miller pub. Then back to the boat to pack up, ready to glide happily back into the ABC marina before 9.30am. The end of another wonderful week on a fabulous canal.

Chapter 19

Lower Heyford to Inglesham, the Source of the River Thames 2017

Map 11

This trip would complete our navigation of the entire length of the non-tidal section of the River Thames from Inglesham to Teddington.

The only remaining section not explored thus far was from Inglesham, the effective source of the Thames for powered craft, to Abingdon.

We began on the South Oxford Canal at Lower Heyford. We had hired 60-foot narrowboat 'Rousham' from Oxfordshire Narrowboats. She had been built in 2016 so would be in good order, we thought. Not quite – we had to crawl on hands and knees to light the gas grill or oven. Turning on the hot tap was a dangerous activity since it came with an explosion of steam and bullets of scalding water that bounced back off the sink into our faces.

As we were unloading the car with a week's worth of stuff, we noticed two other boats being loaded. Actually, there were many more, but those two caught my eye. They were each crewed by half a dozen or so young men who were already drinking and making merry. I guessed they were a stag party. The boatyard did the usual handover, which didn't take long since they knew we knew the ropes. We wanted to leave before the stag do – their handover was going to take forever.

The first task was to turn the boat around. That went well thanks to the winding hole next to the boatyard. There was no wind either – which helped because there were moored boats on both sides of an already narrow canal. Our plan was to set off, go through the first lock and then moor for the night in the countryside. There is something special about being on a narrowboat, out in the middle of nowhere, under a starry sky.

We found a good spot on a grassy straight bit of bank. The mooring pins provided by the boatyard were poor, without top loops. Luckily, we had brought our own, including a solitary banking clip (mooring hook). One of the pair got lost somewhere along the way. These are useful on the South Oxford because it has trunking (steel piling) along most of its length. So I moored with a banking clip at the stern and a mooring pin at the bow. We put the kettle on and rummaged around for the doughnuts.

We heard them coming before we felt anything. The first of the stags. They swished down our port side faster than the Flying Scotsman. Incredibly close. Engine roaring. Our boat first moved back, then sideways, then catapulted forward. I was waiting for it to stop. There was an almighty crash from the stern as the banking clip was forced off the trunking and catapulted onto the deck, still attached to its rope. Tea, coffee and doughnuts went flying. We were moving forward now faster than the speed limit, or so it seemed, floating completely free. When I got out onto the stern, a passer-by had managed to capture the bow line that had come off its mooring pin and was being dragged along the bank. The stag was already 200 yards ahead. I yelled – we got a cheery wave. The passer-by and I managed to stop our boat, pull it into the bank and think about putting in mooring pins at bow and stern. Then along came stag number two. Not so close and not so fast. But we took off once more. Only superhuman effort by my new friend and I got us back under control. We all shared the doughnuts.

A banking clip is made of half-inch mild steel. Hydraulic forces had fully straightened the hook that goes under the trunking. The trunking was undamaged.

The next morning we cleared up after the mandatory eggs and bacon and then set off south. After Thrupp progress was slow because of all the boats moored on both sides. We were running on tickover most of the time, but that didn't stop the locals seeing we were a hire boat and yelling that we should slow down. I think they meant stop and clear off. We turned right at Duke's Lock so we could take the short cut off the South Oxford Canal and get onto the Thames without going on into Oxford.

It was now about 3pm, gloomy and starting to rain. So on with the Hi-Viz, life jackets and wet gear. We came out onto the Thames ahead of King's Lock then set off northwest towards Eynsham Lock, after which we planned to moor at The Ferryman pub for the night. There were storm clouds on the horizon, and it was windy. It was now about 4.30pm and getting dark even though it was still early autumn. The river was wide and deep, so the boat moved along sweetly.

I saw the lock about 500 yards ahead, could see the lock keeper moving and assumed he was getting ready to open up and let us in. I made my usual straight on approach. To my left, just within my peripheral vision, I noticed the landing stage and what looked like green and red builders' buckets floating in front of that staging. Channel markers flashed into my head. Surely not, too far left, too far out of the main channel. Too near the landing stage. I couldn't see a fez or a church steeple bobbing about in the waves so carried on. Big mistake – we stopped dead.

We had hit a sandbank about 300 yards from and directly in front of the lock gates. The landing stage was to our left, about 40 yards or so away. An almighty weir was directly to our right, about 600 yards distant. We were marooned.

We ran aground in the middle, opposite the weir. Lock channel is to the left.

I first tried to reverse off, but we were stuck fast. The stern was floating, and the rudder was free, but she would not move. The lock keeper walked to the edge of the landing stage and shouted across to us. "I tried to warn you." He hadn't, or we hadn't noticed. He just let us come on. "I could do with a tow," I said. "Do you know of any cruisers in transit?" "Huh" was the reply. "You will need something bigger than a cruiser." He then said we were not his responsibility and that we should contact the hire company.

A young woman attending to a group of children on the riverbank about 40 yards to our right said she could go and get her boat. I thought about that, but it was getting gloomier, and I wondered if she would be able to return before dark. So I said I would call the boatyard first, since their office should still be open. I got through to the office manager. By chance a rep from River Canal Rescue (RCR) was with him.

It was now gone 5pm. The boatyard manager said there was nothing he could do as he was going home. He suggested I call the Environment Agency. RCR said there was nothing they could do until tomorrow and that we should be prepared to stay in the middle of the river overnight.

Lindsay and I were horrified. He did suggest we pump out the water tank, which was at the bow, so we set about turning on all the fresh water taps in the bathrooms and galley. He also suggested we deploy the anchor. I was not at all happy about this because I knew the anchor chain and warp would be around 30 yards long for a Thames craft. I also knew that weir heights could be adjusted overnight. This might mean we start to float in total darkness, tethered to a 30-yard line with the weir current pushing us left onto the landing stage.

Lindsay was sitting at the bottom of the galley steps, crouching over, holding her head in both hands. I felt so sorry for her. I tried to use the long pole to push us sideways. I tried hanging off the side, feet on the gunwale, rocking the boat with the engine in reverse. Nothing worked.

I called the Environment Agency emergency number. Without knowing precisely where we were, they decided we were not in any personal danger, not a danger to other boats and so there was nothing more they could do *or were prepared to do*. I called the boatyard, only to find an answer phone that cited their out-of-hours emergency number. I called that and got an answer phone. They had all gone home. We were marooned. Everyone had gone home.

But suddenly, help could be at hand or so we thought. The lock gates opened, and a large narrowboat came through and tied up on the landing stage. It was an Anglo Welsh 'Constellation Class' boat based in a marina just the other side of Eynsham Lock. A crew of four emerged and I shouted over to let them know we were marooned and would appreciate a tow. They ignored me. They would not make eye contact. They tied up and went inside.

After the lock closed, the lock keeper came over and shouted that he was going off duty. He turned round and merged into the gloom without further ado.

We were completely alone in front of the lock, with that weir roaring away to my right. It was now about 6pm and starting to drizzle. I carried on poling, rocking, reversing and pumping for the next half-hour or so. Suddenly, two of the narrowboat crew emerged from their boat, towed along by a small dog. Without looking at us, without looking over, they climbed onto the landing stage and left for a walk. They came back about 15 minutes later. I shouted over to them – again no response of any kind.

I began to plan for a night on the river. We had torches, so we would be able to see if we had floated free. One of us would have to remain awake all night. Lindsay still had her head in her hands. Water was still pouring from all the cold taps. We dug out blankets since I was unsure about having the heating on with an empty water tank.

Out of the gloom I saw a small white shape that gradually got bigger. It was a small cruiser coming upstream from Oxford. It came right up to us. It had a crew of two, a couple, with the lady already standing on the bow. They had sussed our situation immediately. I asked for a tow, they happily obliged, and I threw over our stern line. The lady tied our line to their bow T-stud. The captain gently reversed to take up the slack. It was not a large boat – maybe 20 feet long but with a wide beam. He increased power, the line flicked tight and with the lightest of touches, we were off and free. So much for needing a 15-ton narrowboat as a tractor!

Lindsay and I thanked our new friends. They said they had thought nothing of it – it's what anyone would do to help, wasn't it? They tied up next to the Anglo Welsh boat, opened the lock gates and went on their way. We gently reversed, then manoeuvred past Anglo Welsh then tied onto the landing stage. I resisted a somewhat overwhelming temptation to give them a side clout on our way past.

We always plan for unscheduled stops on our boating holidays. There are always unpredictable delays, but of course the boat has to be back at its base at the agreed date and time. So we knew that tomorrow we would need to make up about two hours on the river if we were to keep a date with our friends at Lechlade. We crawled on the floor to light the gas oven, shoved in our ready meals, filled the kettle with the water we had kept in saucepans and sat quietly for some while.

I began to think about whether one has any right to ask another for help. I could imagine a scenario in decades' time where crews passing through Eynsham Lock were asked to avoid the sunken rusting hulk of narrowboat Rousham. In 2017 it had got stuck on a sandbank, they said. The bodies of Mr and Mrs Hills were never recovered because nobody wanted to help them. They say that only their skeletons remain on board now – that of Mr Hills has its head in the gas oven, adjacent to a decomposed chicken arrabbiata, with a gas lighter clutched in its bony hand.

We were up at first light the next day because we had a date with the water hose located on the far side of the lock. We drained and entered the lock, closed the gates and waited for it to fill. I wandered over to the hose and looked around. To my amazement, there moored on the lock side was a powerful wide-beamed Environment Agency cruiser. The lock keeper had said that our demise was for the hire company to solve, knowing full well that a rescue boat was on his patch – literally around the corner.

So watered and breakfasted we struck off towards Lechlade. Our first port of call was Pinkhill Lock, where I had to stop and buy a Thames licence. I took the opportunity to talk to the lock keeper about yesterday's experiences. I asked why the downstream side of Eynsham Lock had not been dredged. The Environment Agency has no money and no longer undertake dredging on the Thames above Oxford, he said. I told him I was beating myself up about the grounding and had not expected to see red and green channel markers in those positions so close to the landing stage. He told me that the sandbank had been created by severe storms some years earlier. Many boats had become grounded since then, so I wasn't to take it too personally. I told him I *had* studied the Environment Agency Thames guide book – indeed had a copy on the boat with me. But I had not noticed until last night the 'builder's bucket' type of buoy. There they were, shown as ludicrously small images, not much bigger than a blob of ink. (See what I mean from the diagram at the end of this piece.)

Lassoing bollards at locks when going uphill is not so simple, especially somewhere like Sandford, which has the deepest fall of all locks on the

Thames at 8 foot 9 inches (2.69m). The key is to bring the boat in on the side the lock keeper is standing, but not close to the lock wall, i.e., not right under a bollard. A couple of feet out or so is ideal. Stop the boat. Hold the rope in a coil about two feet diameter. Trap its free end using the third and fourth fingers of one hand folded into your palm and hold the coil in both hands. Make sure there is a good bit of slack at the end tied to the boat. Then 'broadcast' the coil outward from your body, straight ahead of you, using both hands, aiming for a bollard, making sure you keep hold of the free end. With practice the coil will fly straight ahead, up and over a bollard. Then pull in the boat. If it doesn't, the lock keeper will wait until you have tried twice more, develop a kindly smirk, grab the rope with his long pole, loop it around a bollard and chuck you the free end.

It took us two hours to reach Bablock Hythe, where we had planned to moor the previous night and then eat later at 'The Ferryman' pub. It's a delightful spot in the sunshine. Then through Northmoor Lock and on to Newbridge, where 'The Rose Revived' pub was to be our destination on our return from Lechlade. The river is wide at this point but, although we were pushing on, it was against the current and a headwind, so 5mph felt about right on this boat. We had a marine GPS speedometer with us as a precaution since it's difficult to gauge speed on a wide river.

After Shifford Lock the river narrows and the meanders begin to kick in. The loading on the tiller really ramps up as the boat pirouettes its way upstream. There seem to be an endless succession of hairpin bends that actually fold back within themselves, creating an illusion of going round and round in circles. 'Full lock' on both sides of the tiller was therefore the order of the day, taking its toll on the shoulders. The scenery is pretty bland because the Thames is contained between banks gouged out of an extensive flood plain. I was conscious of needing to make sure I drove the boat around the outside of the meanders. On the insides of many were those red builder's buckets. I was careful to keep red on my left going upstream.

We have always found that 'Pearson's Canal Companion' guides provide the best commentary for inland waterways cruises. They provide good descriptions and accurate timings but, as sod would have it, an error in the timing between 'The Rose Revived' and Tadpole Bridge added an hour to our already fraught day. Our attempt to make up time was not helped by many of the locks being unmanned and set against us. How our spirits were lifted when we saw a boat emerging from a lock, allowing me to drop Lindsay off onto the landing stage, me to drive right in and her to close the gates. All the Thames lock gates we traversed were invariably beautifully balanced and easy to close.

The meanders returned in earnest between Tenfoot Bridge and Radcot Lock. This section feels isolated from civilisation, so lack of visual stimuli helped me concentrate on getting Rousham smoothly around each bend. It was windy and gloomy with a thin misty rain. Lindsay sat beside me on her fold-up chair, allowing me use of the full tiller arc. She didn't steer – it required too much effort, not just from arms but also from whole body weight shifting constantly from one foot to another. We had lunch on the fly. We lost a lot of cherry tomatoes when they shot off plates as we turned left then right then left…

St John's Lock, highest on the River Thames

St Lawrence Church, Lechlade, in the distance.

Around 6pm we had reached St John's Lock. We could see the church spire at Lechlade in the distance. On a sunny day this would be a beautiful spot, but we hardly noticed. We were wet and tired and had been on our feet for over ten hours. We moored up at 7pm just before Halfpenny Bridge in Lechlade. Ground level was a large field, with public access, at Rousham's roof height. She was pointing upstream into a light flow, so I planned to knock three mooring pins into the turf. Lindsay held the bow firmly against the bank, but not so tight that it pushed out the stern, while I got the centre line pin into the ground. That stopped the boat drifting backward. I next got the stern line tied off, then back to secure the bow. I was really tired at this point. I was bent over lump-hammering the mooring pin, Lindsay next to me holding the bow rope. I happened to look back between my legs. There was a small dog peeing over the far mooring pin, its large owner attached to it on the end of a long lead.

I am normally a mild-mannered person but erupted into a foul-mouthed tirade, which startled the dog and then its owner, both of whom scuttled off into the gloom. I needed to remember to bash out that pin and dunk it in the river before setting off in the morning.

We didn't have the energy to cook on board that night, so we made a hot drink, locked the boat then set off along the field towards the bridge. It was a dark, wet and windy night. The field was covered in cowpats and dog mess. We walked through the tunnel under the bridge, then up the steps onto the road and then headed into Lechlade town centre for 'Monica's Plaice' fish and chips.

We sat in silence at the back of the restaurant for some while contemplating the past two days. We were due to collect two friends, Steve and Sandra, tomorrow and proceed upstream to Inglesham – the limit of navigation for powered craft. However, I knew that turning the boat round to head downstream might be problematic because there are two sandbanks to avoid. And I was now nervous of sandbanks.

We were up early the next day. Our friends got on board, they donned life jackets and we set off towards Inglesham. It's only half a mile or so from Lechlade. Soon the footbridge over the Thames came into view and behind it one of the five 'Round Houses' on the abandoned Thames and Severn Canal. The Cotswold Canals Trust, in association with the Waterways Recovery Group and other partners, are restoring the canal right through Stroud and onto Saul Junction and the River Severn. Inglesham Lock has already been largely restored, but it is still currently on private land, meaning we couldn't decamp and take a look.

Inglesham – as near to the source of the Thames as a powered craft can get

The River Coln comes into the Thames from the right.

We all agreed this was a beautiful place to be. The flood plain on our left was level with Rousham's roof. Erosion had exposed a sandbank that swept gently into the fledgling Thames. Mature willow trees dangled their fronds into crystal clear water.

The Round House could be seen behind Inglesham Wharf Warehouse, now a private residence. There was a gentle flow downstream – I had been concerned about that because a strong flow would have made turning the boat more difficult. The Thames comes in from the left here and flows past the old wharf, before turning right towards Lechlade. We took photographs and loitered a while.

The reconstructed lock at Inglesham in 2022

A fledgling River Thames flows past the far arch. There are no lock gates yet. Reconstruction has been a joint venture between Cotswold Canal Trust and Inland Waterways Association volunteers.

Steve and I had decided earlier how we would turn around to head off downstream. The River Coln joins the Thames on the right here but is quite narrow. I turned right into the Coln, but with the bow about 30 feet in, the crew noticed sandbanks ahead and to the left, blocking further progress. The water was sparkling and translucent, so the obstructions were very evident. There was a strong breeze coming from the west, but the old wharf building nullified its effects. I had turned through 45 degrees at this point and so began reversing gently back into the Thames. However, I could not go straight back, or I would end up on that sandbank. So I made a series of back and forward shuffling movements, using the boat's rearward motion to gradually push the stern over to the left, away from the obstruction. Eventually I was able to go straight back across the wharf and into the Thames's unnavigable section. With the engine in forward gear tickover, I let the breeze and the current take us slowly round to the right, the flow from the Coln giving the bow another gentle nudge, then past the erosion sandbank and we were on our way downstream.

St Lawrence Church, Lechlade, completed in 1476

Rousham is 60 feet long. I am pretty certain that with gentle handling it would be possible to wind a full-length narrowboat here.

I had first learned the trick of reversing a narrowboat during our Warwickshire Ring adventure a decade earlier. I had been waiting mid-stream for a lock to empty and there was a strong crosswind that kept blowing the boat onto the offside of the canal, into the shallows and onto a mass of tree roots and brambles. We were south of Rugby and the canal was wide and exposed at that point. I remember the bow got stuck on the roots, so I couldn't go forward. The wind was trying to push the stern over, trying to get me onto the vegetation from which I would not escape easily. I put the engine into forward gear and drove the stern to the right against the wind, then into reverse so I could get back across the canal to the towpath side. I ended up going back a bit too fast. So then quickly into forward gear – and suddenly realised that I was able to position the stern with some accuracy, just so long as the boat was going backwards. In other words, a narrowboat can be manoeuvred in reverse by using a series of 'long back' and 'short forward' shuffles, the stern being positioned during the 'short forward' bursts. (Each 'short forward' burst is conducted while still going backward of course.) A narrowboat rotates about its centre of gravity, so once the bow is rotating, each shuffle gives it another kick. With practice it's possible to very nearly rotate on the spot. This technique has proven immensely useful – open water 360-degree turns, for example. Or having gone too far in search of an overnight mooring, having to reverse back to the gap you passed a quarter of a mile ago. There is no need to use lots of power during these manoeuvres – slow and gentle is the order of the day. Unless you hadn't noticed that weir…

So we had now been as far as possible towards the source of the Thames as can be achieved in a powered craft. Rousham began to retrace her steps back to Oxford.

My friend Steve took over the helm and drove the boat for the rest of the day. I was very happy with that. Sandra and Lindsay mostly stayed at the bow, chatting and taking pictures. With the wind behind us, and heading downstream, Rousham moved easily through deep water. It would have been easy to exceed the 5mph speed limit, were it not for the meanders, so we checked the GPS speedometer every now and again. Going downstream I was acutely aware that this time we had to keep green buoys to our left and red buoys on our right. We saw many, usually on the insides of the meanders where the river deposits its silt.

We had time now to stop for lunch. We found a spot where the flood plain had come down to river level, not roof level, near Tenfoot Bridge close to Duxford. Steve got the boat in close to the water's edge and although it looked reedy it was solid enough for us to hammer in bow and stern mooring pins. There was little wind and no other boats ready to rip out those pins. In fact, it was a very isolated spot and therefore a joyous location. The four of us prepared lunch and then sat around the galley table for an hour, in the warm, enjoying good food and swapping stories. How very different from the previous day.

Our destination that day was 'The Rose Revived' pub at Newbridge. Steve and Sandra had left their car there overnight. We got in about 6pm and looked for the pub's moorings. What we found was a very high bank at the end of their beer garden, a gigantic willow tree shrouding the entire riverside and fallen masonry that prevented us getting in close. We decided to put Steve ashore by reversing onto the riverbank at 90 degrees, between lumps of rock, so that he could jump off. We then proceeded downstream and then reversed back gingerly beneath the willow, getting as close as we could to the underwater obstructions. We threw all three lines onto the bank. Luckily Steve could use the remains of a concrete bollard to secure the centre line. He pulled the boat in sideways as close as she would go. There was little flow to complicate matters. He used mooring pins for the bow and stern. All three lines were literally at the end of their tethers – there was no question of looping through and tying them off on the boat. And of course, this left us vulnerable to drunken yobs casting us adrift during the night – a risk we had to take. The riverbank was level with Rousham's roof, so our gangplank ended up at a substantial uphill angle, not to mention it bridging over an uncomfortable expanse of the River Thames. I did worry that our walking the uphill plank skills might prevent us getting a meal in the pub that night, but in the end we all got off safely, had dinner and said goodbye to our friends.

However, Lindsay and I had to get back on the boat and it was now dark. We did have some residual garden light to guide us, but getting on board was going to be far from straightforward. For a start the gangplank rocked sideways when it was stepped on. Secondly, we could not see the river below or anything much within peripheral vision. Thirdly, it was very much downhill. And it was a big gap. And I had enjoyed a glass or two of Beaujolais Village. We stood and pondered a while, even thinking we might decamp to a pub room for the night. Eventually, with my shoulder bag around my neck, Lindsay's handbag in one hand, using the other arm to balance, I stepped onto the gangplank, paused and then shuffled downhill as straight as I could – all the time looking at the handhold on the boat cabin side. I was on. I turned around to help her summon the courage to do the same. She didn't feel secure aiming for my outstretched hand, which from her point of view was moving up and down with the boat. She preferred to focus on that handhold. She made it too.

I pulled in the gangplank. We went inside, made a hot drink and then opened the cabin side doors. It was a cool starlit night. The river glided peacefully by. The only sounds were a gentle babbling plus an occasional soft scrape of willow fronds across the roof. What a fantastic day.

The garden at The Rose Revived Inn

Rousham was moored just off to the left, under the willow.

Next morning, I put out the gangplank and Lindsay and I went to 'The Rose Revived' for breakfast. The pub only has nine rooms, so it was a relaxed and delightful affair. The sun was shining. We wittered away over bacon, eggs, toast and coffee. From the dining room window, we could see the Thames ambling by. There was Rousham, resplendent in yellow and blue, secured on its tethers, moored under that glorious willow. We were in no rush because Lindsay and I were due to meet our cousins Robert and Virginia for the next stage of our journey.

Robert and Virginia arrived around 10am. They are experienced sailing craft folk so skipped down the gangplank. Robert threw the bow and centre lines on board then quickly untied the stern line and got on before the boat had a chance to move. He hauled in the gangplank, and we were ready to continue eastward towards Oxford once we had all donned life jackets.

The Thames is wide at this point with few meanders. Although Robert has decades of boating experience, this was the first opportunity he had ever had to tiller-steer a heavy craft over 60 feet in length. He took to it like duck to water of course, so the plan was for him to drive the boat most of the day.

We had to wait at Northmoor Lock while the lock keeper had fun and games trying to shoehorn in two narrowboats and a large fibreglass cruiser. We were very near the rear gates. Thames locks are large. One does not normally worry about keeping forward of the cill since we are usually towards the front of a lock or at least near the middle. However, the lock keeper did remind me, because we were within a foot of the cill, and I was glad he had. Northmoor Lock weir is famed for having one of only two operational paddle and rhymer (or rimer) manually operated weirs – there are no others worldwide.

After an hour we were passing by Bablock Hythe and 'The Ferryman' pub. There used to be a ferryman at this point, but his rowing boat has long gone. Our cousins had parked in Abingdon that morning, then got a taxi to 'The Rose Revived'. We planned to arrive at Abingdon that evening. The Thames begins to flow north at this point, making a wide loop up to Oxford and round to Abingdon. Robert and Virginia's taxi journey had been just eight miles, but it would be nearly 30 miles by boat.

The meanders made a return over the next few miles. Big switchback loops of water, wide flood plains and many green and red buoys. We passed through Pinkhill Lock with the familiar procedure of lassoing bollards from both bow and stern, pulling the boat in, turning the engine off and waiting for the lock keeper to close the rear gates. The Thames was, of course, flowing downhill now all the way to the English Channel, so all the locks were 'downhill'.

After Pinkhill we passed Anglo Welsh's narrowboat hire base – the very one that disgorged the boat that refused to assist us two days ago. And soon we were into Eynsham Lock where, I'm glad to say, the lock keeper who did so little to help us was not on duty. He would have got a dose of Sir Alex Ferguson's hair-dryer treatment. His colleague admitted that many boaters get marooned on that sandbank and that I shouldn't continue to beat myself up about it. He said the Environment Agency no longer dredged the upper Thames. Nor did they see fit to erect warning signs on any of the approaches to Eynsham. And in any case, everyone knew about the sandbank at Eynsham. Mmm.

After that comment, it dawned on me why I had made that mistake. On our journey back from Inglesham, we had seen many red and green buoys but none of the design in the Thames river book. Had we come up from Oxford via King's Lock, we would have seen red, green and orange buoys and got used to their 'builder's bucket' or 'football' forms. But we didn't – we came to Eynsham Lock from Duke's Cut Lock, after Duke's Lock on the Oxford Canal. This bypasses King's and takes you straight into Eynsham. If there are frequent groundings there, why has the Environment Agency not erected a warning sign at Duke's Cut Lock? Or warnings at King's and on the upstream side of Eynsham for that matter. And if everyone knew about Eynsham, why did Oxfordshire Narrowboats not warn me?

Robert waited for the lock keeper to open Eynsham lock gates. The correct channel was clearly and obviously marked by green and red floating builder's buckets, close to the landing stage on our right.

We went through King's Lock, which has a fall of only 2 feet 6 inches, so no trouble hooking a bollard. The river had turned east by now and we moored for lunch just before Godstow Lock. Godstow Lock is the first hydraulically operated lock on the upper Thames. All locks above Godstow are manual. All locks below it are hydraulic.

After Godstow we began to see members of the numerous Oxford University and local schools' rowing clubs, out training on the river in their singles, pairs, quads and eight-person craft. There were as many female crews as male. We were not concerned about the coxed crews, but uncoxed boats were a hazard. They came onto us at an unseeming lick, often forcing us to take avoiding action. Rowing coaches buzzed around in two-person twin-hulled skips with outboard engines. These are fast manoeuvrable little craft, generally respectful of us.

Oxford City beckoned next. We slowed and drifted past 'Sheepwash Channel' on our left. Down that short channel is an ugly rusty railway bridge and beyond that Isis Lock, the current terminus of the South Oxford Canal. It was at this very point all those years ago that Jonathan and I shot out from Sheepwash Channel across the river and buried our bow and its occupants deep into the vegetation. I swear I could still see the dent in the riverbank to our right. Osney Bridge was now ahead of us. This is a low structure that limits the height of powered craft on the upper Thames. The river had narrowed at this point, with Osney Lock next.

Osney Lock and its omnipresent weir are not pleasant places to be. The landing stage is a rickety wire mesh grid. The weir takes the Thames, very narrow at this point, into the suburbs of Oxford, under an ornate railway bridge and around the castle and cathedral. It's possible to see at least three generations of building styles on this section as the river, a little wider now, meanders its way to Folly Bridge. This spot is well known locally for the 'Head of the River' pub and 'Salters Steamers' – which provide tourist trips to Staines and back. These boats are huge and take no prisoners, completely ignoring the speed limit from our own observation and creating a substantial wake to boot. On the approach to Folly Bridge, the river had split into two channels. A line of orange 'football' buoys closed off the right-hand channel, although Robert noticed a gap and was tempted to go that way. There was construction work in progress, so that might have meant testing his reversing skills.

Once past Salters boatyard, the Thames really opens up. It's wide and has endless college rowing club premises along its banks. We got up a head of steam, through Iffley Lock, under Isis Bridge and Kennington Railway Bridge and then onward to Sandford Lock. We found Sandford Lock unmanned but with a bit of a kerfuffle going on around the nearest control console. It appeared that a boat was stuck in the lock with the water level at half-mast. The lock had got itself into a quiescent state and was refusing to cooperate no matter who pushed the console control buttons or how often or in what sequence. Sandford Lock is absolutely huge with a nine-foot fall – the biggest lock until Teddington and pretty intimidating. We sent Robert down to sort out the mess while I held the boat on a bollard using the centre line. I have to say it's another place one does not want to be. The scenery is pleasant enough, the King's Arms pub close by, but the waiting area for the lock was almost completely covered in Canada goose droppings, dog faeces, pigeon poo and the like.

Robert eventually got the lock to cooperate. The sluices appear to be interconnected with a pre-programmed time delay that kept being reset by impatient operators. All of a sudden, uncommanded, the upper sluices began to open, the lock began to fill, the upper gates opened, and our stuck friend came out. We could then continue on our way to Abingdon.

There then followed nearly two hours of frankly memorable boating. The river was wide and deep and Rousham got into her stride. We saw no other boats. There were no people. There were no buildings – maybe an occasional boathouse. A sense of isolation crept upon us. The wind was in our faces, making the water blackish and a bit choppy. Dusk was beginning to close in. Woodland areas on each bank looked black and menacing, many with inlets concealing hidden weirs waiting to plunge us all into oblivion. There were huge flood plains on both sides. And it was starting to get cold.

The huge arc we were traversing on our way to Abingdon just went on and on. We knew that Abingdon Lock was somewhere out there, but the river just kept on turning right. We were quite frankly relieved to see Nuneham Railway Bridge in the distance. We had begun to think we might have somehow gone the wrong way.

We passed uneventfully through Abingdon Lock and found a spot to moor just before the bridge. It was nearly dark. Lights twinkled all over the town and along the bridge. We all decamped to a restaurant and then said our goodbyes. It had been another memorable day.

In the morning Lindsay and I took the boat downstream a little, past the old entrance to the Wilts and Berks Canal and along Abingdon's inspiring waterfront. So many wonderful chimneys atop graceful architecture. We retraced our steps back to Oxford, turned right into the Sheepwash Channel, went through Isis Lock and were then back on the South Oxford Canal.

There then followed the somewhat gloomy task of crawling in tickover through mile after mile of narrow canal with boats moored on both sides. And locks with rickety gates and hardware, lift bridges that didn't lift too well and vast concrete structures overhead that carry the A34 around Oxford. Past the entrance to Duke's Cut, a brief stop in Thrupp and then back to Lower Heyford.

Our adventure down the Thames from the river's source at Inglesham to Teddington Lock was now at an end. It had taken place over a five-year timescale, using five very different narrowboats. There had been hair-raising moments for sure, but Lindsay and family members and I would not have missed a second of all that messing about on boats on that wonderful river.

How obstructions are marked on Inland Waterways

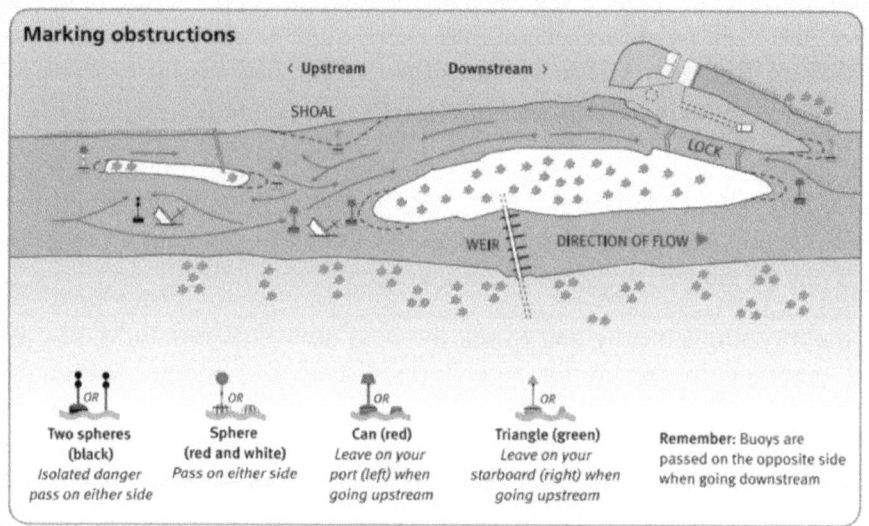

For more detailed information about boating on the River Thames visit **www.environment-agency.gov.uk/boating**

Environment Agency

The diagram above appears in the Environment Agency (EA) Rivers Handbook 2013.

Note how all the examples in the blue river schematic are of a floating stake topped by a red 'can' or a green 'triangle'. Note that 'builders' buckets' are indicated as an alternative form but shown only in the tiniest of print.

I hope that EA put warning signs at Duke's Lock so that boaters coming off the South Oxford Canal and onto the Thames are pre-warned of the sandbar in front of Eynsham Lock.

Eynsham Lock in 2020

The first image below shows the approach to the lock coming upstream from Oxford and Duke's Cut – as we did. The two green buoys were not there then. There had been no warning to boaters at Duke's Cut. It was late and gloomy. I didn't see the red buoy and ended up with the boat too far towards the middle of the channel.

Eynsham Lock looking east towards Oxford

The two (left hand) green buoys were not present or were not visible given the conditions, when we came upstream to Eynsham Lock. There had been no warning at Duke's Cut Lock as there had been for other boaters coming upstream from Kings Lock.

Eynsham Lock looking west

Hindsight

What I should have done upon getting marooned was to call 999 and ask for Fire and Rescue. All fire crews near rivers, especially the Thames and the Severn, practise rescue of people and boats. In our case, a messenger line thrown, canoed or fired over to Rousham would have enabled her to be quickly pulled off the sandbank.

Author's Note: An abridged version of this article was printed by 'Waterways World Magazine' in their September 2023 issue.

Chapter 20

A Day on the River Thames with Robert and Virginia 2018

A gentle cruise up and down a short section of the Thames between Temple Lock and Cookham Lock. Robert and Virginia keep their boat, an ex-fishing vessel, in Marlow Marina, just a few hundred metres from their Thames-side house. We went up to Temple and had lunch, then back through Marlow Lock and down to Cookham.

Virginia, Lindsay and Robert and their fishing boat at Temple Slipway, Bisham

Robert very kindly let me drive the boat which, like most cruisers, has wheel steering. It was very responsive, with a powerful engine. The only issue I had was not knowing where the rudder was pointing. At Marlow Lock I was too far out and needed to get the stern over to the right. With tiller steering that's easy, move the tiller right, apply some power and the stern goes right. I found I had to jog the boat a few times to see where it would go and then turn the wheel in the direction I wanted. Clearly, I'm

251

a novice at the technique, but I got into the lock and the lock keeper helped tie us to a bollard.

We motored down a wide river to see Cliveden House up on the horizon. Then moored for tea and lemon drizzle cake in the stern. All in all, a lovely day.

Cliveden House from the River Thames

Chapter 21

Worcester to Stratford-upon-Avon via the River Severn 2018

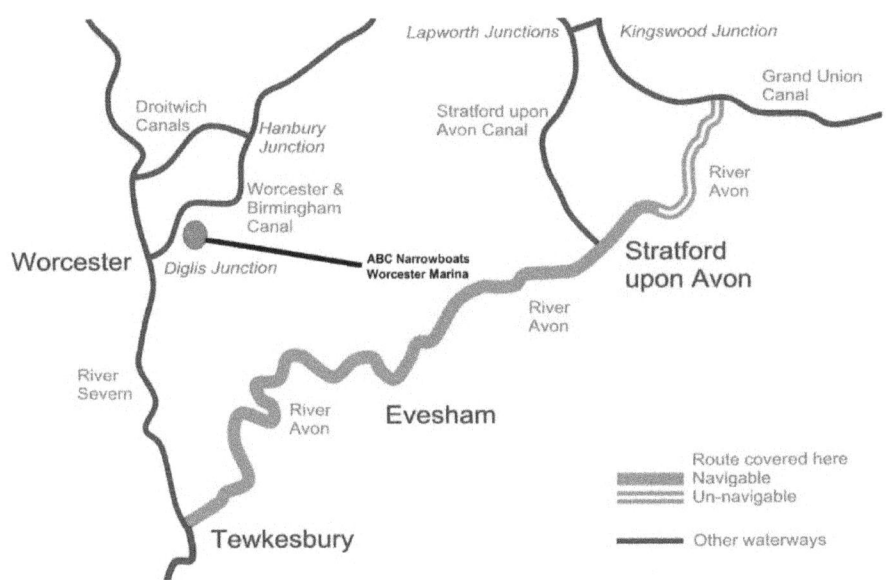

© Copyright waterwayroutes.co.uk

Map 13

Lindsay and I had been to Stratford-upon-Avon by narrowboat once before in 2009, but we now wanted to do the same using the alternative route via the River Severn. That river is a mighty and potentially dangerous beast, with the journey not to be taken lightly.

We did have considerable experience of narrowboating on rivers by then, having navigated the entire length of the non-tidal River Thames from its source at Inglesham in the Cotswolds to London at Teddington Lock. But on that journey there were no gigantic river locks, apart from the one above Abingdon, no deep water, apart from the approaches to London, and no real risk of being caught out in flood conditions – apart from when we did at Sonning Bridge in 2012. Oh well, take it all back. But actually, the Severn was a project to be taken with eyes wide open and brain fully engaged at all times.

ABC Narrowboats' Worcester marina

We began at ABC's Worcester marina, where we hired one of their newest boats – Ash's Lark. She was 62 feet in length, reverse layout with two bedrooms, each with their own bathroom. The galley layout in the stern encompassed an L-shaped dinette with seating for six people. The only quarrel we had with the boat was that the two single berths in each bedroom had been made with a width of 2 foot 6 inches, meaning the gap between the berths was not enough to walk right through – you had to turn sideways and shuffle. That was downright annoying after a few days.

Lindsay's sister and her friend George would be coming with us as far as Tewkesbury, where we would leave the River Severn and continue to Stratford on the River Avon. Note that this is not the same River Avon we met in Bristol. 'Avon' is an Anglo-Saxon word for 'River'. There are several Avons in England. It would be the Warwickshire Avon that we would be exploring.

Lindsay and I drove to the marina and parked the car more or less right next to the boat. It's a compact, enclosed marina with workshops and offices at one end and the other leading directly out onto the Worcester and Birmingham Canal. Sue and George could not get there until early the next morning, so we went through the handover procedure, moved the boat nearer to the entrance and then spent the night in the marina – not an uncommon practice, the staff told us. They have one regular couple who hire a boat for a week, and it stays there moored the whole time. Floating Hotel.

Diglis Marina and Canal Locks

Sue and George arrived at 9am the following day. The first task was to don life jackets. I was determined to let George drive the boat this time, hoping he had got in a bit of practice at his boat club in Anglesey. However, getting out of the marina is tricky because of the 90-degree turn needed with hardly any manoeuvring space, so I did that for him.

The Worcester and Birmingham Canal was completed in 1815 and has 58 narrow beam locks. It runs from Worcester to Birmingham's Gas Street Basin. Edging out onto it from the marina and going left takes you up to Birmingham via the Tardebigge flight of locks. Thirty narrow locks over 3.5 miles raise the canal by over 220 feet. We did not want to go there. We turned right and headed for Diglis Marina and the locks that lead out to the Severn.

I had been concerned about the Diglis canal locks because of their size – two consecutive wide locks and the only broad-beam locks on the canal. I understood that CRT volunteers manned those locks, but no one there that day.

If there is one section of canal anywhere on the network that makes you feel you have gone back 200 years, it's the stretch down to Diglis. It's dark, narrow and in a cutting beneath the streets of Worcester. Once on the canal proper, George took the helm, with Lindsay to assist. Sue and I walked down to the lock, windlasses in hand. It took George a while to find his steering legs, giving Sue and me plenty of time to prepare the narrow locks and have a chance to take in the atmosphere.

Sue waiting for George at The Commandery, pike and helmet to hand

The canal runs alongside 'The Commandery', a historic building open to visitors. It was as a museum in 1977 and was for a while the only museum in England dedicated solely to the civil wars. Set adjacent to the canal in Worcester centre, The Commandery is most famous for being the Royalist headquarters during the deciding battle of the English Civil War – the Battle of Worcester 1651.

Waiting for the lock to fill at The Commandery

George made his way down to Diglis Marina, a modern development in Worcester, with the first Diglis canal lock (Diglis number 2) straight ahead and the marina off to the left. It was windy and George had trouble getting the boat in the lock, but with patience and with no help (deliberate policy), he made it. Unfortunately, so did a family of swans with their brood, much to the consternation of bystanders, who foresaw them getting squashed when the boat drifted towards the side of the lock where they were. However, we kept the gates open and grabbed a handy pack of swan food there for this purpose. A few minutes of bribery did the trick, allowing us to shut the gates smartish. We had opened both gates to give George more room.

Two big canal locks at Diglis before reaching the River Severn

Before opening the second Diglis canal lock (Diglis number 1), the four of us gathered together for a briefing. There is no landing stage after the second lock and hence no opportunity to get back on the boat before hitting the River Severn. In addition, river traffic going upstream, including fast passenger craft, come right across the bottom of the lock and it's a blind corner. The landing stage is on the river itself, around the corner to the left.

I asked Lindsay and Sue to take charge of the lock, filling it as necessary. They would open a single gate, since the lock is huge. I would drive the boat in, and George would go onto the bow to act as a lookout. Once the lock had been emptied and opened, I would drive the boat out and onto the river, with George calling the shots, then head for the landing stage. Lindsay and Sue would close the lock and walk round to the landing stage. It happened just like that.

I tied up at the landing stage for another briefing. Ahead of us and to the right was an enormous weir, protected though by a string of floating barrels strung together like a row of beads. Ahead were two gigantic river locks, one smaller than the other, controlled by traffic lights. Maximum boat length is 135 feet, maximum beam 22 feet and height of the gates above the cill 23 feet. Ash's Lark was 62 feet long and 6 foot 10 inches wide – should fit in fairly easily then. The lock keepers are housed in a control room high up on the top of the island formed by the locks. There was no question of handling the locks ourselves; everything was automated on a gigantic scale. And we were now on a river with a huge flow even though we were on the non-tidal part, upstream of Gloucester.

The procedures inside locks are different from those on the Thames. There are no bollards to lasso. Instead, at intervals down the lock sides, are vertical bars set in the chamber walls. Boat control is achieved by looping a boat's bow and stern lines behind these bars and then holding fast as the boat sinks or rises in the lock. The ropes just slide up or down the bars and do not therefore lengthen or shorten, unlike locks on the Thames. It's a good system where the rise or fall can be substantial. On the Thames it's mostly around four to six feet per lock. On the River Severn locks, it can be around 10 to 20 feet.

I asked George if he would take charge of the bow line once we were inside the lock. I would drive the boat in and look after the stern line. It was not necessary to turn off the engine – undesirable in fact.

After we had all clambered aboard and checked that our life jackets were in place and secure, I pushed Ash's Lark away from the landing stage and into the river. The lock keepers must have seen me because the traffic light went green straight away. The two gigantic gates opened with a hushed hydraulic sigh to reveal a cavernous space. In we went towards the far end. George was on the bow, rope in hand.

However, all did not go well. I made a Horlicks of it by not bringing the boat in parallel to the right-hand wall, resulting in the bow drifting out. I backed up but became aware of another series of hydraulic sighs and a gentle clunk behind as the upper gates shut. We didn't have a bow thruster. The only way to get the bow in was to back up a bit and push the stern over to the left and try again. But, unlike on the Thames, the lock keepers are 30 feet up in the air and cannot offer assistance. I messed around for what seemed ages, with George now clambering up on the gunwale, trying to get his rope under the bar in the wall.

He did so just in time, because, without warning, we began to descend. I don't know if the keepers could see us on CCTV and had got fed up with us fiddling about or were just not looking, but we were going down whether we were roped or not. We ended up with the bow pulled in but the stern sticking out. I had been able to use the engine to keep the stern in somewhat but couldn't use too much engine power because George, bless him, was hanging onto the rope at the other end.

Diglis River Severn lock – the smaller of the two at Diglis. Looking back as the gates closed.

Out of the lock and onto the river. What a glorious experience. George joined me at the stern, and I handed control to him. We passed MV Conway Castle, the largest passenger vessel on the River Severn, licensed for up to 195 passengers.

Out on to the River Severn on a glorious morning

I had a GPS speedometer with me so we could measure our speed over the ground. We were permitted to go at 8mph downstream. The boat wasn't too sure about that with the tachometer at around 2,000 rpm and a great deal of vibration through the tiller arm. George steered the boat well but had to exert a deal of force on the tiller. Sue appeared on the counter with us and wanted a go – George said no, it needed too much strength. He could have been right, but I suspect he was having too much fun.

We stopped for lunch at some riverside steps at Upton on Severn. That was about two hours downstream. There had been little other chance to moor because the banks either side of the Severn are typically ten feet or so high.

After lunch, we pushed off and made our way around the big loop towards Saxon's Lode, Malvern Hills to our right, then a sharp turn left around the lower slopes of Bredon Hill. At that point we were confronted by an enormous barge full to the brim with aggregate. We had cut the corner and were on the wrong side. George responded admirably and got us over to the right and out of harm's way. That barge was not going to take prisoners.

Near miss on the River Severn

Another hour and a half until we met the Mythe Bridge. At this point I advised George to watch out for the turn left towards Avon Lock at Tewkesbury. It was important to steer a wide arc all the way round to avoid getting grounded on the sandbar there.

After getting the lock keeper's permission, we moored the boat on the floating pontoon.

Moored for the night on a floating pontoon just outside Tewkesbury Lock

Note how high the pontoon can reach from the length of the guide poles.

Then powered up the iPad to watch 'Strictly Come Dancing', after which George and I walked into town to get fish and chips for us all.

Lindsay and I were going to go up the River Avon the next morning. Sue and George left us that night to find their hotel and then look around historic Tewkesbury the next day. We said our goodbyes. George had made a good job of getting the boat from Worcester Marina down to Tewksbury, and I was pleased to have got to know him that bit better.

Towards Evesham

We have used 'Pearson's Canal Companion' guides over all these years. They have rarely let us down. But they did on this trip because some timings were very wrong.

We left Tewkesbury, having gone through Avon Lock, and set off for Bredon. That should have taken one hour, but it took us one and a half hours going at the 4mph upstream limit. That rather set the tone for the rest of the day. We needed to be at Evesham before dark because Sandra and Steve were joining us the next morning. It was going to be a long day.

The first lock was Strensham Mill. It's one of those you don't see early enough. It's disguised by the mill building and all the trees and shrubs around. We had not seen another boat up to that point, but all of a sudden, we came up to the lock entrance to find it full, with one coming our way, another one waiting to come down and one up our backside, who materialised from nowhere. That lock is small and tight and has a swing bridge over the lock chamber. The lock landing stage is almost non-existent. I had trouble getting us in tight enough to let the other boat out. I ended up using the centre line wrapped tightly around a nearby tree.

We lost a lot of time at that lock. Next up, the big loop round Eckington and under that wonderful stone arch bridge dating from the 1720s.

1720s Eckington Bridge – Grade II listed

Nafford Lock was up next. That really was a beast. We met it in benign water conditions. In strong flows, it would be impossible in a full-length boat unless it had a powerful bow thruster. We didn't have a bow thruster.

Going uphill, as we were, the problem is the lock has the weir immediately to the left of the exit gates and potentially therefore a strong flow across the gates. A 62-foot boat like ours can barely make the right turn necessary, simply because it's almost impossible to get the stern over to the left in order to make the boat go right. We got very close to snagging our bow on the weir barrage. If I did the trip again, once the lock had filled and both gates were open, I would push the boat over against the right-hand chamber wall by using the long pole. Then come out under power with the tiller hard left. In that way the stern has more room to get left before the boat is out of the lock.

We were upset and somewhat shocked to see a sunken narrowboat at the lock exit. Quite why that has not been removed yet goes unanswered.

Sunken boat at Nafford Lock which had somehow managed to go over the weir – probably during flood conditions

Then came a long loop up to Pershore. That was supposed to take two hours but took nearly three. As we approached Pershore New Bridge, a fibreglass cruiser came out ahead of us – they had been on the public moorings there. We were close enough for a chat. Were we aware that Pershore Lock was difficult and potentially dangerous if the paddles were not operated in the correct order? Plus, they told us, the gates are heavy and stiff. I had read the guide books and had expected some issues, but they seemed quite concerned for our safety. I don't know if they had looked at Lindsay and me and formed the impression that we were old, doddery and past it. We were certainly old, but they volunteered to do the lock for us. In all our years of boating, that had never happened before. We were a little nonplussed.

And that's what they did. We waited for them to go through the lock and emerge on the other side. There did seem to be a lot of cranking and moving around going on up top, but they seemed to get through just fine. They then took their boat up to the public mooring on the other side of the lock, tied up and jogged back towards us. They emptied the lock and opened the gates so we could get in. More jostling around up top – it's deep, so we could hear but not see much. Then we began to rise in the lock, but we could not see anyone on the gate paddles. I understood though because Pershore Lock has a ground *and* gate paddles. The ground paddle must be used first when filling the lock. Up we went, the gates opened, and we chugged out with much waving and blown kisses. What lovely people.

Next up was Wyre Lock, a peculiar diamond shape and very shallow. There are numerous theories about its shape – the one I like is that it can hold a greater volume of water that way. However, it's not easy to use a standard-length central line once inside.

There's no getting away from the fact that the Warwickshire Avon is a sight to behold, especially on a cloudless sunny day. The section around Fladbury is typical. There were two mills there, one naturally called Fladbury Mill and another close by called Chadbury. Fladbury Mill is a 17th-century Grade II listed brick building. It still contains electrical generations machinery from its time as a hydro-power station. The Fladbury Electric Light and Power Company operated between 1920 and 1925.

We eventually made it to Evesham around 8pm. It had been a very long day. Probably more than two hours longer than estimated in Pearson's guide. However, it was a joy to find such good moorings, all on rings, and so close to the town. Lindsay and I had a quick clean-up and then trotted off to a nearby Indian restaurant.

The River Avon is wide at Evesham. We were pretty much the only boat around, making a return after dark a spookily enjoyable experience. The river shimmered in the lights reflected from the opposite bank, with its frequent plops and slurps and sighs adding to the atmosphere. It could have been Halloween.

Sandra and Steve arrived next morning for the journey up to Stratford-upon-Avon. They had been with us before when we went to Stratford via the Stratford Canal. They had driven there the previous day and had spent time exploring, including doing a bit of William Shakespeare.

We donned life jackets and set off under Workman Bridge and through Evesham Lock. Steve drove the boat while Sandra and I cranked the paddle gear and heaved at the gates. Lindsay's hips were worrying her after the previous day's stresses and so she would be an observer all the way to Stratford.

Navigation was not possible on the River Avon section from Evesham to Stratford before 1974, when a major restoration exercise finished. The waterway with its locks and weirs had been abandoned by 1860 due mainly to the impact of the railway network. The concept of building new locks and weirs, with most of the work being undertaken by volunteers, was new. Negotiation with the Severn River Authority led to an agreement that was eventually formalised by Parliament. That became the Upper Avon Navigation Act 1972.

Funding came from landowners, private benefactors and the Inland Waterways Association (IWA) restoration fund. The section from Evesham to Bidford Bridge was opened by 1971. The estimated cost for the complete restoration was £250,000, most of which was raised by public subscription. The complete project, which involved the construction of nine new locks and associated weirs, was completed on 1st June 1974 and declared open by Queen Elizabeth the Queen Mother.

All locks on the Warwickshire Avon are broad types, maximum craft dimensions being 70 feet by 14 feet. All have paddles mounted at the bottom of chevroned double gates. The gates are mostly made of steel, with steel balance beams, a function of the need for minimal cost during rapid restoration. As a result, the gates are heavy and the water flows within each lock can be violent if boaters proceed recklessly.

Sandra working very heavy paddle gear

The locks above Evesham are named after people who played a significant role in restoration. The 'Robert Aikman Lock' at Offenham is a good example.

Anyone who enjoys the inland waterways today owes Robert Aikman (1914–1981) a great deal. Without his 'unreasonableness' we would have lost the Oxford Canal south of Banbury, the southern Staffs and Worcs Canal, and perhaps the Leicester summit as well. And without his tenacity in saving the Macclesfield Canal, the restorations of the Peak Forest and Ashton canals would have been much less likely. Aickman's finest hour was the reopening of the South Stratford Canal by the Queen Mother in July 1974. Aikman said it was, "*a pivotal moment – conclusively demonstrating that volunteer-led restoration was a viable model for the recovery of the waterways".* (Text based on that from the IWA website.)

The upper Avon is a wonderful waterway. It's narrow and twisty – reminded me of the upper Thames between Inglesham and Oxford. The section between Bidford and Weston was particularly memorable.

We stopped for lunch as usual on these trips and then made our way towards Stratford under Stannals Bridge. Steve told me that he and Sandra had walked the previous day to the bridge along 'Stratford Greenway', the track bed of the single-track railway built in 1859.

Stannals Bridge carried the GW Railway from Stratford-upon-Avon to Cheltenham

Stannals Bridge was built originally in 1859 to carry the 'Honeybourne Line', a single-track railway linking Oxford, Worcester and Wolverhampton. It was doubled in 1908 for the Great Western Railway but was never a commercial success and closed in 1975. The bridge looked in poor condition as we glided gracefully under its rusty girders.

Next along past Shakespeare's Avon Way to our left, through Gordon Gray Lock and C P Witter Lock and past Holy Trinity Church, where William Shakespeare is buried. Up next the Royal Shakespeare Theatre and Stratford waterfront. Ahead we could see Tramway Bridge, which marked the end of our journey.

All that was left was to get through Stratford Basin Lock and get moored up for the night. That proved tricky, however, because it was a windy day, and the basin was crowded. Steve had managed the lock and so I was on the tiller. I found a spare slot on the pontoon, tried to reverse, but the wind kept pushing me sideways. I was dangerously near a heritage narrowboat with one of those huge wooden tillers. Steve got me to throw him the stern line and with a lot of his muscle power, I got Ash's Lark backed up and secured.

Stratford's Tramway Bridge (1526) in the foreground with Clopton Bridge (1480) behind

These two bridges mark the limit of navigation for powered craft on the Warwickshire River Avon.

Ash's Lark moored in Stratford Basin

The boat name has incorrect spelling – it should be Ash's Lark or
Ash's Bushlark. The bird is a species of lark native to Somalia.

Sandra, Steve, Lindsay and I ended our day at an Italian restaurant
opposite the basin. It had been a hugely enjoyable journey up from
Evesham, but hard work, I have to say, with all those heavy gates. Our
friends left us to drive home while Lindsay and I had a quiet walk around
the town. Then back to Ash's Lark, a nightcap and a good rest ready for
the trip back down the Avon to Evesham in the morning.

It was going to be just Lindsay and me on board Ash's Lark all the way
back to Worcester, via Evesham and Tewkesbury. It has never ceased to
amaze me how retracing one's steps has never been a boring exercise –
nothing looks the same as on the outward journey and that has to be one
of the joys of the canal network. Out and back trips are just as enthralling
as the popular cruising rings.

We got to Evesham without much drama, just a lot of hard work on those
heavy and stiff gates. Lindsay drove the boat most of the way while I did
all the cranking and pushing and walking around up top. There had been
a fair amount of rain over the week, and I was not thrilled having to moor
at the landing stage sited right on top of the weir at Evesham. There are

so many warning signs there. It's a scary place to be. Good job it was not Halloween. The river was flowing strongly, always wanting to push the boat back, making the tying of lines somewhat tricky. I put on bow and stern lines just to be sure, bow line first to avoid the flow pushing the bow out. I made sure the boat was tied securely and that Lindsay was happy to remain on board before I left to prepare the lock and open both top gates. Getting into Evesham Lock meant turning left a full 90 degrees, right across the river current. It would mean going in fast and then slowing quickly to avoid hitting the lower gates. There was also the complication that Ash's Lark was slightly too long to fit in the lock straight – it would have to be on a diagonal.

Evesham Lock landing stage right on top of the weir

As I walked down the landing stage to deal with the lock, I was not aware I was being watched. The lock keeper's house is right by, and above, the top gates. I opened the top gate paddles to fill the lock, then closed them, before walking round to open both gates. Then back to the boat. Lindsay had been driving Ash's Lark into and out of every lock on the way down from Stratford but felt nervous of the manoeuvres needed to get into this lock. So I took over the tiller.

I recovered the stern line and walked forward to untie the bow. The boat began to drift backward quite quickly but kept straight, allowing me to get on. What I had not realised was that the river was flowing along past but also under the landing stage, keeping me pinned to it – I could not get the bow out. Then, luck or was it by design, the bend in the landing stage (see above) allowed the stern to get caught by the current, which did push the bow out. I was then able to make a wide arc, under power, and get into the lock chamber.

Lindsay took over the tiller and I got off to close both top gates. The lock keeper made his appearance. He began to criticise her for not setting the boat on a diagonal. Actually, the Pearson's guide book does not mention the need for this – the stern was still forward of the cill and the bow was tucked just to the left of the arrowhead, but he was unhappy. I closed the top gates and walked forward to open one of the lower paddles.

I was followed by the lock keeper. I tried to make light conversation and mentioned how I found a number of the locks downstream of Stratford somewhat 'brutal'. Red rag to a bull. He exploded with a tirade of invective, defending the locks. He said a lock could not be brutal because that was a human characteristic. I was tired and decided not to up the ante – I don't think he would have welcomed, or indeed understood, the point that I was using the word brutal as a metaphor. I gather this man had been retired as lock keeper, having been there for a decade or more. Probably a good public relations move.

Back to Tewkesbury

Lindsay and I spent the night on Ash's Lark at Evesham, the only boat there that night, resisting the temptation to revisit that Indian restaurant across the way. The next morning began calm and warm and sunny. I sat by myself on the wooden bench that crossed the boat's cruiser stern, sipping my tea, chatting to the swans, listening to the Avon slopping and slurping against the boat's hull, wondering what dramas the day would bring.

Lindsay took this fabulous picture as we headed back to Tewkesbury

It was going to be a long haul back to Tewkesbury. Lindsay's hips were hurting; she was becoming less mobile by the hour or so it seemed. In the event the only issues occurred at Pershore Lock, where reconstruction of the weir was just beginning, together with a rebuild of the downstream landing stage. That meant no place to get on the boat after coming out of the lock. Pershore Lock is over nine feet deep. The only way to get back on board was to climb down the lock chamber ladder. I could have got onto the roof but actually climbed right down to get onto the gunwale and then shimmy along to the stern. The penalty paid for that was a copious covering of green slime on my jacket and trouser legs. Out of the lock we went, leaving the gates open since we had no easy way to get off, get back up there and close them.

Moored in Tewkesbury on our final night before going back to Worcester

Return to Worcester

The public moorings in Tewkesbury were in good use on our last night afloat – there were four boats including Ash's Lark wanting to lock down onto the River Avon the following morning. Tewkesbury Lock is awkward and small, requiring a 90-degree turn to get in. A boat ahead tried, but he made a hash of the turn and had to back out a few times. He got in eventually but then had trouble getting over to the left chamber wall. With the lock keeper's permission, I gently used our bow to creep up alongside and push him over. It was a tight fit – we both had to watch that our sterns were clear of the cill as we descended to the river.

I was first out the lock. I turned left and prepared to go with the flow down the Avon about half a mile before joining the River Severn. It was at that point our engine began making a shrieking sound. I put the gearbox in neutral to stop the propellor, but the sound persisted. I pushed the button on the Morse lever to disengage the drive and revved the engine. The sound increased with engine speed. The problem therefore was with the engine itself and not the gearbox or prop shaft or final water seal.

I was fairly sure the noise was an alternator or water pump bearing issue, which *was* a cause for concern. If a bearing had seized but the engine alternator/water-pump belt continued rotating, friction might cause an engine fire and that was very much a worry. There was a fire extinguisher on board of course, but would that cope with an extensive oil fire? I didn't know. I suspected not.

Lindsay and I were both wearing automatic life jackets and so could get off the boat should an uncontrollable fire develop.

I decided to keep going. Approaching the River Severn, I kept to the left and only turned right when I could see Mythe Bridge on my right. There is an extensive sandbar on that corner and by delaying the turn towards Worcester until the bridge is in view is recommended procedure.

We set off upstream towards Worcester, the shriek not seeming any worse. However, the more I thought about our situation, the more concerned I became. There were several issues. First, Lindsay has poor mobility and would not be able to get off the boat in a hurry, especially if she were down in the cabin. Second, we were both wearing substantial walking boots which would impair our ability to swim or even prevent the life jackets keeping us afloat. That's not an issue on canals of course where good boots are protection from the rough ground around locks. But on deep rivers, especially the lower Thames and the Severn, it could be and that was not something I had considered until now. It would be darn near impossible to get those boots off once in the water. I toyed with the idea of taking them off right away and padding around in socks or bare feet – but was that sensible? I didn't know. I thought about calling 999 at that point, fearing the worst. But didn't, not wanting to make a fuss.

We carried on up river. The little person in my head kept nagging away. Could I get the boat onto one or other bank? Could Lindsay get off there and would she be able to climb up said bank, given that most of the River Severn is contained in a channel about ten feet deep all the way to Worcester? In the end I decided on a wait and see policy. It was unlikely the engine would have stopped dead. From then on I kept Ash's Lark as far right as I could. If the engine failed, I knew where the anchor and my mobile phone were.

Aggregate barges blocking our path

A distraction I could have done without was being chased up the river by aggregate barges. These are gigantic, powerful barges that operate between Queenhill and Upton Ham. They are fast – meaning looking over my shoulder every ten minutes or so. They are named after fish native to the Severn – Elver, Perch and so on.

After a couple of hours, I spotted the pontoon at Upton and decided to cross over and moor there for a while. It would give me a chance to raise the engine cover and have a good look around down there. It seemed OK, no burning smell, just a bit hot and that constant noise. We sat on the bow, boots still on, and had tea and jam doughnuts. That was nice.

Monster barges on the River Severn

With hindsight, I could have left the boat on the pontoon and called a taxi to get our stuff back to the marina. But that seemed a bit selfish. I could also have phoned ABC at Worcester and got them to come to us prepared for emergency repairs. In the end I decided we would try to get the boat back to the marina.

Two hours later, Ash's Lark sailed under Diglis footbridge, and the river lock came into view. I was surprised to see it open and assumed the lock keepers had seen me coming. The sun was directly behind me and quite low on the horizon, making it impossible to see which lock traffic light was illuminated. In I went, only for a head to appear way up yonder, asking that I back out and wait for another lock cycle – a boat coming down has priority apparently. I moved the boat to the right-hand side of the river, looped the centre line around a handy rusty pole and waited.

Eventually, a boat came out and in I went, only for that head to re-appear and give me another bollocking. I should have waited for the light to go green apparently. Yelling skyward, I tried to let it know that the sun's position made that impossible, but the head had no truck

Under Diglis footbridge on the approach to Diglis River lock at Worcester

with that. Finally, I was beckoned in, and the gates closed behind us. Lindsay was at the bow during all this and must have wondered what I was up to. I had begun to wonder myself.

Going upstream into the smaller of the two River Severn locks

The lock began to make purring sounds and soon we were going up. A few sighs and moans later, those big gates opened to reveal a beautiful blue river.

Worcester Cathedral from the River Severn on the right turn into Diglis canal lock

It was then necessary to leave Lindsay alone on the boat – I had tied up at the landing stage and needed to walk around the corner to get the Diglis canal lock open. I turned the engine off, which was still creating a racket. My God, that lock is a beast, with huge heavy gates and paddle gear. Once the lock had emptied, it took all my strength to get just one of those gates moving. I left it like that. I was certain I could get the boat around the corner, off the river and into the lock via one gate, whatever the state of flow.

I made sure another boat was not coming down from the marina, then walked back to collect Ash's Lark and bring her around the corner into the lock. I had to get off the boat of course and shinned up the nearest lock ladder. At that point a friendly CRT volunteer lock keeper appeared, allowing me to shin back down – he would do all the work from now on.

Back to Worcester Marina

We would stay in the marina for our last night on board, mainly because the boat had to be returned by 9am the next morning and us off it 30 minutes later. Plus, Ash's Lark had to be reversed into its mooring slot and I didn't want to do that with too many other boats around in that very tight space. Lindsay and I had our customary fry-up, packed what stuff we could and settled down to review the week. It had been hard work. The engine noise had been a worry – I reported that as soon as we were back at Worcester – but overall, a fantastic adventure was had by all of us.

Chapter 22
Honeystreet Café to Crofton 2019

Map 10

The Kennet and Avon Canal arrived in Honeystreet in 1810. Victorian entrepreneur Samuel Robbins saw an opportunity for a wharf and timber yard there. His Honeystreet business thrived and became all things timber, including building barges for timber transport. The buildings on the wharf often caught fire – mainly as a result of embers from Robbins' steam-engine-powered machinery. The iconic chimney, still there today, was built in 1859 to act as an extractor fan, removing fumes from the sawmill's engine house and hence reducing the fire risk. In 1860 Robbins was joined by his son-in-law Ebenezer Lane and by Henry Pinniger. The company Robbins, Lane and Pinniger (RLP) was born. It lasted until 1933, when it delivered its last barge. Like so many canal-based businesses, it was doomed by the coming of railways.

The Kennet and Avon Canal at Honeystreet Wharf by Joseph Barnard Davis.

Honeystreet Wharf in the 1820s – looking north, Devizes to the west.

Note the still-present chimney now of Honeystreet Boats and Café.

© Copyright Wiltshire Museum, Devizes

Lindsay and I collected 'Honey Rose' from Honeystreet Boats for a week on the Kennet and Avon Canal. It was early September – an Indian summer at that time of year had blessed us over two previous decades and we looked forward to that pattern continuing.

This was going to be a trip on which we would be on our own. The various groups of friends who had been with us before were all unavailable. Lindsay's hip problems would mean most of the hard work resting on my shoulder, but I was still enthusiastic.

The Barge Inn at Honeystreet

Still a very bohemian place. Good simple food, ales and live music.
Take your dancing shoes and a violin. Campsite and facilities.

We had been this way before of course, having cruised the entire length
of the Kennet and Avon over several sections in previous years. What
was different this year was firstly that Honeystreet is close to home and
secondly that previous visits had always been in transit, passing through,
not allowing much time to explore a very historic section of countryside.

Who knew for example that Wolf Hall, lionised by Hilary Mantel's epic
trilogy about Henry VIII's right-hand man, Thomas Cromwell, was just
eight miles along the canal near Crofton? Wolf Hall was the family home
of the king's third and favourite wife, Jane Seymour. She died in October
1537, shortly after giving birth to the son the king had craved. She was
the only one of his six wives to be given a full queen's funeral. She was
later exhumed and re-buried beside the king in St George's Chapel,
Windsor.

Honey Rose was a narrowboat, not to be confused with the broad-beam boats from Moonraker's on the other side of the canal. She was not the usual kind of hire craft. She was a private boat used by the owners for the early part of each year and then made available for hire during the rest of the season. She is 55 feet long with a cruiser stern, had the galley at the rear and the main double bedroom at the front. A large walk-through bathroom and lounge were in the middle section. The galley had gas hob and oven, microwave, toaster, coffee machine, filtered water, sinks and fridge. There was Eberspächer central heating.

All the boats we have hired over the years have, without exception, had diabolically uncomfortable, bolt upright, bench seating in their lounges. This boat was no exception, but at least she had a four-seat dinette which converted to a double bed.

Honey Rose moored on rings outside the Barge Inn at Honeystreet

I don't normally use the centre line when mooring overnight, especially when the boat is on rings as here. I think I put it on first when trying to control the boat in windy conditions and then forgot to take it off.

And she had a pair of 'Stressless' lounger chairs, complete with footstools, from Norwegian firm Ekornes. Bliss. No backache when watching TV or reading or listening to music.

We decided Lindsay would sleep in the front double bed[13] because it was only four feet wide, and she often thrashed around while dreaming. I was happy to make up dinette, but in the end that was too much of a faff, so I just kipped on the lounge sofa – which worked rather well.

The plan was to go east up to the canal summit at Crofton, turn around and come back past Honeystreet and go on then to Devizes. We got away quite late at about 4pm. The first task was to find a place to moor for the night. The first visitor moorings are at Pewsey, about three hours away. That seemed fine; we would arrive about 7pm – our rule of thumb was to get tied up by 7.30pm at that time of year.

The boat was already pointing east when we set off. Lovely calm afternoon, motoring slowly past moored boats. Onto the 'long pound', under the White Horse to our left up on Woodborough Hill. Then over 'Wide Water', so called because it looks like a wide lake, an extensive mere even, but it's shallow and essentially unnavigable. Boats have to keep close to the towpath side. When the canal route was being planned, the landowner Lady Wroughton insisted the canal over her land had to be made to look like an ornamental lake.

---

[13] Double beds on hired narrowboats are generally only four feet wide (1200mm) and usually arranged longitudinally - that is head and toes are parallel with the boat's longitudinal axis. A further inconvenience is that the double bed will have one side up against and slightly underneath a gunwale, making it impossible for the person on that side to get out at night without clambering over their partner. And the boat's toilet tank will usually be sited under the bed. Fortunately, modern tanks and seals are leakproof – not the situation when we began our narrowboat adventures in 2010.

A solution often adopted by private narrowboats and hire boats offering a higher quality fit-out is to have a double bed arranged across the boat where it can be wider. A fold-away extension allows the bed to be up to 6 foot 3 inches in length without blocking daytime access to bow or stern. That was the arrangement on 'Kingfisher' described in Chapter 16.

However, most hire boats also offer single beds and those were the options Lindsay and I always went for.

At Wilcot, the canal buries itself in an extensive patch of woodland. I thought I might be able to moor there for the night. I tried but could not get the boat close enough to the towpath side. There were underwater obstructions and too much vegetation.

Moored as close to the bank as possible – note the gangplank at full stretch

Pewsey Wharf

Pewsey Wharf emerged from a deep cutting ending at Bridge 114. That bridge carries the A345 between Marlborough and Salisbury over the canal. The old wharf is to the right. Wharfinger's house and store, a large, now Grade II listed building, lies set back end-on from the canal. It was built of brick around 1810. The wharf would have been a hive of activity with goods and travellers wanting to take advantage of this new form of transport. It didn't last though, as along came the railways in 1862, leaving the canal just 50 years free from competition.

There are visitor moorings at Pewsey, only there aren't. They are there, but permanently occupied by liveaboard boaters who most definitely do not move on every five days as required by CRT regulations. I had hoped to get a slot at Pewsey, but it was impossible. The canal is lined by every kind of boat, narrow, broad, long, short, fat, steel, fibreglass, wooden, Dutch barge, Kennet barge, new, derelict, part sunken and just about floating. Most piled high with logs, bits of tree, coal, bikes, flowers and pots, trash in old coal bags, old motors, generators, tools, furniture, washing, paint tins, TV aerials on poles, windmills, fold-up chairs, old barbies (cookers, not dolls that is, although that wouldn't surprise me), canoes, coracles, painters dangling with and without their craft, dinghies, fenders, rope, chains, solar panels and foredecks strewn with blackened aluminium foil and trays. Very few looked occupied. Just the occasional smoking chimney. Curiously, most had up-to-date CRT licence plates. So, no mooring spaces for over a mile.

The issue there is that right by the bridge and only 50 yards or so from the Waterfront Pub and Bistro is a CRT sanitary station – a most unsanitary, disgusting place, I have to say. Lindsay and I had the misfortune to walk by it on our pre-hire survey. It is the only one between Devizes and Great Bedwyn and therefore the centre of social activity for all those quasi-static boats. And the place really stinks, way past the pub – don't go there if the wind is from the west. Fish and chips in a lavatory – no thanks.

Finally, just past bridge 113, at the start of the embankment, there was a space. I got the boat into the bank pretty well, but the towpath was high up behind me. I jumped off with the centre line and held the boat until Lindsay had managed to throw me a mooring pin and the hammer. She could not get off the boat of course. Another boat came by a bit too fast – its suction pulled Honey Rose out. It was all I could do, marooned on the bank, high up and looking down on her roof, to keep hold. It was touch and go. I nearly went in. The boat nearly broke free and would have dragged her centre line into the water. I remember thinking, *I can't do this anymore.*

I managed to hold on and secure the boat by the centre line. Then clambered down from the towpath to hammer in both bow and stern lines. It was now nearly 8pm and way past acceptable closing time. We were a long way from any pub and so fired up the microwave for dinner and rest. Oh, those Stressless chairs.

Wootton Rivers

We were late getting away the next morning, but that was fine because a week was plenty of time to complete the trip. So a quick shower, then a cooked breakfast as usual, followed by washing up, tidying the lounge and generally making good.

The boating day began with us journeying eastward on 'the long pound' towards Wootton Rivers Bottom Lock. Salisbury Plain stretched far out to our right, the Marlborough Downs to our left. I don't suppose many folks have ridden horses all over Salisbury Plain and have driven narrowboats all the way across its northern extremes.

WWII gun emplacement at Wootton Rivers
© Copyright Brian Robert Marshall

On the left, just before the Wootton flight, is a 1940s 'pill-box' gun emplacement built to defend Southern England from an invasion by the German army. The land invasion never happened, but the defences remain.

The Wootton Rivers flight has four broad locks, the first of which is lock 51. This structure, together with adjacent bridge 108 are listed buildings according to Historic England. The road bridge is the only way of getting from one side of the lock to the other and it's not too close. I was going to have to work all the locks during the week because of Lindsay's hip problems, and the sheer dimensions of the lock and bridge dampened my spirits. In the end it took about four hours to get through the entire flight but including a stop for tea and doughnuts.

Crofton Summit

The Kennet and Avon Canal summit pound at Crofton is about two miles long. It includes the Bruce Tunnel, about 500 yards long and wide enough for two narrowboats to pass inside. Beyond the tunnel are the nine locks of the Crofton flight – all going downhill now of course, all the way to Reading and the River Thames.

Crofton Pumping Station was built in 1812 to pump water from Wilton Water, a natural spring-fed lake, up to the summit pound at bridge 103. From 1959, diesel and then electrically powered pumps took over, leaving the steam-powered beam engines at Crofton to provide a historic attraction. Having already been at the summit in 2013 and spent time at the engine house, I turned the boat at the winding hole below the bottom lock and Lindsay and I set off back westward.

Drained pound below Wootton Rivers Top Lock 54

I had planned to cruise gently through Savernake Forest, past Burbage Wharf with its historic crane, and then try to find a spot to moor for the night, hopefully before Wootton Top Lock. That section of canal needs dredging. It was nearly impossible to get the boat near enough to the towpath, even using the gangplank. I stopped several times and tried to get in, eventually succeeding but much closer to the lock than I had wanted.

Towards Devizes

We got up late the next day, but it didn't prevent that cooked breakfast. Lindsay and I were chatting away when a young female face appeared at the window, clearly distressed. I went outside to help. She said she and her boyfriend had been coming up the Wootton flight, but their boat was now stuck inside lock 53 (Brimslade). I asked her what she meant by 'stuck'. She said they had moored at the landing stage as usual, walked up to the bottom gates of the lock and opened the paddles. That emptied the lock and they had driven their boat in. After closing the gates and closing both paddles, they walked up to the top gates. They did not notice anything unusual until they cracked open one paddle – no water came in. They thought there was maybe a defective paddle and had walked round to open the one on the other side. Only then did they notice there was in fact no water in the pound beyond. The image above depicts the scene from the bridge across lock 54.

CRT clearing an obstruction from under the gates at Brimslade Lock, Wootton Rivers

We had experienced a very similar situation during our visit to Bath, again on the Kennet and Avon. I was tempted to use the same trick as then, which was to run water into the empty pound from the pound above lock 54. Simply open both upper and lower gate paddles and let it flow. However, it seemed that there might be a bigger problem here. I decided to call out CRT.

Along they came – they clearly knew what the issue was. They drove straight to lock 53 and, after about an hour, appeared at our lock to perform the 'let it flow' technique. I was surprised how quickly the pound filled. The distressed lady had gone back to her boat by then. We got into lock 54 and motored on down to lock 53. There we met up with a different CRT team who were going to try to remove rubbish from under the gates and an obstruction stuck in a ground paddle. We were there for about two hours.

In January 2021 CRT closed the Wootton Rivers flight for major repairs:[14]

Devizes via Honeystreet

The remainder of the week saw us get back to Honeystreet, where we stopped overnight on those glorious rings. The Barge Inn there is still a very bohemian place, frequented by the narrowboat community that has been developing to the west of the pub for many years. It had once been acquired as a community asset following a national charity grant but eventually went bust. It's in private hands now and hope springs eternal that it succeeds.

It was then down to Devizes for a couple of days. Nice place to stay with good boater facilities. No locks, just a couple of swing bridges. On the way, there are miles of moored boats that never move on. Most seem in a dilapidated state, many occupied by down-on-their-luck or anti-social or just plain lazy individuals. There are a few clearly genuine liveaboard boats, clean, well maintained with wafts of smoke emerging from their chimneys.

I do wonder how many of these craft make the journey to a CRT septic tank disposal point or pump-out station. On that stretch of the Kennet and Avon, that would mean a trip to Devizes or Pewsey every week or so. In all probability, it's too easy to dump sewage overboard. I have never seen a report of the level of dangerous pathogens in canal water, but I'm sure it would not make good reading. So whenever you or your crew come into direct contact with canal water, make sure all hands are washed, especially any little ones.

The same applies whenever you have been down a weed hatch and emerged to be ravaged by a big black dog.

---

[14] While it is tempting to traverse a double-width lock via one gate, that should only be attempted by an experienced skipper who can be confident of not hitting the other gate on the way in or out. Hitting a closed lock gate will form a groove and over time lead to extensive leakage.

And Finally

This was to be our final narrowboat holiday. They had lasted 15 years, with 30 individual adventures. But in 2020 the world was hit by Covid.

I was now 76 years of age and finding the day-to-day activities around handling a typical 15-ton narrowboat a bit of an effort. Lindsay had become less and less active. In the early and middle years, she managed most of the locks and had enjoyed that, especially chatting to other boating enthusiasts. But now it was down to me. More or less single-handed had become the name of the game. And now that had become too much.

I did think about hiring a 'helper' to accompany us. We had seen that on the first Mon and Brec trip. An elderly couple recruited a fit young man to live with them on their boat for a couple of weeks. He did all the hard work while the owners enjoyed the cruise. The gentleman owner had a nasty-looking injury to his face which I assumed was due to a fall – and that becomes a big risk around canal infrastructure in later years.

Lindsay and I very much enjoyed our canal and river adventures. And there was so much more pleasure to be had by sharing them with family and friends.

Looking back, my overall impression of our waterway years is that there exists out there a parallel universe - one where 200-year-old stuff can still be cranked, where people actually talk to each other, where smartphones are a rarity, where eyes are focused on the horizon and not on a pavement, where help rushes in when one is in need and where the slow pace of life refreshes one's soul.

Lindsay's father Sam, old salt that he was, would have loved his time in and around narrowboats – in all probability hosting a perpetual ear-to-ear grin and humming a happy tune.

Bibliography and Acknowledgements

Resources referenced with thanks:

Warwick Castle website.
Wiltshire Times newspaper.
Daily Mail newspaper archives.
British Listed Buildings website.
Grace's Guide to British Industrial History.
BBC website.
Derby News website.
Historic England website.
Waterways Routes website.
Britain Express website.
Web Aviation website.

Environment Agency.

Pearson's Canal Companions. A set of paperback books covering all navigable canals and most rivers throughout Britain.

Colin Edmondson's 'Going it Alone' notebook published in 2003.

'John Knill's Navy' published in 2020.

Black Prince narrowboats, Bradford-on-Avon.

ABC narrowboats, Worcester.

Castle Narrowboats, Gilwern, Wales.

The author apologises for any references used without an acknowledgment. Wikipedia text and images are assumed to be public domain material that can be reproduced via the terms of a 'Creative Commons Licence'.

Images not owned by the author have been given citations stating their originators. Every effort has been made to contact all image owners and obtain agreement to use their work herein. Where it has not been possible

List of Route Maps

Map 01

Llangollen Canal

Map based on an original by Waterway Routes

© Copyright Waterway Routes 2022

Map 02

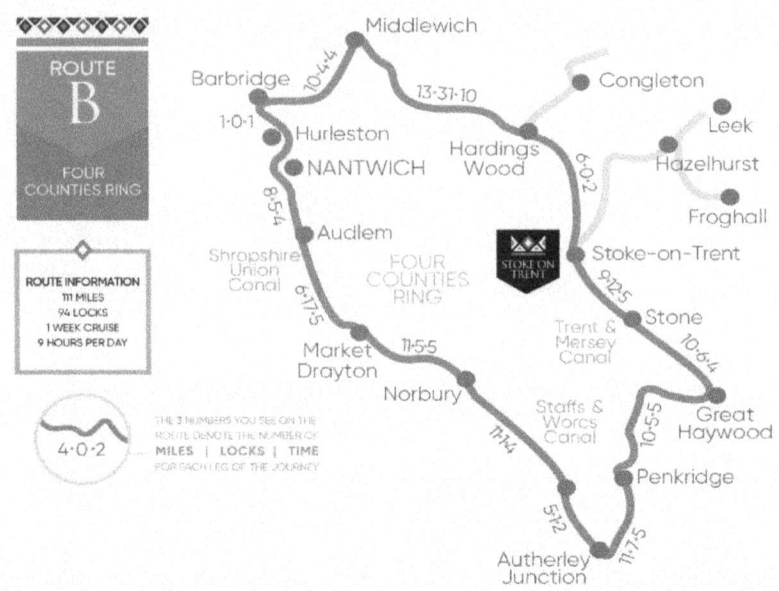

Four Counties Ring

Map 03

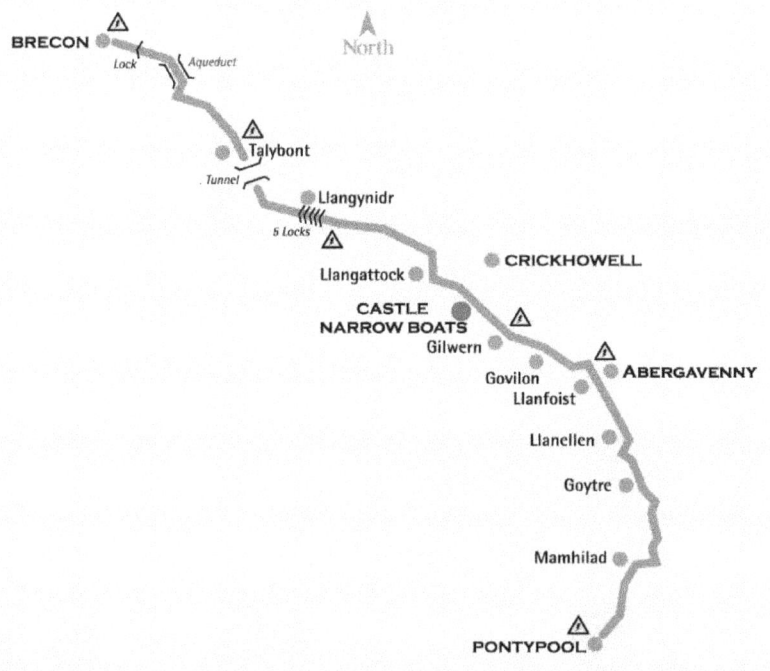

Monmouthshire and Brecon Canal

© Copyright Castle Narrowboats 2022

Map 04

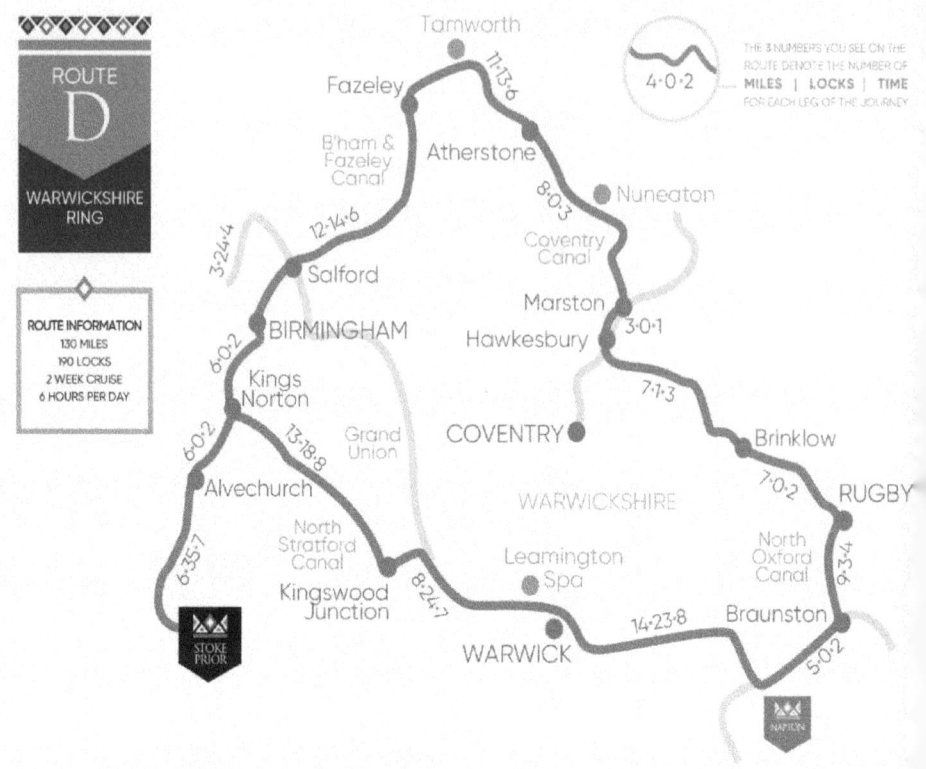

Tamworth

Fazeley   11·13·6

B'ham & Fazeley Canal   Atherstone

3·24·4   12·14·6

Salford   8·0·3   Nuneaton

Coventry Canal

BIRMINGHAM   Marston

6·0·2   Hawkesbury   3·0·1

Kings Norton

6·0·2   13·18·8   Grand Union   7·1·3

COVENTRY   Brinklow

Alvechurch   WARWICKSHIRE   7·0·2   RUGBY

6·35·7   North Stratford Canal   Leamington Spa   North Oxford Canal   9·3·4

Kingswood Junction   8·24·7   14·23·8   Braunston

WARWICK   5·0·2

ROUTE D WARWICKSHIRE RING

ROUTE INFORMATION
130 MILES
190 LOCKS
2 WEEK CRUISE
6 HOURS PER DAY

THE 3 NUMBERS YOU SEE ON THE ROUTE DENOTE THE NUMBER OF
MILES | LOCKS | TIME
FOR EACH LEG OF THE JOURNEY
4·0·2

STOKE PRIOR

NAPTON

Warwickshire Ring

© Copyright Black Prince Holidays 2022

Map 05

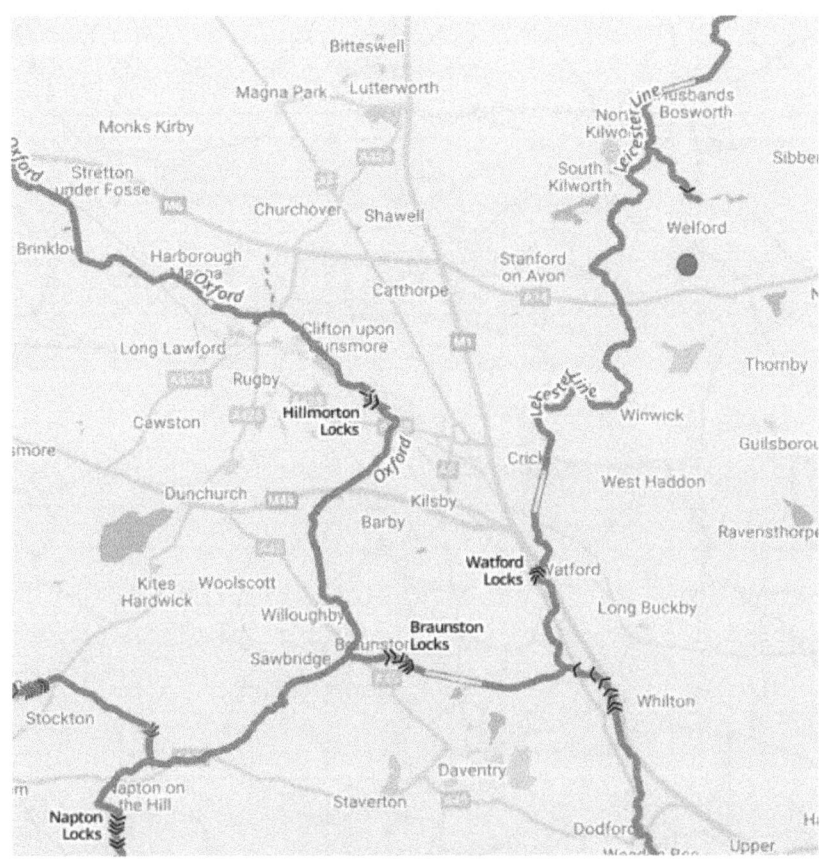

Welford Arm of the Grand Union Canal

© Copyright Ordnance Survey 2022

Map 06

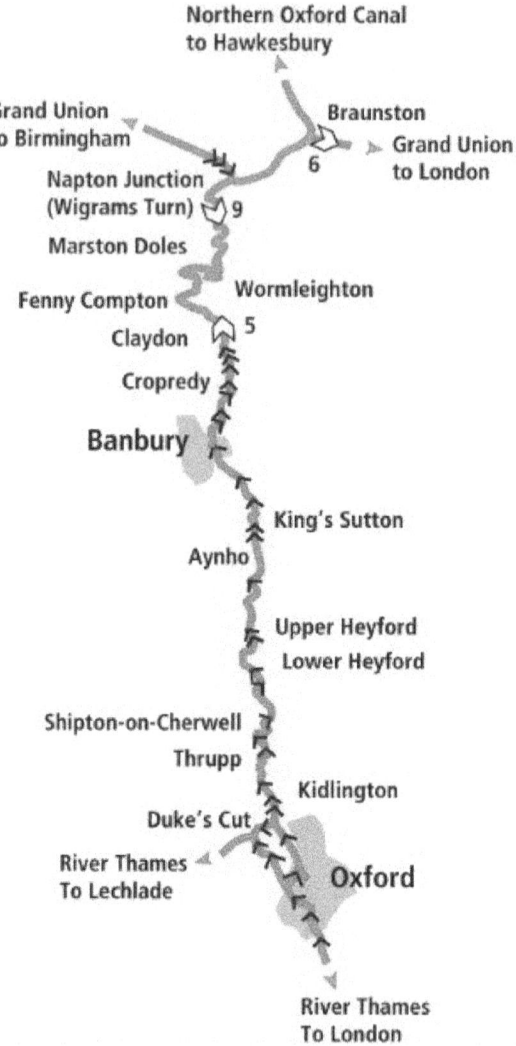

Northern Oxford Canal
to Hawkesbury

Grand Union
to Birmingham

Braunston

6

Grand Union
to London

Napton Junction
(Wigrams Turn) 9

Marston Doles

Wormleighton

Fenny Compton

5

Claydon

Cropredy

Banbury

King's Sutton

Aynho

Upper Heyford

Lower Heyford

Shipton-on-Cherwell

Thrupp

Kidlington

Duke's Cut

River Thames
To Lechlade

Oxford

River Thames
To London

South Oxford Canal

© Copyright Kelsey Media 2022

Map 07

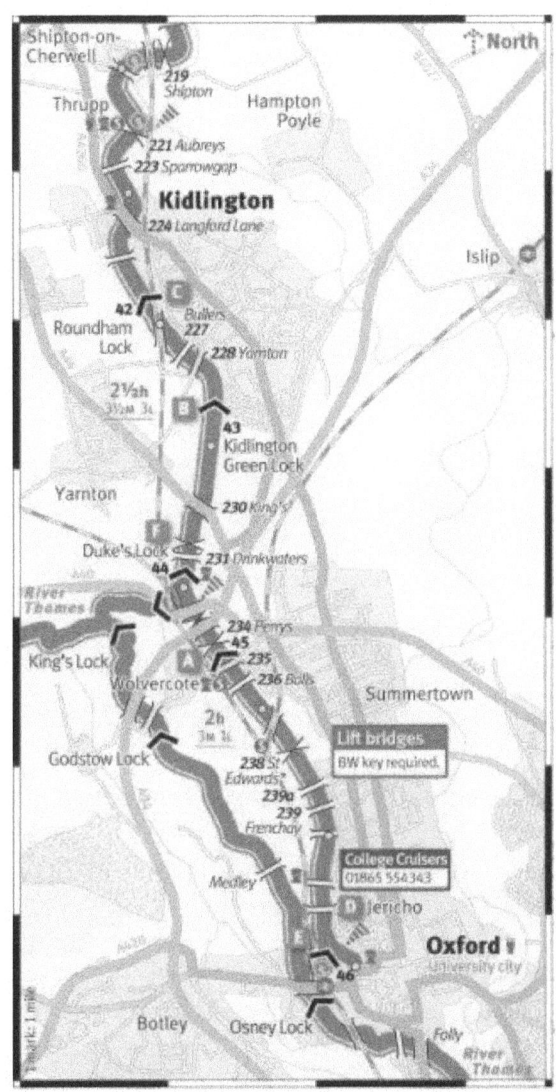

Thrupp into Oxford and back via King's Lock and Duke's Cut

© Copyright Waterways World 2022

Map 08

Route covered here
Other waterways
Derelict waterways

Leek

Hazlehurst   Hazlehurst
Junction   Aqueduct

Leek Branch

Endon

Cheddleton

Trent & Mersey
Canal

Baddeley
Green

Caldon Canal

Stoke-on-Trent   Caldon Canal

Consall Forge

Froghall

Hanley

Etruria
Junction

Froghall Junction

Uttoxeter Canal

Caldon Canal

Map based on an original by Waterway Routes

© Copyright Waterway Routes 2022

Map 09

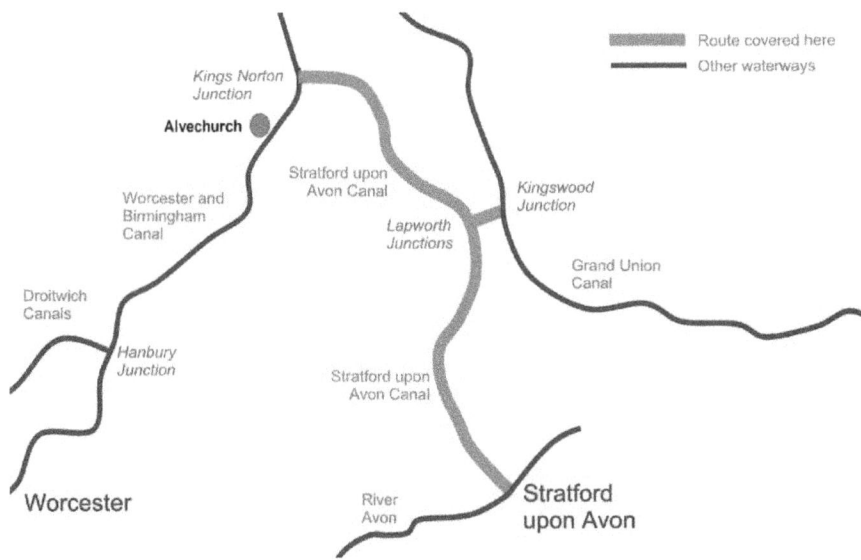

Kings Norton
Junction

Alvechurch

Worcester and
Birmingham
Canal

Stratford upon
Avon Canal

Kingswood
Junction

Lapworth
Junctions

Grand Union
Canal

Droitwich
Canals

Hanbury
Junction

Stratford upon
Avon Canal

Worcester

River
Avon

Stratford
upon Avon

Route covered here
Other waterways

Stratford-upon-Avon Canal

Map based on an original by Waterway Routes

© Copyright Waterway Routes 2022

Map 10

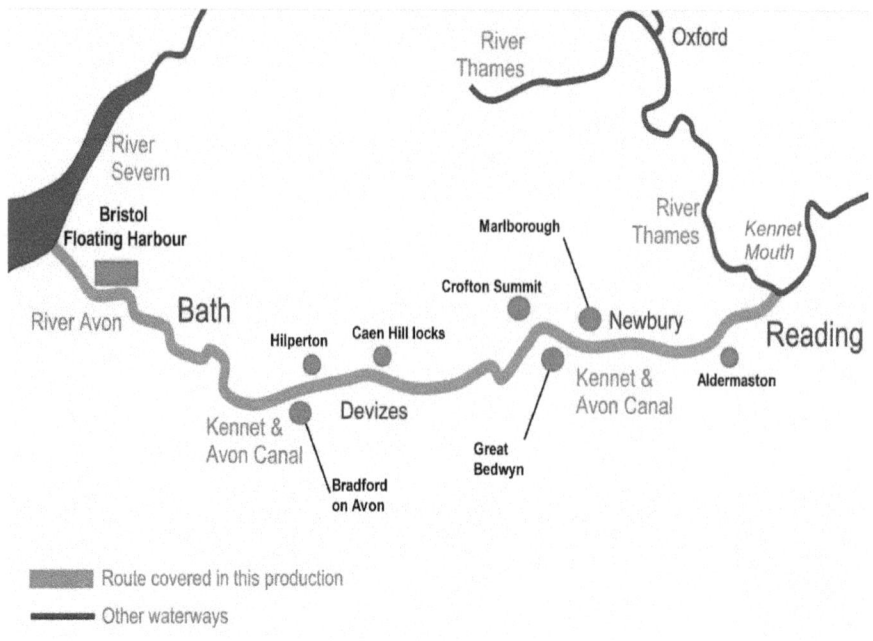

Kennet and Avon Canal

Map based on an original by Waterway Routes

© Copyright Waterway Routes 2022

Map 11

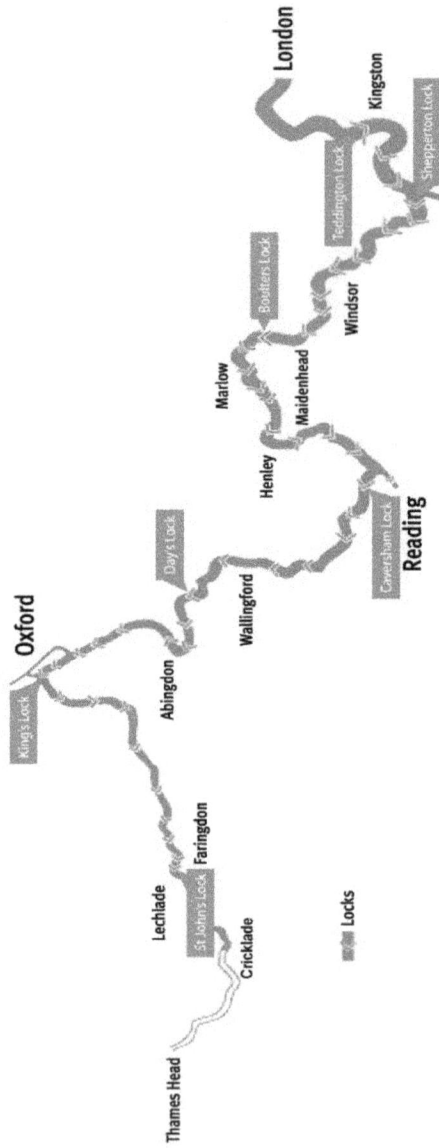

London

Kingston

Shepperton Lock

Teddington Lock

Boulters Lock

Windsor

Marlow

Maidenhead

Henley

Day's Lock

Caversham Lock

Reading

Oxford

Wallingford

Abingdon

King's Lock

Faringdon

Lechlade

St John's Lock

Cricklade

Locks

Thames Head

River Thames (non-tidal)
© Copyright Environment Agency 2022

Map 12

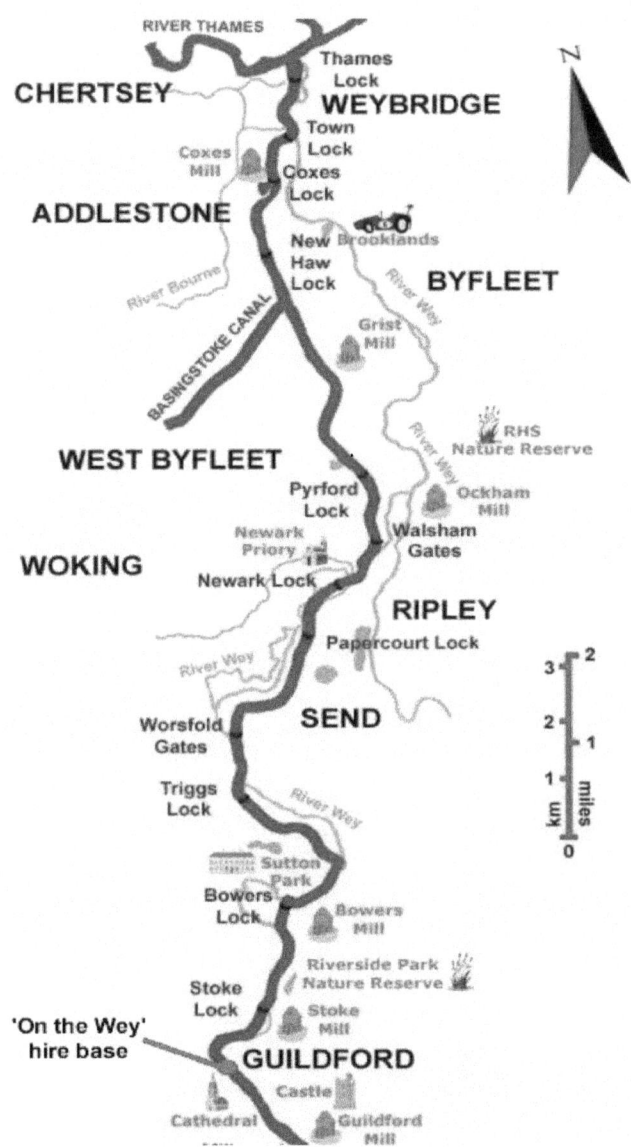

RIVER THAMES

CHERTSEY

Thames Lock

WEYBRIDGE

Town Lock

Coxes Mill

Coxes Lock

ADDLESTONE

New Haw Lock

Brooklands

BYFLEET

River Bourne

River Wey

Grist Mill

BASINGSTOKE CANAL

WEST BYFLEET

RHS Nature Reserve

River Wey

Pyrford Lock

Ockham Mill

Newark Priory

Walsham Gates

WOKING

Newark Lock

RIPLEY

Papercourt Lock

River Wey

SEND

Worsfold Gates

Triggs Lock

River Wey

Sutton Park

Bowers Lock

Bowers Mill

Riverside Park Nature Reserve

Stoke Lock

Stoke Mill

'On the Wey' hire base

GUILDFORD

Castle

Cathedral

Guildford Mill

River Wey Navigation to the Thames
© Copyright Wey River Freelance Community 2022

Map 13

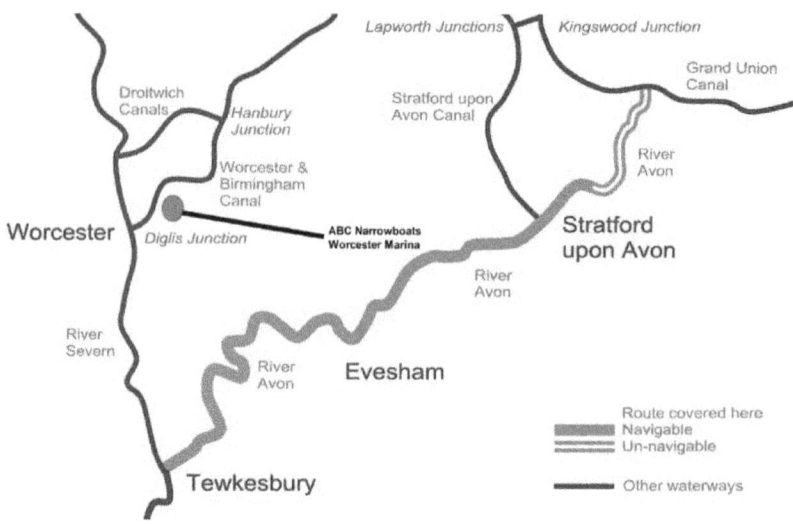

River Severn Worcester to Stratford-upon-Avon

Map based on an original by Waterway Routes

© Copyright Waterway Routes 2022

About the Author

In 1969 Peter Hills graduated from Surrey University with an MSc degree in computing, control and systems engineering.

He initially worked for Sperry Gyroscope, later British Aerospace, in Bracknell and played a leading role in three major projects for the Royal Navy. Those projects all involved the Sperry 1412 computer, for which he was one of a five-strong 'skunk works' development team. He was made a Chartered Engineer in 1975.

Peter stayed in military systems and software engineering for fifteen years – at which point he set up Pacts Auction Systems and in so doing switched from military to commercial systems and software development.

Over the next 30 years, Pacts became the pre-eminent supplier of back-office technology for regional auction houses. It was installed at more than 200 locations in Britain and Europe and processed over £300 million of auction sales each year.

Peter retired when Pacts was acquired by Bidpath Corporation in 2016.

He remains a member of the Institute of Engineering and Technology (The IET) having first joined as an Associate Member in 1966. Peter is a guest contributor to the Archives section of the IET website.

www.ingramcontent.com/pod-product-compliance
Ingram Content Group UK Ltd.
Pitfield, Milton Keynes, MK11 3LW, UK
UKHW030626300425
5690UKWH00001B/96